Corporate and white-collar crime in Ireland

Manchester University Press

IRISH SOCIETY

The Irish Society series provides a critical, interdisciplinary and in-depth analysis of Ireland that reveals the processes and forces shaping social, economic, cultural and political life, and their outcomes for communities and social groups. The books seek to understand the evolution of social, economic and spatial relations from a broad range of perspectives, and explore the challenges facing Irish society in the future given present conditions and policy instruments.

SERIES EDITOR
Rob Kitchin

ALREADY PUBLISHED

Public private partnerships in Ireland: Failed experiment or the way forward for the state? *Rory Hearne*

Migrations: Ireland in a global world
Edited by Mary Gilmartin and Allen White

The economics of disability: Insights from Irish research
Edited by John Cullinan, Seán Lyons and Brian Nolan

The domestic, moral and political economies of post-Celtic tiger Ireland: What rough beast?
Kieran Keohane and Carmen Kuhling

Challenging times, challenging administration: The role of public administration in producing social justice in Ireland
Chris McInerney

Management and gender in higher education
Pat O'Connor

Defining events: Power, resistance and identity in twenty-first-century Ireland
Edited by Rosie Meade and Fiona Dukelow

Corporate and white-collar crime in Ireland

A new architecture of regulatory enforcement

Joe McGrath

MANCHESTER UNIVERSITY PRESS

Published by Manchester University Press
Altrincham Street, Manchester M1 7JA, UK
www.manchesteruniversitypress.co.uk

British Library Cataloguing-in-Publication Data is available

ISBN 978 0 7190 9066 0 *hardback*

First published by Manchester University Press in hardback 2015

This edition first published 2018

Printed by Lightning Source

For my parents, Mary and Bill

Contents

Tables and figure

Tables

Figure

Series editor's foreword

Over the past twenty years Ireland has undergone enormous social, cultural and economic change. From a poor, peripheral country on the edge of Europe with a conservative culture dominated by tradition and Church, Ireland transformed into a global, cosmopolitan country with a dynamic economy. At the heart of the processes of change was a new kind of political economic model of development that ushered in the so-called Celtic Tiger years, accompanied by renewed optimism in the wake of the ceasefires in Northern Ireland and the peace dividend of the Good Friday Agreement. As Ireland emerged from decades of economic stagnation and The Troubles came to a peaceful end, the island became the focus of attention for countries seeking to emulate its economic and political miracles. Every other country, it seemed, wanted to be the next Tiger, modelled on Ireland's successes. And then came the financial collapse of 2008, the bursting of the property bubble, bank bailouts, austerity plans, rising unemployment and a return to emigration. From being the paradigm case of successful economic transformation, Ireland has become an internationally important case study of what happens when an economic model goes disastrously wrong.

The Irish Society series provides a critical, interdisciplinary and in-depth analysis of Ireland that reveals the processes and forces shaping social, economic, cultural and political life, and their outcomes for communities and social groups. The books seek to understand the evolution of social, economic and spatial relations from a broad range of perspectives, and explore the challenges facing Irish society in the future given present conditions and policy instruments. The series examines all aspects of Irish society including, but not limited to: social exclusion, identity, health, welfare, life cycle, family life and structures, labour and work cultures, spatial and sectoral economy, local and regional development, politics and the political system, government and governance, environment, migration and spatial planning. The series is supported by the Irish Social Sciences Platform (ISSP), an all-island platform of integrated social science research and graduate education focusing on the social, cultural and economic transformations shaping Ireland in the twenty-first century. Funded by the Programme for Research in Third Level Institutions, the ISSP brings together leading social science academics from all of Ireland's universities and other third-level institutions.

Given the marked changes in Ireland's fortunes over the past two decades it is important that rigorous scholarship is applied to understand the forces at work, how they have affected different people and places in uneven and unequal ways, and what needs to happen to create a fairer and prosperous society. The Irish Society series provides such scholarship.

Rob Kitchin

Foreword

Rare is the study that makes economic crimes by high-status individuals the subject of criminological research and criminal law theory. Rarer still is the study that does so in the context of a globally influential model of economic development in the neoliberal age such as Ireland. When work of this scientific and legal significance is written in an engaging, historically informed narrative that can be accessed by the widest audience of lawyers, criminologists, business leaders and concerned citizens, you have the makings of a future classic. Joe McGrath's study of corporate and white collar crime in Ireland is just that.

This is a study of the evolution of Irish corporate criminal liability, and its enforcement, from independence through the financial crisis of 2008. The author argues that for most of the twentieth century Ireland addressed corporate and business wrongdoing more generally through a model that was heavily reliant on conventional criminal law, policing and prosecution and which, somewhat paradoxically it might seem, were remarkably lenient. Starting in the 1990s, the architecture of enforcement changed. The monopoly of criminal law authorities, the *Garda Siochana* and the government's central prosecution service was broken up in favour of a number of regulatory agencies. This new model was much more reliant on cooperative efforts to encourage compliance, as well as civil sanctions and orders. Paradoxically, the new model also appears to have been more punitive (or at least less lenient) toward corporate wrongdoers (both companies and company officers). This new model is expressly compared to the responsive regulatory model that has been promoted as a restorative justice approach to business crime and which is an innovative international model. Since 2008, the architecture is possibly being shifted once again through the introduction of a layer of new legislation reflecting an expressive objective of denouncing corporate wrongdoers as the moral equivalents of traitors and terrorists, and to highlight the tough on crime credentials of government.

The research behind this monograph is impressive and comprehensive. The author has canvassed the reported case law regarding Company Act enforcements since independence, all the major governmental reports issued concerning corporate or business wrongdoing, all legislation adopted or contemplated concerning corporate criminal liability, and reviewed newspaper coverage of corporate crime in all the major newspapers again since independence. While statistical data about corporate wrongdoing and enforcement is sparse (indeed, the very lack of governmental interest in such statistics is a telling feature of the inertia with which Ireland addressed corporate wrongdoing in the traditional model) the author presents what is available in clear and helpful ways. The author combines legal analysis of the statutory and case law regarding company wrongdoing, including the emerging European law framework, with socio-legal analysis of institutional structures, the historical record of enforcement, and the social and intellectual context in which company law has been formulated and interpreted.

Drawing on a rich body of sociological, criminological and political science literatures concerning crime, risk and governance, the author develops a sophisticated and convincing interpretation of the two models, why the first model remained so stable for so long despite its clear failures, and what has driven the change in the architecture of enforcement. The first model of formally punitive but practically lenient criminal law enforcement belongs, first of all, to an Ireland whose overall political economy is one of austerity, relative isolation from global capital, and a generally constrained and contained corporate sector (especially financial services). The rationalities of governance in the regulatory field reflect a clear priority of reinforcing the sovereignty of the state and guarding against foreign intervention or domestic subversion. The anchoring of enforcement power in the *Garda* and prosecution service is designed to effectuate those ends, and arguably does. If this leaves corporate wrongdoing under-deterred, it is also the case that the corporate sector is minor and within the context of a highly agrarian economy, not of much threat to state stability.

This model begins to come under pressure as Ireland shifts toward economic liberalisation and global trade in the 1970s, but remains largely intact because liberalisation itself is promoted through the premise of a light touch regulatory strategy. Only in the 1990s, when the economic take-off facilitated by liberalisation is in full swing do corporate scandals and the increasing vulnerability of the larger economy to business misconduct begin to problematise the criminal law based architecture of the traditional model. The new model formulated in the 1990s and implemented in the first decade of the twenty-first century is balanced in favour of cooperative regulation and civil enforcement. It reflects a governmental rationality far more attuned with global liberalism and the logic of governing at a distance through embedded actors – what some following Foucault call 'governmentality'. Most recently this new architecture is being stressed by the powerful reactive response of the public and politicians to the devastating financial crisis of 2008 and the profound losses it has imposed on the Irish economy overall. Pursuing a pattern observed in the USA and the UK as well, Irish politicians are governing through crime, seeking executive power and legitimacy by expressively denouncing corporate wrongdoers. This may ultimately undermine the new architecture which paradoxically relies on effective but highly constrained criminal law enforcement.

This monograph presents original and well-developed findings that make important contributions to the fields of criminology, criminal law and business law, and the contemporary history of Irish law and governance.

Professor Jonathan Simon, University of California, Berkeley

Acknowledgements

First and foremost, I am most grateful for the support and guidance I received from Professor Shane Kilcommins. This book commenced life as a PhD thesis I completed under his supervision at the School of Law, University College Cork. That thesis, and the foundation for this book, would not have been completed without his expertise, insights, patience and good humour. I hope that one day I will be as inspirational a lecturer and academic as he is now.

I am also grateful for the insights on corporate theory provided by Professor Irene Lynch Fannon. This expertise complemented the expertise of Professor Kilcommins in his fields of regulatory theory, criminology and penology. I am grateful to have had the benefit of their different perspectives on corporate and white-collar criminality.

I also express my sincere thanks to Professor Jonathan Simon of University of California (UC) Berkeley for his kind, generous and thoughtful foreword. My only regret in having the endorsement of such a prominent and insightful scholar is that he easily manages to better express my own research findings than I do. It is an immense honour to have his encouragement and assistance.

I gratefully acknowledge the financial support I received from the Irish Research Council and the Millennium Research Fund at National University of Ireland (NUI) Galway. These sources allowed me to pursue fellowships at Harvard Law School, the Centre for the Study of Law and Society at UC Berkeley, and the Centre for Irish and Irish American Studies at New York University. I am grateful to each of these institutions for hosting me and providing me with experiences that enriched my research.

Institutional support from my former employer NUI Galway was generous and forthcoming. I also thank my current employer, the Sutherland School of Law at University College Dublin, for its support. I am very grateful to my students and colleagues at both institutions for allowing me to canvass their views on white-collar criminality. All of these experiences have positively informed my research for this monograph. I am also grateful to Dr James Cunningham for reading early versions of the proposal for this book and for his constructive suggestions on improvement. Tatiana Kelly proofread and checked the references for this book while completing a summer internship and I am thankful for her care and attention in doing so. I am also grateful to the team at Manchester University Press for all their assistance.

There are numerous friends and colleagues that provided enjoyable distractions and diversions while I was researching this book. These include: Alan Desmond, Eoin Daly, Eilionoir Flynn, Paul Fuller, Diarmuid Griffin, Ronan Hoare, Lughaidh Kerin, Tom O'Malley, Sinead Ring and Gerry Sadlier. In particular, Paul and Ronan visited me when I conducted research in the USA and our epic road trip from the West to East coast and back again will not be forgotten (or repeated).

Finally, this book is dedicated to my parents, Mary and Bill. As a child, they brought me to the library during the day and later confiscated my books at bedtime so that I would sleep at night. I am grateful to them for stimulating my interest in reading and for supporting my studies for longer than they probably thought was necessary. My godmother, Imelda, was also generous in her support and my godfather, Felix, kindly read an earlier (and much longer) draft of this book. In addition, I also want to thank my brothers Liam, John and Tom for their support. In particular, I thank John who encouraged me to pursue a career in academia because, he said, 'it would beat working for a living'. To the extent that I have found this path extraordinarily rewarding, he has proven correct.

Dr Joe McGrath
Sutherland School of Law
University College Dublin

Introduction

Description of project

This monograph argues that a new regulatory architecture started to emerge in the 1990s to address corporate and financial wrongdoing in Ireland. Many aspects of this new architecture are analysed, including its design, features, structures and mechanics; both the product and the process that created it; and its cultural, political, practical and symbolic elements. It is argued that for much of the twentieth century, Ireland was economically dominated by its agricultural sector. In the decades following independence, rural Ireland was romanticised as 'poor but happy' in a celebration of anti-materialist values. The State did not seek to develop a vibrant business community in Ireland and actively sought to dissuade foreign companies from establishing within its borders. It initially advanced protectionist policies as an assertion of sovereignty to prevent any attempts by the British to subvert and control the Irish economy. A corporate culture, as we now understand it, simply did not exist. These restrictions on business stifled economic growth long after they were abandoned.

Moreover, even when the State opened up its economy and embraced free trade, it still had little experience of how to effectively regulate corporate activity. This period was characterised by political inertia in corporate affairs. Members of Parliament openly professed their lack of interest in corporate regulation, finding company law to be complicated and of little personal or national interest. As a result, Irish company law review and reform was irregular and rare. For the most part, the legislature adopted a culture of policy imitation, replicating English company law without any particular consideration as to whether this legislation suited the Irish corporate context. The lack of reflection on corporate regulation is unsurprising because the ability to perceive risk is culturally contingent. The risks we identify, and do not identify, reveal as much about society at a given time as they do about hazards in our environment (Douglas, 1992). Corporate and white-collar crimes did not animate a State with a stagnated economy that was largely agrarian in orientation, with relatively low levels of incorporation and low levels of crime. Instead, increased corporate activity was positively associated with wealth creation, employment, and as a way to escape economic stagnation. The State was not concerned with protecting general society from corporate harms because 'the race between perceptible wealth and imperceptible risks cannot be won by the latter' (Beck, 1992: 21). The interplay of these social, political and economic factors had a particular impact on policy choices in the State. Corporate wrongdoing was criminalised, not because it was viewed as morally reprehensible or because it was a threat to the security of the State, but because it was a ready-made system of enforcement which had already been used to address ordinary crimes, and which could, it was thought, be easily and uncritically adopted to police the corporate sector. Preventing corporate wrongdoing was not a priority and criminal sanctions were a form of 'damage limitation "retrofitted" after the fact' (Garland, 2003: 51).

However, addressing 'crime in the suites' with a 'street crime' model of criminal liability, without reflection or adjustment, created difficulties at all stages of the criminal process, including policing, prosecution and punishment. Conventional policing and prosecution authorities monopolised most of the policing and prosecution of corporate wrongdoing in the State, even though they were unsuited to these tasks. These agencies were orientated to policing conventional crimes, were under-resourced, had little experience or training in dealing with corporate wrongdoing, and complained that they were hamstrung by weak powers and outdated laws. Addressing corporate wrongdoing within the conventional crime model also meant that alleged wrongdoers were able to use the due process safeguards that applied to 'ordinary' criminals. The regime respected general criminal law defences and typically demanded both a conduct and a fault element (intent). The accused was presumed innocent and the prosecution had the burden of proving its case beyond a reasonable doubt. This model was informed by the liberal legal tradition which championed the use of fair and just procedures to achieve the goals of the criminal law. Nevertheless, despite these protections, politicians and the public did not seem to support the prosecution of corporate wrongdoers. The application of the criminal law was associated with *mala in se* crimes, such as violent and sexual assaults, not wrongs that were considered *mala prohibita*, such as false accounting. Consequently, the law was rarely enforced even though the penalties on conviction were relatively mild. Only a handful of the 280 criminal offences proscribed by the Companies Acts 1963 to 1990 were prosecuted. Of these, the failure to file annual accounts was the only offence to be prosecuted with any regularity. A culture of corporate non-compliance and non-enforcement reigned.

Since the 1990s, however, a new 'logic of action' appears to have emerged to address the growth of business. This is evidenced by the new ways of thinking about corporate wrongdoing, in the content and scope of corporate regulation, and in the enforcement of law. The changed perception of corporate wrongdoing can be located in the changed nature of Irish society generally. Supranational influences like the EU and globalisation opened up the marketplace and provided wider access to more consumers and easier access to foreign capital. Ireland seized the opportunity to market itself as an attractive place in which to do business. It was no longer willing to define itself in opposition to its British counterparts or by reference to its rural identity. It wanted more. Ireland embraced free market capitalism and assumed a corporate ethos: lowering corporate tax, championing facilitative light-touch regulation and embracing materialism. The dominant culture became one of entrepreneurship rather than agrarianism, as more people became highly educated, hard-working, white-collar workers. By the 1990s, Ireland had experienced spectacular economic growth. Unfortunately, the growth in big business had out-paced the maturity of Irish politics which was unable to maintain the necessary distance to govern it properly. High-profile public tribunals established in the 1990s revealed the corporate corruption of politics at the highest levels. In addition, State-owned banks were encouraging their customers to cheat the State, while also stealing from their clients' accounts. A series of reports also highlighted extensive problems with the structure, content and enforcement of company law. International corporate scandals, resulting in hundreds of millions of euros in losses for investors, kept public attention focused on corporate wrongdoing.

The interplay of changed social, political and economic conditions produced a new generative structure of company law. Specialist agencies were established to police and prosecute corporate wrongs, colonising functions formerly held by government departments and conventional crime fighters. These regulators were given extensive powers in their respective areas. Unlike previously, corporate compliance and enforcement are the core objectives of these agencies. Though residual problems still exist, their officers are better trained, better resourced and enjoy more political support than ever. By 2001, the Companies Acts contained over 400 criminal offences. As criminal and evidential procedures had posed problems because of the difficulty in proving that company law offences had been committed, the State expanded out instrumental regulatory crime stratagems to streamline accountability and make it easier to prove wrongdoing. Strict liability and reverse onus provisions were increasingly used to make it easier to secure convictions for offences contrary to the Companies Acts. The decline in due process protections was accompanied by higher penalties on conviction.

Furthermore, administrative sanctions were created which blur the distinction between criminal and civil jurisdictions. These sanctions carried significant fines, fewer procedural protections, and can sometimes be applied in the absence of judicial involvement, unless appealed. In addition, the legislature sidestepped criminal due process safeguards entirely by channelling corporate wrongdoing into the civil jurisdiction of law. While a number of civil sanctions did exist prior to 1990, the main civil order of significance was arguably the disqualification of an individual from managing a company and this order could only be employed on the criminal conviction of the accused. Since 1990, however, civil sanctions, like restriction orders, can be triggered for events that are not necessarily considered blameworthy, imposed for mandatory periods, with limited judicial input, and in circumstances that are considered non-adversarial. The use of regulatory crime initiatives, administrative sanctions and civil orders reflected the new emphasis on streamlining accountability and instrumentalism.

The departure from the conventional criminal model had a significant impact on corporate enforcement. Enforcement became much more sophisticated, moving away from the 'command and control' model to a compliance-orientated, 'tiered' or 'responsive' model of enforcement. Enforcers first educated company officers about their responsibilities and encouraged them to comply with their obligations. Corporate and financial regulators generally adopted a collaborative and conciliatory approach, accepting voluntary rectification of wrongs in preference to punishment. If this approach was unsuccessful, regulatory responses escalated to civil sanctions and ultimately to criminal liability. Criminal sanctions were used as a last resort and there was a particular reluctance to prosecute cases on indictment. Most prosecutions took place in the District Court where punishments were limited. Offenders generally received neither prison sentences nor criminal records. Therefore, despite the establishment of specialised enforcers with enhanced powers, the reversal of settled patterns in criminal justice to streamline sanctioning, increased punitiveness and multi-layered diversification of enforcement stratagems, there was still some reluctance to criminally punish corporate wrongdoers in practice.

However, the tipping point arrived in 2008 when major irresponsibility in the Irish banking sector caused the economy to free-fall and threatened the stability of the common currency of Europe. Political apathy was replaced by activism and politicians competed to be more outraged by corporate wrongdoing. Politicians stated that bankers were guilty of economic treason, did more damage to the State than the IRA, and should be treated like terrorists. Corporate and white-collar crimes became politicised and the State demonstrated a tendency to 'govern through crime' (Simon, 2007). Developments which had previously been introduced under the blanket of instrumentalism, to surmount the problem of attributing guilt to company officers, were more expressive, introduced to boost executive power, to 'act out' for public approval, and to be 'tough' on corporate and white-collar crimes. There was also a greater commitment to more readily enforce the severe sanctions which have existed for some time. This was evinced by the willingness to escalate from compliance to sanctioning approaches, by the severe penalties actually imposed in practice and by the investigation, prosecution and conviction of senior bankers for indictable offences.

Corporate and white-collar crimes were being governed in new ways combining both dimensions of thought and action in a form of 'governmentality'. Governance was being shaped 'by the institutions, procedures, analyses and reflections, the calculations and tactics that allow the exercise of this very specific albeit complex form of power, which has as its target population, as its principle form of knowledge political economy, and as its essential technical means apparatuses of security' (Foucault, 1991a: 102). Though the State had initially governed under the cover of protectionism, to resist British influence, it subsequently employed the 'art of government' to escape economic stagnation, embracing competition and light-touch regulation to promote itself as an attractive location for foreign investment. In order to facilitate the intensification of industrialisation, increasingly detailed legal provisions were introduced to regulate commerce and the markets. This manifested itself in the 'juridification of social relations': a recognition of the growth in scale and scope of corporate regulation in the modern State (Habermas, 1987: 357). More recently again, the 'regulatory impulse' has been employed to restore international confidence in Ireland's regulatory regime since the financial crisis (Vaughan, 2009). However, governance in Ireland needs to be understood not just in terms of regulatory intervention; governmentality shows that Ireland's way of solving problems is political (Rose, 1999). It is a 'way of knowing' that affected how the State recognised harm and therefore how it defined crime and enforced the law.

Furthermore, the 'art of government' now extends beyond the boundaries of the Irish nation State. Increased Europeanisation and globalisation have broken the State monopoly on governance. The State is now the object and subject of regulation from the EU, ECB, IMF, Moody's and WTO, among others (Braithwaite and Drahos, 2000). Additionally, governance also extends to new sites within the State. Braithwaite (2008: 13–14) notes that though local policing was once concerned with regulating trade and commerce to create an orderly society, the police subsequently became preoccupied with the 'punitive regulation of the poor' so 'business regulation became variegated into many different specialist regulatory branches'. Similarly, policing corporate wrongdoing in Ireland became more disaggregated, parcelled out among different regulatory institutions, private actors and even the regulatees themselves who are educated, encouraged and therefore expected to internalise compliance with the law. All of this results in more 'government at a distance' from centralised nation State power (Rose, 1999: 49). The constitution of the markets and the just regulation of commerce are back on the criminal justice agenda, albeit in a fragmented way.

Need for this project

Corporate crime and white-collar crime are notoriously ambiguous concepts. Sutherland (1949: 9) first coined the term white-collar crime when he defined it as being 'committed by a person of respectability and high social status in the course of his occupation'. However, Nelkin (2007: 738) has suggested that: 'If Sutherland deserved a Nobel prize, as Mannheim though, for pioneering this field of study, he certainly did not deserve it for the clarity or serviceableness of his definition ... The apparent success of the label in finding public acceptance may testify less to its coherence than to its capacity to name a supposed threat.' Difficulties may also arise in distinguishing white-collar crime from corporate crime. In general, white-collar crime is considered to be crime committed by the natural persons, those capable of wearing white collars, while corporate crime is committed by artificial legal persons, corporate entities. However, the terms are used so interchangeably that this distinction can also be confusing and the contemporary approach is often to abandon it and take an all-encompassing approach (Mcguire, 2010), or to use 'corporate crime' as an umbrella term for all such crimes (Horan, 2011).

Definitional issues are complicated further by differing positivist and sociological approaches to the definition of crime. The positivist construction centres on conduct defined in law as crime while the sociological perspective of law recognises that crime is behaviour which society deems morally reprehensible, reflecting the values of society. The core contribution of Sutherland's work, for example, was to show that white-collar wrongdoing was a serious form of crime which was not defined or enforced as such by the legal system. Following his lead, criminologists have typically not been concerned with whether or not the wrongdoing was defined in law as a crime, preferring instead to define it as any breach of criminal, civil or administrative law (Box, 1983; Pierce and Tombs, 1998; Schrager and Short; 1977; Tombs, 2005). This approach was taken to overcome labelling issues, whereby powerful corporate players had their breaches of the law classified as somehow less serious than ordinary crime (Pierce and Tombs, 2003). Nevertheless, conceptual difficulties remain as to its unifying core, especially when corporate and white-collar crime involves a whole range of misconduct including financial offences (e.g. false accounting), offences against consumers (e.g. selling adulterated food), offences arising from the employment relationship (e.g. breaches of health and safety laws) and offences against the environment (e.g. pollution), among others (Tombs, 2005). In one instance, urinating in public was added to the list of white-collar crimes because the perpetrators were more likely to be stockbrokers from Manhattan than homeless people (Kahan and Posner, 1999).

Though corporate and white-collar crime is a broad area of inquiry, this monograph is restricted to an analysis of the enforcement of criminal offences in the Companies Acts and matters which have had an impact on their enforcement. This restriction facilitates a manageable but broad-ranging inquiry, rather than a sectoral approach, because the Companies Acts generally apply to all companies and their officers, including banks and their officers. It is also an area of considerable scholarly neglect. When analysing the criminal justice system, criminologists and penologists most frequently analyse 'real' or 'serious' crime (such as homicides and sexual offences) but ignore regulatory crimes that do not capture public imagination and are often enforced by specialised agencies (Campbell, Kilcommins and O'Sullivan, 2010; Hanly, 2006; McAuley and McCutcheon, 2000). Publications on regulatory crime are exceptional (Kilcommins, 2011; Kilcommins and Kilkelly, 2010). Irish company law textbooks document doctrinal legal changes to certain criminal offences, like insider dealing and fraudulent trading but they pay little attention to increased criminalisation or the use of regulatory strategies (Courtney, 2012; Forde and Kennedy, 2008; Keane, 2007). Few articles exist on the issue of corporate enforcement and even these are now dated (Gallagher, 1999; Lynch Fannon, 2002). The study of corporate governance is at an early stage of development in Ireland, particularly by international standards (Brennan, 2010) though some valuable textbooks are starting to emerge on corporate regulation (Cahill, 2008; Connery and Hodnett, 2009). Horan's work, *Corporate Crime* (2011), is an especially valuable and detailed analysis of contemporary corporate legislative provisions. By their nature, however, these books do not occupy the same territory as this monograph because they are reference works aimed at legal practitioners. They do not seek to place changes in a broader jurisprudential or sociological context.

Similarly, most academics researching criminal procedure do not incorporate any discussion on changes in the criminal law through regulatory crime initiatives (Fennell, 2009; Hamilton, 2007; Healy, 2004; McGrath, 2005; O'Malley, 2009; Walsh, 2002). Kilcommins *et al.* (2004: 132) have called for further research in the regulatory area, arguing that 'restricting focus to police-generated crime statistics … ignores the harm and anxiety caused by those against whom police activity is typically not directed, which must surely constitute a large part of the challenge to contemporary society'. Unfortunately, however, this call has gone unanswered and 'much of the literature on white-collar crime continues to be concerned to demonstrate the seriousness and diffuseness of such offending, and to show that its costs and damages dwarf those of conventional or ordinary crime' (Nelkin, 2012: 625). Unlike this project, such work does not analyse the practicalities of enforcement or even acknowledge an emerging new legal architecture.

International research on the sociology of punishment continues to predominantly focus on 'crime in the streets' rather than 'crime in the suites' (Braithwaite, 2003). Nevertheless, there is useful literature on corporate and white-collar crimes (Box, 1983; Fisse and Braithwaite, 1993; Sutherland, 1949). In Ireland, however, it has tended to be preoccupied with 'the punishment of the poor' project (Bacik and O'Connell 1998; McCullagh, 1995, 2002; O'Donnell and O'Sullivan, 2001; O'Mahony, 1998). This literature concentrates on contrasting the preferential manner in which middle-class offenders are treated as compared with those of more limited means. The extent of even this research should not be over-emphasised, however, given that criminology has been an 'absentee discipline' until recently in Ireland (Kilcommins *et al.*, 2004: vii). In addition, this sociological research is, by its nature, non-legal. Though some American scholarship has recognised the increasingly prominent role of regulatory criminal law in society, and the move towards criminalisation and instrumentalism in problem-solving (Mann, 1992), that work does not cover the same terrain as this monograph which employs legal analysis. Moreover, the distinctive contribution of this project is not in the analysis of the nature of corporate or white-collar crimes themselves but rather in its analysis of the emerging new architecture in Ireland that attempts to manage rather than punish corporate wrongdoing. This new system of administering justice uses criminal law to control social relations and yet steps outside paradigmatic criminal law, using regulatory stratagems, to do so as a last resort where monitoring, advice, informal warnings and civil measures have failed.

Regulation is not a new field of inquiry but it 'has long been monopolised by economists with some occasional contributions by students of public administration in the public law tradition' (Baldwin *et al.*, 2010: 4). Political scientists, for example, have produced valuable literature on corruption (Byrne, 2012; Collins and O'Shea, 2000). By its nature, this body of work naturally tends to focus on political wrongdoing rather than business wrongdoing, which is not the subject of this inquiry, though it is considered where it has had an impact on the enforcement of the Companies Acts. Lawyers have been particularly late to arrive on the scene but have benefited enormously from the work completed by others in the social sciences. Consequently, international dialogue has matured beyond 'command and control' versus 'compliance-orientated' models of enforcement. Regulation now is 'responsive' (Ayres and Braithwaite, 1992; Black and Baldwin, 2010), 'smart' (Gunningham and Grabosky, 1999), 'decentred' (Black, 2001), 'supra-national' (Braithwaite and Drahos, 2000), orientated to address 'risk' (Black, 2005), and has also incorporated behavioural economics (Thaler and Sunstein, 2008). Though this international work is useful, it does not map the Irish tradition and the Irish study of regulation is still in its infancy. The first research centre in Governance and Regulation was established at University College Dublin in 2010. Only very recently have Irish scholars discussed the arrival of the 'regulatory State' (Scott, 2008; Vaughan and Kilcommins, 2008), and not without disagreement (Scott, 2010;

Kilcommins and Vaughan, 2010), when such observations had been made somewhat earlier in other jurisdictions (Braithwaite, 1999, 2000; Majone, 1994, 1997; Moran, 2003).

Nevertheless, despite its slow start, the study of regulation is becoming a phenomenon in Ireland. The State advanced a 'Better Regulation' agenda and committed the State to subjecting legislation to a Regulatory Impact Analysis (Department of An Taoiseach, 2004, 2009). However, these latter developments seem more concerned with reducing 'red tape' for business than developing new regulatory technologies. This gives credence to the view that 'regulation is acquired by industry and is designed and operated primarily for its benefit' (Stigler, 1971). Moreover, the public demand for books on corporate and financial crime in Ireland is significant. This is evidenced by contemporary publications on this topic by Cooper (2009, 2011), Ross (2009, 2012), Ross and Webb (2012), O'Toole (2009), Kelly (2012), Lyons and Carey (2011), Carswell (2011), McDonald and Sheridan (2009), Murphy and Devlin (2009), McDonald (2010), Lewis (2011) and Lyons and Curran (2013). Most of this research, however, is anecdotal (O'hOgartaigh, 2011). The sudden surge of interest in regulation in academia, government and journalism lacks a tradition of scholarship or any deep empirical and contextual analysis in Ireland. This book provides that foundation. It is the first dedicated examination of the practice of corporate regulation and enforcement from the foundation of the State to the present day. It provides the definitive case study of a State at a critical stage of its economic development, trying to cope with the negative aspects of increased corporate activity, having experienced an economic boom and depression in a remarkably condensed period of time.

Structure of this project

This monograph does not analyse the emergence of a new regulatory architecture along a linear narrative of progress and rationality. Instead, a socio-legal 'history of the present' is constructed, taking 'an analytical rather than archival' approach to 'understand the historical conditions of existence upon which contemporary practices depend' (Garland, 2001: 2). Legal instruments and regulatory responses are ordered into contrasting traditional and contemporary models, putting shape and order on varied regulatory measures that are sometimes contradictory, incoherent and disordered. Each model is not merely a space of time or state of affairs, but rather a series of problems and questions to be investigated. In the Foucaultian tradition, these regulatory paradigms are packaged as separate mechanisms housing the internal interaction of many moving parts, and then set in juxtaposition to facilitate the search for discontinuities (Foucault, 1991b). This approach may be subject to the criticism that it lends itself to excessive generalisation and simplification but it is necessary to reveal broad structural patterns and new ways of thinking about corporate wrongdoing which would not otherwise be revealed or examined.

The physical structure of this monograph is divided accordingly. Part I (Chapters 1–4) captures the traditional approach to addressing corporate and white-collar crimes in Ireland in the twentieth century. These chapters explain how inertia in corporate affairs supported a legal system that was orientated to addressing 'street crime', the use of inappropriate legal mechanisms to address corporate wrongdoing, and the lack of corporate enforcement. These threads are then drawn together in a brief summary. Part II (Chapters 5–7) explore the emergence of a new logic of action in addressing corporate wrongdoing, grounding this in an analysis of changed ways of thinking about corporate wrongdoing, new legal structures and their enforcement. The monograph then summarises the main threads of the traditional and contemporary approaches and juxtaposes them to capture changed sentiments, legal patterns, continuities and discontinuities that may not otherwise be visible.

Part I

THE TRADITIONAL ARCHITECTURE OF ENFORCEMENT

1

Defining crime: the 'real' crime obsession

Introduction

In December 1985, the Revenue Commissioners commissioned billboards which stated that '[t]ax fiddlers are going to have to face the music'. Rottman and Tormley (1986) observed that the purpose of these billboards was to remind the general public that tax evasion was a criminal offence, a reminder that would not have been necessary for more conventional wrongdoing. Similarly, Box (1983: 1) argued that the public conception of criminality was driven by a fear of conventional or so-called 'real' crimes, like offences against the person and property-related offences. These offences 'form the substance of the annual official criminal statistics ... [and] constitute the major part of "our" crime problem'. This message, he said, was reinforced 'daily by politicians, police, judges and journalists who speak to us through the media of newspapers and television. And most of us listen. We don't want to be murdered, raped, robbed, assaulted or criminally victimised in any other way.' To what extent, however, was the entire Irish legal system, and not just the popular conception of crime, also driven by a 'real' crime perspective?

This chapter illustrates that the Irish courts adopted a positivist approach which tended to define crime in terms of characteristics of 'real crimes'. The characteristics of regulatory crimes, like corporate and white-collar offences, were not sufficiently recognised. By contrast, the European Court of Human Rights (ECtHR) adopted a more progressive approach, asking what kinds of wrongdoing ought to be crimes. In doing so, it was much more willing to recognise both the regulatory and conventional strands within criminal law. Given the increased tendency to employ regulatory initiatives to enforce corporate obligations, discussed later in this monograph, it is especially unfortunate that the definition of crime in Ireland has not grown sufficiently to accommodate corporate wrongs. However, the sociological approach to defining crime clarifies this longstanding marginalisation. It explains that crime must be deemed morally reprehensible by society and that this operated to reflect and reinforce social mores and values at particular points in time (Durkheim, 1964). Irish society was simply more concerned with tackling 'real crimes' than regulatory wrongs and this marginalised corporate wrongdoing from the crime debate.

Defining crime – the procedural and purposive approach

Melling v. *Ó Mathghamhna* ([1962] I.R. 1) was the seminal case defining crime in Ireland. Melling was accused of smuggling butter contrary to section 186 of the Customs Consolidation Act 1876. This was punishable by a £100 fine or a fine in the amount of treble the value of the smuggled goods. If unwilling or unable to pay the fine, offenders could be sentenced to twelve months in jail. Melling claimed that this was a criminal charge so he had the right, under Article 38 of the Constitution, Bunreacht na hÉireann, to trial by jury. The court adopted a strictly neutral and formal approach to crime, described by Kingsmill Moore J. (24), 'as meaning no more than an accusation in proper legal form of having committed a criminal offence'. The judges unanimously held that crime should be defined in accordance with the activities of the criminal courts. Lavery J. (9) emphasised the criminal nature of the proceedings involving detention, examination while in custody, trial, and the imposition of a pecuniary penalty and potential imprisonment. In this respect, the proscribed behaviour must be a crime, according to Kingsmill Moore J. (23), because the offender was treated like a common criminal. Ó Dálaigh J. (48) stated that the procedures specified in the legislation (relating to imprisonment, entry, search and seizure, and withdrawal by *nolle prosequi*) were expressed using 'the vocabulary of the criminal law'. Gathered together, the evidence suggests that the court was defining crime in procedural terms.

In addition, however, the court also stressed the public, expressive and punitive nature of criminal law. Kingsmill Moore J. (25) prioritised the punitive nature of criminal law as a defining characteristic, stating that the indicium of crime is that the 'sanction is punitive and not merely a matter of fiscal reparation'. O'Dalaigh J. (40) also stated that the primary purpose or goal of criminal law was punishment and the primary purpose of civil law was compensation: 'One of the chief characteristics of civil liability (as contrasted with criminal liability) is the obligation to make reparation and, in our times, not to have to suffer imprisonment if unable to make such a reparation.' Furthermore, Lavery J. (17) stated that the primary punishment did not need to be a custodial sentence in order to be punitive. Sanctions that purported to be civil because they merely imposed fines could not continue to pretend they were civil when failure to pay resulted in imprisonment. Moreover, culpability was also emphasised as a significant feature of criminal liability. As observed by the court, criminal offences often require *mens rea*; misbehaviour must be done knowingly with intent to evade the law. While it was noted that *mens rea* may also be an element in civil wrongs, Kingsmill Moore J. (25) emphasised that it was a feature most associated with criminal law, by stating that *mens rea* 'is not a necessary ingredient of a criminal offence ... but where *mens rea* is made an element of an offence it is generally an indication of criminality'.

In *McLoughlin* v. *Tuite* ([1989] I.R. 82), the Supreme Court had to determine whether the failure to provide information to the Revenue Commissioners contrary to sections 500 and 508 of the Income Tax Act was a crime. It echoed the purposive and procedural approaches taken in *Melling*. The court agreed that the primary purpose of the criminal law was to punish the wrongdoer but it unanimously held that the penalty in this case was not a criminal sanction. Finlay C.J. (90) stated that the penalty was not a punishment; it was merely a deterrent or incentive. The court also held that the sanction had none of the procedural characteristics of a criminal offence, as elaborated in *Melling*. In particular, the offender could not be taken into custody or searched for failure to make returns. No question of petitioning the court for bail arose and he could not be imprisoned for failure to pay any penalty imposed by the court. The court also reiterated the emphasis on culpability as a significant element of any criminal offence. The court held that the sanction was civil because it did not require *mens rea*, unlike the criminal offences in the same Act.

The above examination reveals a positivist approach, one that defines a crime as a 'legal wrong that can be followed by legal proceedings which may result in punishment' (Williams, 1955: 107). The courts defined crime in terms of traditional criminal procedures like arrest and imprisonment, the role of the State as prosecutor, the presence of culpability requirements, criminal law as strictly punitive in purpose, the vocabulary used in the construction of the offence, and the severity of the sanctions. These common threads were those most readily associated with conventional criminality. Though this monograph is primarily driven by an Irish perspective, the jurisprudence from the European Court of Human Rights (ECtHR) on the categorisation of sanctions is also instructive in a modern Irish context. Since the enactment of the European Convention on Human Rights Act 2003, the Irish courts must, where possible, construe Irish law in accordance with Articles 6 and 7 of the Convention – the right to a fair trial and the right not to be punished unless for breach of law. An analysis of the ECtHR jurisprudence determining criminality is therefore instructive and is considered below.

The European Court of Human Rights jurisprudence

In *Engel and Others* v. *The Netherlands* ((1979) 1 E.H.R.R. 647), the European Court of Human Rights had to determine whether military disciplinary proceedings involving arrest and detention were criminal in nature because they resulted in serious punishments including the deprivation of liberty. The court, emphasising its supranational or 'autonomous' approach to defining crime, noted that while the categorisation of offences under national law was helpful, more relevant factors were the nature of the proscribed conduct, and the nature and potential severity of the penalty. The court, no doubt influenced both by the procedures involving arrest and detention and their punitive purpose, stated that the disciplinary sanctions 'did indeed come within the "criminal" sphere since their aim was the imposition of serious punishments involving the deprivation of liberty' (para. 85).

The criteria used by the court in *Engel* were developed in *Benham* v. *United Kingdom* ((1996) 22 E.H.R.R. 293). The applicant was subject to a 'community charge' of £325. He did not have sufficient assets to satisfy the debt so the local authority sought a purportedly civil order from the magistrate's court committing him to prison on the basis that his failure to pay was due to wilful refusal or culpable neglect. This was granted and the applicant was imprisoned for thirty days. The ECtHR held that the nature of the proceedings and the potential severity of the penalty were persuasive evidence that the applicant was charged with a criminal offence. On the nature of proceedings, the court noted that the law was of general applicability to all citizens and enforceable by a public authority using statutory enforcement mechanisms. The court also emphasised that the applicant had to be found culpable to be subjected to the imposition of a custodial sentence. Finally, the court stated that the potential severity of the penalty (potentially up to three months imprisonment) also indicated the criminal nature of the sanction.

Once again, a number of common threads are visible in these judgments, relating to the nature of proceedings and the nature of the potential penalty imposed. Summarising these threads, Ashworth (2006: 3) suggested that misbehaviour was considered a crime if a public authority brought proceedings; the wrongdoer was found culpable; and if the finding of wrongdoing resulted in potentially severe consequences, like imprisonment or a significant financial penalty for the wrongdoer. Expressed in this manner, the approach of the ECtHR shares remarkable similarities with that adopted by the Irish courts, which also emphasised the central role of the State, culpability and severity of penalties, among other things. The European Court has, however, gone further than the Irish courts in recent case law. We therefore turn our attention to this jurisprudence which recognises regulatory crime as an important feature in the landscape of the criminal law.

In *Ozturk* v. *Germany* ((1984) 6 E.H.R.R. 409), the ECtHR re-examined the categorisation of civil and criminal behaviour in light of 'regulatory' road traffic offences. The German authorities contended that they had decriminalised road traffic offences and moved them into the civil sphere. The court, following *Engel*, distinguished criminal from civil offences using purposive and procedural techniques similar to those employed by the Irish courts. It found that the procedures and purposes of the regulatory sanctions had not substantially changed since the supposed 'decriminalisation'. The new form of regulatory punishment did not actually exclude the potential for imprisonment, for example, because a failure to pay the fine imposed by the German court could have resulted in the imposition of a custodial sentence. The court held that the regulatory sanctions were criminal offences because 'the rule of law infringed by the applicant has, for its part, undergone no change of content' (para. 53).

This analysis was important because it illustrated that obvious attempts to re-brand criminal offences as civil sanctions would not be tolerated. Classifying an offence as 'regulatory' instead of criminal did not in itself operate to evade the rights of accused persons in criminal proceedings. However, it also merely reaffirmed the ideas previously endorsed by both the Irish and European courts. This case would be of limited use, then, except that the court went further than *Engel* and illustrated a more sophisticated analysis of regulation and punishment. In particular, the court appeared to make a number of submissions which could free regulatory criminality from the straitjacket of conventional crime. The court appeared to acknowledge that the criminal law has a regulatory aspect to its character. By stating that the separation of regulatory and criminal law in Germany was not an absolute partition, nor was it in many other States, the court therefore rejected the assumption, often relied upon but never fully justified in the Irish courts, that criminal law was defined by conventional criminality (para. 51). In addition, unlike the Irish courts, the ECtHR did not separate criminal and civil sanctions into mutually exclusive categories of punishment and deterrence. In doing so, the court recognised that sanctions do not only pursue one objective or the other. If law sought primarily to deter rather than punish behaviour, this did not automatically make it a civil sanction.

By making this observation, the court acknowledged that the criminal law also had a compliance-orientated layer to its composition. As with the regulatory sanctions in the case at hand, it recognised that criminal offences could pursue a number of objectives, both punishment and deterrence, for example, and were not any less criminal in character for this. Furthermore, the court suggested that criminality was not necessarily determined by the potential level of the penalty applied. It noted that a relatively low penalty 'cannot divest an offence of its inherently criminal character' (para. 54). Regulatory, compliance-orientated legal sanctions were still crimes, even though such sanctions often only subjected wrongdoers to small monetary fines. Finally, despite the commonly held view that criminal law reflected the moral judgment of the community, the court suggested that stigmatisation of the offender was not the defining characteristic of a criminal offence (para. 53). Commentators often justified lower procedural rights for wrongdoers accused of regulatory offences on the basis that the offences did not stigmatise them, and therefore that they were not truly criminal. By recognising that crime was not determined by reference to stigma, it could be suggested that the European Court was potentially paving the way for a more appropriate recognition of regulatory crime.

The progressive moves made by the court in *Ozturk* were confirmed in *Bendenoun* v. *France* ((1994) 18 E.H.R.R. 54). The French government submitted that charges for failure to pay tax were civil in nature, based on arguments related to the traditional role of the State and the nature and severity of the sanction. The court dismissed these submissions. It advanced a broader conception of criminality encompassing aspects of both conventional and regulatory criminal justice. The court suggested that the offence was criminal because it was a law that applied to all citizens as taxpayers, not a discrete class of a certain status, and because the State imposed penalties for non-compliance. The court emphasised that the important point was not just who enforced the offence but whom it could be enforced against. This could arguably be seen as a movement away from the view that criminal offences must be prosecuted by some sort of centralised state authority. Given that regulatory offences can often be enforced by numerous specialised agencies, rather than a single centralised agency, this approach is potentially broader than the traditional Irish position which often made the role of the State as prosecutor central to the determination of criminality. Furthermore, the court built upon the recognition in *Ozturk* that criminal law sanctions can pursue diverse objectives. The court suggested that the sanctions in question did not pursue the civil law goal of compensation but instead were a 'punishment to deter reoffending' (para. 47). In doing so, the court identified compensation as a civil law characteristic but reclaimed the objective of deterrence for the criminal law. It placed it alongside that of punishment, thereby incorporating aspects of both conventional and regulatory models into a framework of the criminal law, while also distinguishing it from civil law. Finally, on the severity of sanctions issue, the court clarified the flipside of *Ozturk*. While a low financial penalty would not strip the sanction of its criminal nature, substantial fines, in this case almost one million French francs, were an indication of criminality. If failure to pay the fine could result in a secondary punishment of imprisonment, then this also indicated criminality.

The jurisprudence from the ECtHR provides another interpretative layer to defining crime. While taking its own autonomous approach, it echoed, to some degree, the approaches taken in Irish law. It also defined crime in terms of the characteristics of 'real' crimes, emphasising the central role of the State, culpability and the severity of punishment. However, it seemed more willing to recognise that regulatory wrongs could also be crimes, that there was a regulatory strand to the criminal law, and that those accused of such crimes deserved the relevant legal protections which accompanied a criminal charge. This approach was a significant departure from the foundational jurisprudence in Ireland which tended not to fully recognise the characteristics of regulatory crimes in an older analysis of criminality. Therefore, the question naturally arises as to whether the courts were more willing to do so in more recent cases concerning regulatory sanctions. The next section explores whether a fresh perspective emerged in relation to sanctions that seek to enhance and secure corporate enforcement.

The Irish jurisprudence on commercial regulatory wrongdoing

Sutherland (1940, 1949) was among the first to question whether corporate wrongs were crimes or merely breaches of the civil law. Nelkin also noted that it seemed to 'straddle the crucial boundary between criminal and non-criminal behaviour' (Nelkin, 2007: 741). This issue was addressed by the Irish Superior Courts in *O'Keeffe* v. *Ferris* ([1993] 3 I.R. 165 (High Court); [1997] 3 I.R. 463 (Supreme Court)). The liquidator took civil proceedings against Ms O'Keeffe for fraudulent trading to make her liable for the debts of the company. On its face, the Companies Act 1963 appeared to impose a mixture of civil and criminal liability for fraudulent trading, albeit in separate subsections. Section 297(1) imposed civil liability for all debts of the company where the defendant traded with intent to defraud creditors and section 297(3) imposed criminal liability for conduct 'for such purpose as is mentioned in subsection (1)'. Though lawyers for the defence had argued that section 297(1) was a 'criminal offence dressed up as a tort' (172), Murphy J. in the High Court decided that the sanction specified in section 297(1) did not display any of the *indicia* of a criminal offence and that the liquidator could appropriately pursue persons by civil proceedings. He advanced seven grounds to illustrate that the offence was civil: (1) the State was not taking proceedings and was not directly injured by the wrongful activity; (2) criminal procedures such as *nolle prosequi* were not present; (3) the presence of *mens rea* was not conclusive evidence of criminality; (4) unlike ordinary criminal wrongs punishable on committing the offence, this wrong was only punishable following liquidation; (5) the vocabulary of criminal law was not used (specifically the words: conviction, imprisonment, fine, summary proceedings, and indictment); (6) the applicant did not need to be the creditor defrauded because the legislature intended the statute to allow for a class action suit (i.e. the liquidator or individual creditor could sue to recover money for the benefit of all creditors); and (7) the legislature did not intend to create a criminal offence.

The plaintiff appealed the decision to the Supreme Court, submitting 'that the [civil] proceedings [taken under section 297(1)] in substance and in fact are clearly of a criminal nature, impose criminal sanctions and bear all the hallmarks of criminal charges' (470). As such, the proceedings taken were inconsistent with the constitutional requirement under Article 38.1 that criminal charges be tried in due course of law.

Ussher (1986) had already noted previously that the legislation did not create civil liability in the usual sense. It created new liabilities rather than enforcing existing ones, did not enforce private rights, the applicant did not need to be the creditor defrauded, and any money recovered did not necessarily compensate the actual victim of the fraud. In short, he suggested (525) that it did not 'bear the hallmark of civil proceedings', was 'in essence punitive', 'in substance criminal', and that the relevant constitutional protections should apply. On this basis, the defence argued that while the impugned section did not itself create criminal liability, it did seek to 'impose the badge of criminality' using civil burdens of proof in the civil jurisdiction of the court (471). Nevertheless, notwithstanding the language of the offence proscribing wrongdoing, the presence of *mens rea* and the punitive purpose of the sanction, O'Flaherty J., delivering the sole judgment of the Supreme Court, held that the offence did not display the *indicia* of crime, as constructed in *Melling*. Specifically, the court pointed to the lack of a criminal prosecutor, criminal offence, criminal trial and criminal sanction. The narrow focus of the court to the more ostentatious, outward shows of criminality may not be entirely convincing. The court failed to consider that if the legislature were attempting to hide a 'wolfish' criminal offence in 'sheepish' civil clothing, they would be unlikely to call it a criminal offence, have the Director of Public Prosecutions (DPP) prosecute it, try it in front of a jury and imprison the offender. Curiously, the High Court acknowledged that if the offence was a criminal sanction, given the sums of money involved, it would have been considered a serious criminal offence, triable on indictment, and the guilt of the accused determined by a jury of peers. In this respect, it seems unusual that it was not a criminal offence at all, when its effect was so serious, far-reaching and punitive that it had the potential to be an indictable criminal offence. Indeed, given that the ECtHR indicated that subjecting a wrongdoer to a substantial financial fine is a strong indication of criminality, it is particularly surprising that the Supreme Court did not consider the issue.

The Supreme Court stated that avoiding high levels of procedural safeguards by defining this wrong as civil was justified because the court had to balance the protection of the public from fraudulent trading with the rights of citizens not to suffer injustice in the course of proceedings. This argument could, however, be offered for avoiding procedural safeguards for any misbehaviour that affects the public. It is an analysis that fails to appreciate that the rights of the accused and procedural safeguards are institutionalised under an equality of arms framework to protect individuals from the power of the State. These rights act as 'trumps' over policy decisions made by government in the name of public protection (Dworkin, 1987, 1998). Finally, contrary to previous case law, the court acknowledged that a punitive purpose is not the determinative factor in assessing criminality. Punitive damages may, for example, be civilly awarded. The fact that a wrongdoer may have to repay more than she received from fraudulent trading is not in itself materially different from punitive damages and is not unconstitutional. All of this suggests that the Irish superior courts have shown some considerable reluctance to categorise misbehaviours raising jurisdictional ambiguities under the Companies Acts as crimes.

Similarly, in *Registrar of Companies* v. *Judge David Anderson and System Partners Limited* ([2005] 1 I.R. 21), the Supreme Court held that late filing penalties imposed for the failure to file annual accounts with the Registrar of Companies were administrative or civil sanctions that deterred rather than punished wrongdoers. Therefore, the subsequent criminal prosecution for the same wrongdoing did not trigger the rule against double jeopardy. Though *Anderson* was probably correctly decided on its facts, the reasoning of the court was a missed opportunity, both to take on board some of the views of the ECtHR and to rework the criteria provided in *Melling*. Such an approach could have provided real guidance on the nature of regulatory crime and located its place within criminal law more generally. Unfortunately, this did not happen. The Supreme Court drew a sharp two-fold distinction between sanctions as either civil or criminal (in the conventional crime sense). It held that an administrative sanction (civil) and a criminal sanction were distinguishable on the grounds that: (a) administrative sanctions did not involve criminal procedures; and (b) they attempted to achieve legitimate administrative goals through deterrence rather than punishment. With regard to the first limb of the distinction, Murray C.J. (26) held that 'the statutory requirement to pay late filing fees is not in any sense something which involves a criminal process let alone a criminal prosecution'. The court, much like in *Melling*, emphasised that criminal offences involved criminal procedures and processes but that criminal procedures were not manifest in this case and no analogy could be drawn between an increased fee on one hand and imprisonment for default of a fine on another. This logic was circular. The fewer procedural protections given to the alleged offender, the less likely the sanction is to be criminal so the less likely that the court would determine that such procedural protections are necessary. The court also stated that the misbehaviour could not be criminal because the criminal courts were not involved in any determination of the issue. Surely, however, the issue was whether they should be brought within the criminal processes of the courts, not merely to identify the current procedures already in place?

With regard to the second limb, Murray C.J. (26) stated that the late filing penalty was an administrative sanction 'that does not have as its purpose the punishment of an offence but the achievement of a legitimate administrative objective'. Geoghegan J. (29) also emphasised that the sanction is administrative because the motivation for the increased fee was deterrence rather than punishment. Once again, therefore, this involved the strict prioritisation of punishment as the purpose of criminal law. Other objectives (such as reparation, deterrence, and rehabilitation) were marginalised and assumed to be civil law goals. It was also a surprising statement, since it did not appear to conform to the views of the ECtHR that criminal law pursued a number of objectives and did not need to be exclusively punitive in order to be a criminal offence. In more concrete terms, this meant that if in the case at hand, the fines were primarily used to deter wrongful behaviour (late filing of company papers) but still had a punitive element (say, as in *Bendenoun*, by imposing a disproportionately large fee), then contrary to the views of the Supreme Court, this sanction could be considered a criminal offence. Curiously, however, the court did not agree on the categorisation of the sanction if the penalty was excessive and disproportionate to the administrative objective that it sought to achieve. Murray C.J. (26) held that in these circumstances it could be in substance, if not in form, a criminal penalty and he appeared to suggest that the punitive nature and effect of the sanction was a more significant signpost of criminality than the surrounding procedures. By contrast, Geoghegan J. (30) held that though unfair, it would still not be a criminal penalty. The third member of the court, Hardiman J., did not resolve the issue. Instead, he stated that he agreed with both of his colleagues and did not deliver a judgment of his own. The court therefore avoided the thorny issue of when a sanction stops deterring and actually starts to become punitive.

The approaches in both *O'Keeffe* and *Anderson* on corporate misbehaviours and regulatory sanctions seem to reflect and reinforce the approaches in the foundational Irish jurisprudence defining crime. The courts continued to cite *Melling* and have adopted the indicia most associated with conventional crime. Even in regulatory contexts, the Irish courts continued to emphasise traditional criminal characteristics such as arrest and imprisonment, the role of the State as prosecutor, criminal law as strictly punitive in purpose, and the vocabulary used in the construction of the offence. Furthermore, the failure to agree on whether an excessive penalty indicates criminality reflected the court's unwillingness to go beyond the bounds of the positivist, procedural and purposive approach which it used. Unlike the ECtHR, it remained reluctant to address what behaviour ought to be criminal. In general, the courts failed to escape the tautological positivist approach and failed to situate regulatory crime properly within the criminal law (McGrath, 2010).

The marginalisation of regulatory crime

Melling restricted the definition of crime to wrongdoing which bears the more obvious characteristics of crime. Nevertheless, it was consistently cited as an authority and remained the seminal case defining crime. Consequently, Irish jurisprudence failed to fully recognise that the criminal law was a rope of two interwoven strands. The first strand, which was recognised by the Irish courts, was the expressive, symbolic, moral judgement that reflects community values and which inflicts punishment and just deserts on offenders. The second neglected strand was regulatory, instrumental and utilitarian (Lacey, 2003; Lacey *et al.*, 2003). This aspect of the criminal law was often compliance-orientated (criminal law used as a last resort stratagem), aimed to deter offenders to prevent a repeat performance of prohibited conduct, and relied on fines to compensate for wrongdoing – features which the courts more readily associated with civil law. Regulatory crimes also shared procedural characteristics, like being enforced on the basis of strict liability by bureaucratic agencies in the lower courts (Cartwright, 2001; Ramsay, 2007).

Nevertheless, regulatory crime was not a precisely defined concept in Irish law, nor was there a rich common law history in the area. Regulatory and conventional crimes were often distinguished on the basis that the former addressed behaviour which was *mala in se* (inherently wrong) while the latter was *mala prohibita* (merely prohibited). Farmer (1996) explained that this distinction arose from industrialisation in the nineteenth and twentieth centuries when society became more concerned with regulating minor misbehaviours than protecting sovereign power. Certain forms of misbehaviour (snaring game without authority, unlawfully marketing potatoes) were only technically illegal and punished for consequential reasons (mainly to process large numbers of cases quickly and efficiently). Unlike conventional crimes, which were thought to be intrinsically immoral, misbehaviour designated as *mala prohibita* was criminal because the authorities deemed it so and attached a certain procedure to its enforcement. However, this categorisation was problematic. It suggested that regulatory crime was less morally serious, just because it attracted different enforcement mechanisms and procedures. As Wells (2001: 7) observed: 'Morals are historically and culturally contingent; what appears to lie behind the "true" crime/"quasi" crime distinction is an unarticulated argument that, if an activity was not traditionally a matter for the criminal law, then it cannot achieve the status of the "true" crime.'

Conduct is not necessarily moral or immoral, however, just because it is punishable by a particular procedure and not all regulatory offences are addressed as minor matters or punished with small penalties (Mokhiber, 1989). If the Irish courts continue to define crime on the basis of the procedures with which they are enforced, without reflecting on whether the misbehaviour ought to be criminal, then some regulatory offences may not be receiving their appropriate status as 'true' crimes and may be relegated on the basis of ancient procedure, predicated on outdated views. Irish criminal law seems less willing to recognise regulatory crimes, particularly corporate and white-collar crimes, even though it can be argued that society is more willing to recognise the potential harmfulness of corporate irresponsibility to a greater degree than ever before (discussed later). When changed sentiments are not followed by updated procedures and punishments, it can create a lag in what is considered crime. The failure of law to keep up with new moral sentiments by not recategorising certain regulatory wrongdoing as now truly criminal reflects how classifications of *mala in se* and *mala prohibita* are artificially mapped on to legal doctrine to justify particular conceptions and categorisations which may no longer hold true (Lacey, 2007).

In addition to marginalising regulatory crime using procedural distinctions, the purposive approach, whereby misbehaviour is categorised according to the purpose the sanction is trying to achieve, is also inappropriate. The Irish jurisprudence has drawn a stark distinction between criminal and civil sanctions, suggesting that criminal offences are primarily, if not exclusively, punitive while civil sanctions pursue other objectives such as compensation and deterrence. However, criminal offences may also pursue a number of other goals: deterrence, prevention, retribution, just deserts, compensation and reparation. If these objectives are neglected and criminal law is substantially equated with punishment, then it could be suggested that if any provision in the Companies Acts sought to do more than punish an offender, primarily by pursuing compliance-orientated goals, it may not be a crime and is more likely to be classified as a civil offence. The theoretical difficulties aside, it is also complex in practice for the courts to draw a bright-line distinction between punishment and other objectives. For example, in a British fraudulent trading case, *Re a company* ([1991] B.C.L.C. 197), Judge Bromley QC held that the sanction, though civil, also contained a punitive element. He ordered that the wayward director pay £131,420 in compensation and £25,000 as punishment. In reality, it is not difficult to see, regardless of the terminology used, which element really punished him and which was the lesser burden to bear. This must surely raise issues as to whether it is possible to draw bright-line distinctions between punitive criminal offences and supposedly non-punitive civil sanctions. As McGrath (2010: 53) has observed, 'it is not unreasonable to recognise that criminal law is a sanctioning process that punishes offenders but it must be doubted whether criminal law has a monopoly on punishment'.

If the point is taken that punishment is not exclusively a criminal law objective but that its presence may still indicate that wrongdoers deserve the protections of the criminal law, how does this affect regulatory mechanisms that are jurisdictionally ambiguous? The Irish courts suggested that a sanction could be criminal in nature if it was punitive. This is determined by the severity of the sanction and the potential to imprison the wrongdoer. However, it was also suggested that the punitive nature of a sanction could be determined by how stigmatised the wrongdoer was and its effect on his ability to earn a living. When these factors are considered, it is difficult to see why civil orders like restriction and disqualification do not fall within the criminal jurisdiction of the court. In *Tralee Beef and Lamb Ltd (In Liquidation) Kavanagh* v. *Delaney and ors* ([2008] 3 I.R. 347), the Irish Supreme Court described restriction, which prohibits a person from being involved in the management of a company for five years, as highly stigmatising and gravely damaging to the reputation of the restricted person. Though it was an opinion held by a minority, it has been suggested that disqualification from acting as a company director is a penal sanction (Dine, 1995). Even if it is denied that disqualification is a penal order, it was accepted that it was akin to a sentencing process (*Re Westmid Packing Services Ltd (No. 3)* [1998] B.C.C. 836: 837). Therefore, it could certainly be questioned why punishment is the primary purpose of criminal law when certain punitive regulatory sanctions with limited procedural safeguards are often deemed civil in nature. In drawing attention to the potentially punitive and stigmatising effects of civil sanctions, an argument is not being made that such orders are necessarily criminal sanctions but merely that punitiveness and stigma are not always appropriate factors to distinguish regulatory initiatives from criminal and civil law.

In addition, the Irish courts emphasised culpability as a meaningful precondition to criminal liability. In *Melling*, the court stated that *mens rea* was a significant but not definitive indication of criminality. In *Tuite*, the absence of *mens rea* was also a particularly convincing factor to indicate that the provision was a civil sanction. The traditional emphasis on culpability was understandable given that strict liability was more associated with ancient criminal law, when guilt was determined on the basis of the ability of the accused to engage in battle or survive some torturous ordeal (Sayre, 1932). Now, however, criminal guilt is associated with moral blameworthiness and there is a broad legal emphasis on culpability as an inherent 'general principle' of good law (Lacey, 2007). This legal emphasis was evidenced by the fact that the legal maxim *actus non facit reum nisi mens sit rea* has been 'repeated with unbroken cadence' for centuries (Sayre, 1932: 974), and by a presumption in favour of *mens rea* in all criminal offences, unless it was the intention of legislature to impose strict liability (*People (DPP)* v. *Murray* [1977] I.R. 360). As a result of the dominance of culpability requirements, offences not requiring *mens rea* were often regarded as 'not criminal in any real sense but are acts which in the public interest are prohibited under a penalty' (*Sherras* v. *DeRutzen* [1895] 1 Q.B. 918: 922).

Academics have agreed that strict liability 'is now very much the exception to the rule of liability based on fault' (McAuley and McCutcheon, 2000: 313). Nevertheless, despite its uncertain and exceptional status, the empirical dominance of strict liability offences was often greater than conceded (Blake and Ashworth, 1996; JUSTICE, 1980). This led a number of commentators to raise doubts about the centrality of intention to criminal liability (Zedner, 2004: 61). Despite this warning, the Irish courts have continued to emphasise the role of culpability in defining crime. They neglected to consider the role that was played by regulatory criminal law, often enforced on the basis of strict liability, particularly with regard to enforcing legal duties in the corporate context (Wells, 2001: 67–70). Indeed, it may be the case that the failure to recognise that many corporate offences are enforced on the basis of strict liability means that those offences are automatically more likely to be classed as non-criminal. Even recently, where regulatory criminal law is a prominent feature of the criminal law landscape, Geoghegan J. in *Anderson* ([2005] 1 I.R. 21: 30) only grudgingly acknowledged that criminal offences do not always require *mens rea* and still reverted to the traditional position finding that the outward show of criminality must be satisfied.

On the importance of recognising both regulatory and conventional crime, Lacey *et al.* (2003: 5) stated that it was 'crucial to a proper understanding of criminal law to see that it has these two aspects, and that the balance and interaction between them is a key to its historical development and contemporary social significance'. The Irish courts have had difficulties locating the regulatory aspect because it existed somewhere on a continuum between criminal and civil law. Up to now, the courts had only juxtaposed conventional criminal law with civil law when defining crime. They needed to contrast regulatory crime with conventional crime but also regulatory crime with civil sanctions, which was never done. The definitional problems were exacerbated by the use of regulatory mechanisms in 'real' crime contexts and by the use of both criminal and civil mechanisms, expressed in almost identical statutory language, to address the same wrongdoing, as in *O'Keefe*. Ashworth suggested that this unprincipled approach demonstrates 'a blurring of the boundaries between criminal and regulatory and between criminal and civil' and makes the criminal law a 'lost cause' (Ashworth, 2000).

Drawing a bright-line distinction between regulatory and other types of legal mechanisms might be a particularly difficult task but that is not to say that an effort should not be made to understand the nature and characteristics of regulatory criminal law, to study why it is becoming an increasingly prominent tool of enforcement and, in the context of defining crime, to revisit the *Melling* criteria. Unfortunately, tracing the appropriate contours of regulatory crime, and locating its relationship with existing jurisdictional spheres will not be achieved if crime continues to be defined using a positivist lens. This approach defines crime in terms of itself, through procedures, objectives and other characteristics. Viewed through this lens, the positivist approach is a post-hoc rationalisation and tautological because 'it describes form but provides little insight into the substantive make-up of criminal conduct, i.e. how and why particular conduct is designated as a criminal offence' (Campbell *et al.*, 2010: 5). In an effort to fully understand the limits of the positivist approach and understand why the Irish legal system has marginalised regulatory crime from the definition of crime in criminal law, this chapter now turns its attention to the sociological construction of crime.

Explaining marginalisation: the social construction of crime

The sociological approach explains that crime is constructed according the prevailing political and social norms (Morrison, 2013). Social interactions, public perceptions, and community responses are key to understanding this construction of crime. Crime is a label which 'only really exists when there is a social response to particular activity that labels that activity as criminal' (White and Haines, 2000: 4–5). In order for something to be labelled deviant or criminal, some enterprising person, often a moral crusader or someone motivated by self-interest, must take the initiative to publicly identify the behaviour as wrongful and criminal (Becker, 1991). This goes some way to explaining why regulatory crimes and corporate misbehaviours were marginalised from the crime debate. As noted in the Report of the Company Law Reform Committee, authored by Cox (1958: 20), Irish society regarded offences in the Companies Acts as merely 'trivial or technical' rather than criminal, so there was no social response labelling corporate misbehaviours as criminal. Some have reasoned that this is because corporate wrongs tend to lack readily identifiable victims, rendering them 'invisible' or 'victimless' crimes (Box, 1983). Others have pointed to a lack of political will to address corporate wrongdoing, especially when it could inhibit direct foreign investment (Mitchell, 2001). Another significant factor in this marginalisation is that media coverage often focuses on conventional crimes. Even when the media does cover corporate wrongdoing, it is sensationalised and therefore seen as exceptional or it fails to attribute responsibility for it, preferring to describe it instead as an accident or a disaster (Gobert, 1994: 394). Perhaps the most significant factor in the marginalisation of regulatory and corporate wrongdoing from the crime debate is the public conception of who constitutes a criminal. Criminals lurk down dark alleys and perpetrate violence on innocent victims; they are not respectable hardworking executives who generally typify the hopes and aspirations of the middle classes (Croall, 1992). As Kilcommins *et al.* (2004: 102) surmise: 'Society tends to be more concerned about the potential harms caused by drug addicts wielding knives or syringes than by businessmen signing dodgy deals.'

Such techniques of marginalisation help to confirm the public assumption that those who hold privilege and power are honest. The positivist construction of crime fails to consider the role that powerful people, such as captains of industry, play in determining whether something becomes a crime in the first place. Norrie (2001) reveals that regulatory mechanisms departing from traditional criminal law values evolved when systems for inspecting factories were being developed. The structural location of factory owners as powerful and well-respected members of society made it very difficult for inspectors and prosecutors to prove fault before judges who were the factory owners' peers. It was also too easy for a factory owner to deny that he was involved in the wrongdoing when he could show that an employee had committed the fault in question. Regulatory crime emerged when: 'The practical problem of proof merged with the general ideological problem of prosecuting factory owners … The presentation of the offence as 'regulatory' or 'strict' permitted the subtle negotiation of the criminal label … to provide some mode of regulation, however ineffective, of respectable men' (86). So regulatory crime in one sense emerged to enforce laws against powerful individuals but it also helped serve their interests by refusing to label them as 'true' criminals. The 'general part' of the criminal law was reserved for the lower classes that were rigorously policed, while elites were cajoled, advised and persuaded to obey the law with the 'special part' of the criminal law that was rarely enforced (104). In general, as observed by Foucault, the criminal law was designed to punish the poor, stating, 'it would be hypocritical or naïve to believe that the law was made for all in the name of all; that it would be more prudent to recognize that it was made for the few and that it was brought to bear upon others' (1991b: 276).

The sociological approach explains that corporate wrongs are less likely to be considered crimes because there is a perception that they are less harmful than conventional crimes and because of the historical role that particular powerful interests played in corporate enforcement. Legal classifications then reinforce this social perception. Real crimes, like violent assaults and sexual offences, were actively investigated by the police and addressed by the criminal courts. By contrast, corporate misbehaviours were rarely subject to official criminal justice responses in the same way as conventional crimes. For example, the *Report of the Working Group in Company Law Compliance and Enforcement*, authored by McDowell (1998), noted that most criminal offences in the Company Acts had never been prosecuted. In more recent times, when corporate deviancy has been addressed, the preferred techniques was civil orders or regulatory offences enforced by specialised agencies (Vaughan and Kilcommins, 2008: 138–46). Therefore, corporate wrongs were marginalised from crime debates because they were not considered especially harmful and were not addressed by the same machinery as serious crimes. This reinforced the view that they were less harmful than ordinary crimes and that they should continue to be treated differently. Commentators building on this analysis suggested that such perceptions were reinforced again by the under-resourcing of enforcement agencies, through compliance-orientated strategies which reflected a lack of moral condemnation, and by rarely placing white-collar deviants in the public spotlight, as in courts, where they had to explain their behaviour (McCullagh, 1995).

Conclusion

The Irish courts defined crime in narrow terms. They held that the indicia of crimes are traditional criminal procedures like arrest and imprisonment, the State as prosecutor, the requirement of culpability, the vocabulary employed to construct offences, the severity of the penalties, and whether or not they serve a punitive purpose. These matters were more readily associated with conventional crimes than regulatory crimes. Regulatory crimes did not necessarily employ the usual criminal law procedures. For example, they could be underpinned by strict liability mechanisms rather than subjective culpability requirements, were not necessarily punished by periods of imprisonment and could be enforced by specialist regulatory agencies rather than a centralised State prosecutor. They could be designed to deter wrongdoing instead of punishing it. In addition to emphasising traditional criminal characteristics, the courts have sharply delineated sanctions as either criminal or civil. Given that regulatory crimes often shared characteristics most associated with the civil jurisdiction of law, a rigid two-fold classification made regulatory crimes more likely to be categorised as civil wrongdoing. Furthermore, the doctrinal approach taken by the Irish courts, whereby crimes were defined in procedural and purposive terms, was an attempt to define criminal law in terms of itself and was therefore tautological. This approach marginalised corporate wrongdoing, often underpinned by regulatory strategies, from the crime debate.

A fresh perspective on this issue emerged from the ECtHR. While it initially seemed to merely emphasise the foundational jurisprudence from the Irish courts, it seemed more willing to move beyond this approach in disputes regarding less conventional crimes. It seemed more willing to ask what misbehaviours ought to be crimes and what procedural protections individuals should have in these circumstances. The ECtHR has shown a greater willingness to recognise the regulatory strand within the criminal law. It did not strictly characterise crimes as morally reprehensible wrongs or emphasise the criminal law as overwhelmingly punitive in purpose. In Ireland, this approach has not yet fully surfaced. In part, this is because the public perception of crime was also largely driven by a 'real' crime perspective. Regulatory wrongs continued to be marginalised from the crime debate because these misbehaviours were rarely subject to official responses from the criminal justice system. Gathered together, existing sentiments and official responses reinforced the legal approach to the definition of crime. As observed by McGrath (2010: 60–1), 'there must be a greater awareness that the conventional crime model is not a universal crime model. *Melling* and the cases following it speak to real crime, so attempting to make the conventional crime *indicia* fit into regulatory contexts is inappropriate. The jurisprudence needs to be re-evaluated and a new approach needs to be found.'

2

Protectionism and procrastination: the era of inertia in corporate affairs

Introduction

In the last chapter, the issue of regulatory crime was analysed through the lens of doctrinal legal definition. It was shown that the Irish legal system adopted a narrow legal definition of crime, orientated to prioritise conventional crime and one that marginalised corporate wrongdoing from this analysis. This chapter shows that the failure to develop a jurisprudence incorporating corporate wrongdoing into the architecture of the criminal law was premised on a political and social inertia surrounding corporate affairs for most of the twentieth century. It is shown that addressing corporate wrongdoing was not considered a significant issue in an agrarian state, with relatively low levels of corporate activity, where the public was more concerned with job creation than crime, particularly corporate and white-collar crime. It describes the particular framework of social, political and economic factors that led to the marginalisation of corporate affairs within the legal system, thereby giving contextual flesh to the bones of the legal argument made in Chapter 1.

Assumptions, strategy choices and discourses are gathered as evidence and forged together to reveal the particular mindset or 'logic of action' that drove Ireland's approach to corporate wrongdoing for much of the twentieth century. It prompted a distinctive architectural pattern of provisions, policy transfer strategies and enforcement choices. It explains why the criminal law was used to address corporate deviancy, without the appropriate reflection as to whether a model of justice addressing conventional crime was appropriate to the corporate setting. It also explains why liability was structured according to conventional criminal methods and why these criminal law provisions were so under-enforced.

Capturing all of the elements of this configuration would be impossible in this chapter alone. Accordingly, the effectiveness of this architecture and its enforcement are given specific attention in Chapters 3 and 4. This chapter is limited to capturing the mentality underpinning the traditional approach and how this has impacted on policy choices. Though critically descriptive rather than archival, a large amount of information is analysed. By necessity, capturing the political, social and economic momentum of a century of legal history involves some generalisation. Opinions, priorities and legal responses may vary and shift. Discontinuities may occasionally appear. The transition from the traditional to the contemporary approach addressing corporate wrongdoing at the turn of the twenty-first century was not a seamless one; difficulties naturally arise when legal trends are pigeonholed into one period in a particular timescale. Therefore, any features which may more accurately reflect the emerging contemporary approach have been reserved for discussion in Part II of this monograph. Despite these qualifications, however, this chapter is necessary because it attempts to capture the particular character, momentum and personality of the traditional period. It teases out the interaction of social and legal forces, interpenetrating fields that inform each other in ways that are rarely acknowledged, let alone articulated.

Company law in the 'peasant economy'

English legislation substantially influenced the shape and direction of Irish company law. Prior to 1922, all Irish company law was enacted by the British Parliament. It enacted a variety of Companies Acts to regulate the corporate sector and these were eventually consolidated into the Companies (Consolidation) Act 1908. A number of other British Acts enacted prior to Irish independence, and one Irish statute, made some minor additions to the Irish corporate framework in the early 1900s. In essence, however, the 1908 Act was 'for Irish lawyers the bedrock of company law for over half a century' (Keane, 1985: 15). With the exception of a report in 1927 on winding up companies and bankruptcy procedures, a report which was not implemented by the Irish Parliament, Irish company law, as embodied by the 1908 Act, did not undergo any substantial review for fifty years until the Company Law Reform Committee eventually reported (Cox, 1958). The only Irish Companies Act that was passed, the Companies (Re-constitution of Records) Act 1924, addressed the rebuilding of company records when the Companies Registration Office (CRO) was destroyed by fire in Dublin's Custom House.

By contrast, English company law was regularly reviewed and amended following the enactment of the 1908 Act. In 1925, a committee headed by Wilfred Greene was established in England to consider how the Companies Acts 1908–17 could be amended and improved. The recommendations in the Greene Report were implemented in 1928 and the Companies Acts were consolidated by more legislation in 1929. In 1943, a committee chaired by Mr Justice Cohen was established to consider amending the 1929

Act to further streamline company law and to protect both investors and the public interest. Some of the recommendations made in the Cohen Report were later implemented in the Companies Acts 1947 and 1948. In 1952, another committee chaired by Montague Gedge considered amending the 1948 Act. As noted by Gower (1997: 48): 'By the end of the nineteenth century the Board of Trade had established the practice of appointing at intervals of about 20 years a Departmental Committee to review company law, implementing its recommendations by an amending Act which was then repealed and replaced by a consolidation of all company legislation in a Company Act.' Therefore, company law was regularly and thoroughly reviewed in the UK in the first half of the twentieth century. The recommendations of the various committees were considered and implemented by the legislature. In Ireland, by contrast, company law review was non-existent. The reason for the disinterest in corporate affairs was 'due in part perhaps to the lesser role played by industry and business in a predominantly agricultural economy' (Keane, 1985: 15).

For most of the twentieth century, the Irish economy performed poorly. Writing prior to the economic boom of the 1990s, Lee (1989: 521) suggested: 'It is difficult to avoid the conclusion that Irish economic performance has been the least impressive in western Europe, perhaps in all Europe, in the twentieth century.' Though the substantial presence of natural resources (particularly coal and iron) in the Irish State has been doubted, it was in an ideal geographical location with easy access to the British market and it had suffered comparatively little damage following the world wars (Ferriter, 2005: 61, 32; Lee, 1989: 527). So why did the economy perform so poorly for so long? In the paragraphs below, it is shown that the Irish State was agrarian in orientation, had an insufficient knowledge of corporate and economic planning and pursued inadequate economic and corporate policies for the first half of the twentieth century. These policies continued to haunt the State for decades after they were abandoned. In particular, the Irish State failed to promote industry sufficiently, failed to encourage foreign investment and was too committed to the flawed policy of protectionism.

In the early years of the Irish Free State, foreign investment was not encouraged in case overseas investors would gain control of Irish industry and subvert national policies and interests for their own gain. Protectionist policies were advanced as an assertion of the sovereignty of the State and resistance to British influence, to avoid 'contaminating economic contact with a certain neighbouring island race, who, through some unfortunate oversight in divine regional policy, had been located within smelling distance of the chosen people' (Lee, 1989: 187). The Control of Manufactures Acts 1932 and 1934 enshrined the protection of Irish industry in legislation, shielding Irish companies from enormous tariffs and strict quotas that foreign companies were required to observe.

Furthermore, Irish people had to own in excess of half the equity of Irish firms, thereby ensuring that Irish companies were controlled by Irish people (Daly, 1984). Those companies that did not meet this requirement had to receive a special licence from the Minister for Industry and Commerce to operate in Ireland. As observed by the Organisation for Economic Co-operation and Development (OECD, 2001: 18):

> While the rest of Western Europe began a process of trade liberalisation and integration in the immediate post-war years, Ireland maintained a protectionist self-sufficiency strategy. Tariffs on imports were maintained at very high levels until the end of the 1950s and quota restrictions were an important part of the protective milieu in which Irish businesses operated. In manufacturing, much of the sector had developed since the late 1920s under the cover of a very high protective barrier against external competition. With a small domestic market, the granting of protection could ensure a domestic monopoly for production.

Though the legislation resulted in an initial increase in manufacturing output and employment, 'the spurt lasted only as long as it took the newly-founded firms to capture the home market, however, and was already over by the mid-1930s' (O'Grada, 1997: 109). However, the Acts had a number of harmful effects on industry that were more enduring in nature. Irish firms were so sheltered from competition that they were unable to engage effectively in export markets. Furthermore, discouraging foreign corporate involvement meant that Irish industry was denied the opportunity to learn useful skills from businessmen in large, successful and efficient foreign firms. Politicians would later recognise the need to use tax incentives to 'encourage the return from abroad of Irish nationals with managerial experience' (Costello, 1965: 18). In addition, the legislation also stunted the growth and development of licensed businesses because the Acts 'required that most licensed companies supply the majority of their capital from their own resources and this tended to exert a bias in favour of smaller companies' (Daly, 1984: 259).

It is also significant that 'from the 1930s on a series of state-owned companies were engaged in commercial activities that were not being undertaken by the private sector or which were felt to be outside the experience of existing firms' (OECD, 2001: 19). Major investments in enterprise were State affairs, not private initiatives, as evidenced in the establishment of State companies in key areas, like the Electricity Supply Board (1927), the ICC Bank and Irish Life in financial services (1933 and 1939), Greencore Food Processing (1933), Aer Lingus and CIE in transport (1936 and 1944) and Irish Steel (1947), among others (OECD, 2001: 19). Given the bleak economic environment at the time, it is perhaps understandable that private enterprise was not sufficiently developed at this point to perform major corporate activities without State involvement. However, Lee (1989: 390–3) has also argued that the Irish people themselves failed to show entrepreneurial flair. In this early stage of the development of the State, he argues that most rural Irish people were afraid to take the financial gambles that were central to developing businesses. Instead, they desired security and a steady income from managing family farms.

Where farming was not an option, industry and commerce were still avoided. Even in family businesses, parents usually discouraged their children from engaging in commercial trading. The gifted child was encouraged to join a profession while the lesser so continued the family business. Other children with skills were encouraged to join a trade. Even within the small business community that did exist, there still seemed to be a distinct dearth of commercial talent. As Lee (1989: 577) observed of the time: 'most Irish businessmen were simply not interested in ideas. Indigenous industry consisted overwhelmingly of small firms enjoying a captive domestic market and enjoying few competitive pressures … A first-class business mind could be a joy to behold. There were too few of them in Ireland.' Capturing the international view of the Irish as drunken 'spud-gobblers' without any entrepreneurial spirit, he suggested (379) that: 'Industrialisation required sterner qualities of character than Paddy, charming a chap though he could be in his sober interludes, could possibly muster. It is somewhat cruel to impose the strain of trying on the poor fellow.' Domestic financial institutions may also have considered Irish people bad entrepreneurial bets too because 'Irish banks usually found it more profitable to invest their money in bonds in London than lend it to Irish businessmen' (O'Grada, 1997: 231).

Ferriter (2005: 313) has observed that the agricultural sector employed 53 per cent of the workforce in the mid-1920s, when industry employed only 14 per cent of the workforce, compared to 35 per cent employed in industry in Northern Ireland at that time. He stated (313–14) that: 'The idea of promoting industrialisation through a mixture of import substitution and monetary experimentation was rejected, the main focus instead being on the cultivation of a robust agricultural sector … [because] national development was synonymous with agricultural development; that the interests of the farmer and the nation were identical.' Ireland was a rural 'peasant economy' (Lee, 1989: 284), epitomised by the narrow economic plan advanced by the Minister for Agriculture, Patrick Hogan: 'one more cow, one more sow, and a few more acres under the plough' (O'Brien, 1936: 368). The early emphasis on developing a viable agricultural economy, rather than a successful economy more generally, was then enshrined in the Irish Constitution. Article 45.2(v) provided that the State would, as a matter of social policy, secure 'on the land in economic security as many families as in the circumstances shall be practicable'. Notwithstanding its shortcomings, the view of rural Ireland, as poor but happy, was glamorised and romanticised with panache in 1943 by An Taoiseach (Prime Minister), Eamon DeValera (Moynihan, 1980: 466):

> The Ireland which we have dreamed of would be the home of a people who valued material wealth only as a basis of right living, of a people who were satisfied with frugal comfort and devoted their leisure to things of the spirit; a land whose countryside would be bright with cosy homesteads, whose fields and villages would be joyous with the sounds of industry, with the romping of sturdy children, the contests of athletic youth, the laughter of comely maidens; whose firesides would be forums for the wisdom of serene old age. It would, in a word, be the home of a people living the life that God desires that men should live.

Agriculture was supported through programmes to increase tillage in the 1930s, through schemes to improve housing conditions for agricultural labourers, the 1938 Trade Agreement with Britain which ended the economic war and removed certain restrictions and tariffs on Irish agricultural imports to Britain, the Anglo-Irish agreement in 1948 involving British subsidisation of the Irish cattle industry, to mention a few. In 1945, 68 per cent of the total land area in the Republic of Ireland was used productively in agriculture (O'Nuallain, 1946–47). When Ireland did receive foreign assistance in the form of Marshall Aid, a significant portion was invested in agricultural projects like afforestation, land reclamation, and bog land development (Ferriter, 2005: 468). Proposals to build and equip factories for lease to private industry were not implemented. The investments in agriculture, it was suggested, 'brutally exposed the continuing inability of Irish governments to devise a coherent long-term programme of public expenditure' (Lee, 1989: 305).

In addition, it has been suggested that attempts to promote corporate development and increase prosperity may have been stifled by an 'anti-business Catholic ethos' (Ferriter, 2005: 61). Though Kennedy (1978: 52) has claimed that 'the Catholic Church was itself a major consumer of goods and services [so] it is quite probable that the Church contributed to economic growth rather than the reverse', Inglis (1998: 250) has convincingly argued that the 'Catholic Church, because of the nature of its teachings and practices, in particular its opposition to materialism, consumerism and individualism, was an inhibiting factor in modernisation and industrialisation of Irish society.' He argued that the Catholic Church required its flock to prioritise the frugal comfort of religion, family and community over success, economic prosperity and performance. This inhibited the development of a modern industrial economy because 'up to the 1960s and in many cases after then religious belief and practice were not often rationally differentiated from economic and political activity' (253). Daly (1994: 79) has agreed that while idealising spiritual values of rural frugal comfort 'may not provide the major explanation for Ireland's poor economic performance, ideals did influence policies, and, indirectly, performance'. Furthermore, 'the idea that rural life was inherently superior to urban life went back a long way in the Irish Catholic consciousness' (Tobin, 1984: 15). As a result, it 'was committed ideologically to a rural fundamentalism which was suspicious and fearful of the industrial city and it glorified the family farm and the little village as the pillars of social and economic life' (Fahey, 1992: 262). The interconnecting ideas about rural Ireland and the role of religion therein is also neatly encapsulated by the views of Canon Hayes who suggested that 'rural Ireland is real Ireland and rural Ireland is Ireland true to Christ' (Ferriter, 2005: 377).

Nevertheless, contrary to the views of rural Ireland held by bombastic politicians and the clergy, rural Ireland was a 'wasting society' (Lee, 1989: 334). Many farmers had small non-viable holdings (Hannon and Commins, 1992). Mass emigration was so pronounced that the Irish were considered to be 'vanishing' (O'Brien, 1954). Of every five children born between 1931 and 1941 in Ireland, four of them emigrated in the 1950s (Tobin, 1984: 156). It is no wonder that historians have associated this period with terms like doom, drift, stagnation, crisis and malaise, with one Irish writer even describing 1950s Ireland as 'the climate for the death wish' (Cronin, 1954: 7). Crucially, as a result of the various inadequacies and flawed policies in the Irish State, corporate development and growth was visibly stunted. The number of public companies incorporated in Ireland remained relatively static, rising from just 363 in 1925 to 372 in 1956, though the number of private companies (often small and family owned) did increase from 1,088 to 7,385 in the same period (Cox, 1958: 15), relatively modest numbers compared to the 138,215 private companies and 1,103 public companies in Ireland by 2005 (CLRG, 2006: 16). In addition, relatively low levels of commercial activity naturally had knock-on effects on the financial services sector so that 'between the 1920s and the 1950s the banks' business reflected the sluggish nature of economic business generally' (O'Grada, 1997: 175).

In concluding on the social and economic context during the first decades of the Irish State, and the effect this had on business and company law, it is clear to see why corporate issues did not rank highly on the national agenda. The combination of concerns relating to the sovereignty of the new Irish State, poor economic policies (particularly those relating to protectionism), the romanticisation of rural Ireland and political deference to the agricultural sector reduced Ireland to an impoverished State with low levels of corporate activity. In this context, Ireland was inward-looking, concerned more with self-sufficiency rather than attracting investment and promoting enterprise that could compete with players on an international level. Concerns with corporate deviancy and public corporate governance were not significant issues that had to be pursued vigorously in a State with relatively low levels of corporate activity. This would, of course, have implications for the enforcement of company law, but it also affected the substance of the law itself. The low level of corporate activity meant that updating and reviewing company law was not a significant priority for the Irish state.

Post-protectionism inertia in corporate affairs

It is unsurprising that there was so little reflection on the 1908 Act in the decades following independence. To expect the legislature to have updated company law every few years was to demand an experience and understanding of corporate regulatory affairs that, hitherto, the State did not have. Consequently, fifty years after the enactment of the legislation, the Cox Report (1958) detailed the various ways in which the law had naturally failed to keep up with contemporary regulatory challenges. Under the law at that time, auditors did not need professional qualifications to review company accounts. Public companies were not obliged to keep proper records, proper books of account, or file a profit and loss account with the Registrar of Companies. Private companies did not file a balance sheet with the Registrar of Companies and they were not obliged to present their shareholders with a report on the financial affairs of the company. Minority shareholders were particularly vulnerable. Directors could refuse to let them sell their shares and shareholders did not have effective or proportionate mechanisms to resolve their disputes with management. Loans from companies to directors were unregulated and creditors could be defrauded with little fear of reprisal. Shareholders could also obscure the fact that they owned shares in companies and liquidators often only investigated wrongdoing in companies that had sufficient assets to pay them. In highlighting these issues, the Cox Report illustrated that Irish company law lacked transparency, joined-up thinking, and adequate protections for stakeholders and the public generally. Moreover, the existing rules and regulations were aimed primarily at the regulation of public companies while private companies were often provided with exemptions from even the most minimal requirements in the legislation (40–1). Given that there were twenty times more public companies than private companies by 1955 in Ireland, this meant that most regulations did not apply to most Irish companies (15).

Nevertheless, despite being the first substantial review of company law in the history of the State, and despite highlighting significant deficiencies in the law, the Cox Report received relatively little attention. Only one article, consisting of thirty-two words, was written in the leading Irish broadsheet in the weeks prior to its release, perhaps reflecting the depth of Irish interest in corporate affairs among the general community (*Irish Times*, 21 June 1958: 7). Even after the publication of the report, it received a relatively mute and confused reaction, with journalists extracting significantly different conclusions from it. One journalist deduced that the report found the existing framework adequate to address the contemporary needs of Irish companies (*Irish Times*, 4 July 1958: 7), while another journalist in the same newspaper acknowledged that the report found Irish company legislation to be inadequate in 100 different ways (*Irish Times*, 29 July 1958: 11). Additionally, though the *Irish Press* produced a short but accurate account of the key features of the report (4 July 1958: 7), the *Irish Independent* issued a two-part report which seemed to focus more on the 'remarkable' increase in private companies, holding companies, and subsidiary companies operating in the State, rather than the significant scale of corporate governance reforms that the Committee had proposed (4 July 1958: 12; 5 July 1958: 12).

Nevertheless, the inertia in corporate affairs must not be overstated. The State was not so inert that it would not enact legislation to implement the recommendations specified in the Cox Report. Perhaps one reason for this was that its release approximately coincided with the publication of a report entitled *Economic Development* (Whitaker, 1958). Whitaker's report, a 'watershed in the modern economic history of the country' (Lyons, 1973: 628), recommended that the State should abandon protectionism, embrace competition and free trade, and develop indigenous industry so that it could compete in export markets. In addition, Whitaker argued that the State needed laws to protect investments, encourage profit, and attract foreign enterprise. These incentives would be crucial to Ireland's success because 'the real shortage is of ideas, and these are likely to fructify only if domestic conditions favour profit-making … Foreign industrialists will bring skills and techniques we need, and continuous and widespread publicity abroad is necessary to attract them' (217–18).

Coinciding somewhat with this, DeValera – having dominated Irish politics for decades following independence, frequently serving as Taoiseach in the 1930s, 1940s and 1950s – was eventually replaced by Lemass as Taoiseach in 1959. DeValera had idealised agricultural living, frugality and isolationism, but Lemass, by contrast, was pro-competition, pro-industry and pro-European integration, overturning protectionist policies that he had earlier advanced under DeValera (Murphy, 2005). Much like the Cox Report, Whitaker's *Economic Development* 'did not, however, impinge on the consciousness of the body politic immediately. The major newspapers gave it only cursory treatment while the political parties showed a similar lack of interest' (Murphy, 2005: 32). However, Lemass adopted Whitaker's ideas as government policy. While the State was not especially interested in company law, it was interested in escaping its bleak economic situation and it seemed to recognise that company law reform was part of the package that would allow it to do so. Therefore, in both houses of the Oireachtas (Irish Parliament), the Dáil (Lower House) and the Seanad (Senate and Upper House), the Minister for Industry and Commerce, Jack Lynch, recognised that Irish corporate regulation was not only 'seriously out of date' (Dáil Deb 14 November 1962: vol. 197, col. 1174) but also 'scanty in the extreme' (Seanad Deb 13 November 1963: vol. 57, col. 48–49). It will be shown below that the legislature passed new laws to reassure investors that the Irish regulatory environment was modern and secure and that their investments would be safe if companies established themselves in the State.

The legislature enacted the Companies Act 1959 which implemented a large number of proposals suggested in the Cox Report. Company law was then consolidated into the Companies Act 1963, often called the 'Principal Act' or 'Primary Act'. Writing shortly after its enactment, Crowley (1973: 2) suggested: 'The purpose of the Act is twofold, firstly to bring all the legislation on company law together and secondly to bring the law up to date by introducing measures to give protection to shareholders and creditors.' As noted in the Dáil (Norton, Dáil Deb 14 November 1962: vol. 197, col. 1204–1205):

> [R]eforms must be introduced which will have the effect of protecting the public in a much more positive way than they are protected under the existing company law which was introduced in the days of free enterprise and which gave the *entrepreneur* [italics in original] of the day as much freedom as he could wish for himself, while at the same time not providing the adequate protection which the modern state finds necessary in order to protect the shareholders and those with whom the companies trade.

It is interesting to note, however, that the government was not especially concerned with the protection of the general public who could be harmed by corporate irresponsibility, but instead, sought to protect the investing public and the trading public. This corresponds with the two major influences that Levi (2002: 423) identified in the regulation of the corporate sector: reassuring investors that their capital is secure and that the legal system has efficient rules to deal with cases of wrongdoing fairly. However, the Act had more than mere commercial significance, it also had social implications. Emerging alongside the plans proposed by Lemass and Whitaker for economic expansion and progress, the Primary Act was seen as an opportunity to facilitate the development of the Irish economy and boost the confidence of Irish and foreign investors in home industries.

Of course, the new corporate framework was merely one element of enterprise-inducing factors in Ireland (discussed in more detail in Chapter 5), but it did coincide with increased foreign investment from multinational companies in the 1960s. Increased industrial activity at that time resulted in increased economic growth and industrial output (O'Malley, 1992). More people moved from rural communities to live in urban centres and living standards increased significantly, resulting in a nostalgic view that it was 'the best of decades' (Tobin, 1984). It is tempting to form the conclusion that Ireland transitioned from an agrarian to a successful commercial society at this time, but that would be over-stating the case. While impressive compared to previous decades, 'by European standards growth in the 1960s was not that fast and the target set for the decade in the government's Second Programme for Economic Expansion – an average annual output growth rate of 4 per cent – was not quite met' (O'Grada, 1997: 30). Indeed, this programme still prioritised the development of the agricultural sector for 'primary attention', even though it was conceded that the industrial sector was most likely to be responsible for new employment, perhaps reflecting the continued identification of Ireland as a principally agrarian economy. Furthermore, the increased industrial growth experienced in Ireland was attributable to foreign-owned firms, and the performance of indigenous companies in Ireland actually declined during this time (O'Grada, 1997; O'Malley, 1992). This suggests that Ireland's new entrepreneurial spirit was more transplanted than home-grown. In addition, though more people than ever were living in urban centres in the 1960s, industrialisation was relatively well dispersed in Ireland, owing to the availability of government grants to locate in less developed regions and cheaper labour costs in smaller towns and rural areas (O'Malley, 1992: 41–3). As late as 1992, the view remained that 'Ireland as a whole is less industrially developed than most of Europe and this was even more obviously the case in the 1960s' (42). In any event, the increased prosperity was short-lived when the economy declined again in the 1980s, making Ireland's previous successes seem like a 'glorious interlude' (O'Grada, 1997: 30). All of this suggests that the State experienced an incomplete political and economic governance shift in the 1960s, as Ireland 'ceases to be a primarily agricultural economy, but does quite become an industrial one' (Girvin and Murphy, 2005: 8).

Nevertheless, Ireland had witnessed the benefits of increased industrialisation under free-market conditions and the State had abandoned its hostile attitudes to industry. Though the point should not be over-stated, it seems that the State, from about the late 1950s and early 1960s, became more willing to consider the importance of effective company law reform to attract foreign investment and boost the economic prosperity of the State. In doing so, it moved away from the 'comely maidens' approach of the 1930s, when opening Ireland up to foreign corporate activity would not have been countenanced. In this context, however, regulatory reform did not mean tight control over corporate risk-taking. In fact, it sought to minimise any regulatory hurdles that companies might face, cognisant of the fact that 'it would be most unwise to impose on our companies more onerous obligations ... than those which prevail in neighbouring countries, since this would place them at a competitive disadvantage' (Lynch, Dáil Deb 14 November 1962: vol. 197, col 1176–1177). It was concerned that companies might find the cost of compliance too great and avoid doing business in Ireland. Therefore, in accordance with the Cox Report, it disfavoured an onerous corporate governance framework, suggesting instead that 'flexibility' must be maintained in Irish company law (1958: 18).

The increased interest in regulatory governance and the enactment of the Companies Acts 1959 and 1963 in quick succession suggests some departure from the inertia and hegemony of before. However, a closer examination of the content of the legislation and the thoughts of members of the legislature suggest a continued disinterest in issues of corporate governance. For example,

Ireland still had little opinion of its own on how to structure its company law framework so the Companies Act 1959 and 1963 borrowed heavily from the Companies Act 1948 in the UK. When the law needed updating, Ireland followed the route of policy transfer from England and Wales. While creating a shared company law framework made good economic sense, given Ireland's reliance on Britain as a trading partner, it is also submitted that the culture of imitation reflected a lack of innovation and experience in corporate affairs on the part of the Irish State. In creating the corporate framework, Ireland modelled itself so closely on England that it followed English legislation even when that legislation was thought to be flawed and outdated. For example, the Cox Report considered that the *ultra vires* doctrine on corporate capacity had been 'largely defeated', but it did not recommend its abolition because Britain had not done so. Bad law was perpetuated because it was assumed that the British legislature knew best (Delaney, 1959: 305). This suggests that while Ireland was not so inert as to do nothing to update company law, it did not reflect on the propriety of using English law in an Irish context. British legislation was copied and pasted into Irish law; legislative changes were not underpinned by a different way of thinking about corporate affairs in Ireland.

In addition, politicians themselves highlighted their own continued disinterest in company law. They attributed their neglect to the fact that company law was a particularly complicated and technical field (Cosgrave, Dáil Deb 14 November 1962: vol. 197, col. 1193–1194). It was stated that this kind of legislation 'was as dry as dust. Many sections of it could not be less interesting than they were … It will probably be another 50 years before we pass another one' (Norton, Dáil Deb 5 November 1963: vol. 205, col. 821). Although the Primary Act was supplemented and amended a number of times in mostly minor ways over the next four decades or so, it continued to be the foundational framework for Irish company law in the twentieth century. Amendments were introduced in 1977, 1982, 1983, 1986, twice in 1990, and twice in 1999. Most of these statutes addressed specific and relatively minor issues relating to company formations and registrations, acting as a director or secretary, the recognition and qualification of auditors, the distribution of profits and assets, accounting rules, the sale of securities and examinership. The most substantial amendment to the Primary Act in the twentieth century was the Companies Act 1990. This was also heavily influenced by British legislation, specifically the Companies Act 1985, the Insolvency Act 1986 and the Company Directors Disqualification Act 1986 (Appleby, 2005). Ireland continued to imitate the UK, reflecting a lack of original thinking in addressing corporate reform and the same continued inertia in corporate affairs. Furthermore, another committee would not report on reforming company law until 1994, thirty-six years after the Cox Report, and regular company law reform would not be statutorily required until the twenty-first century.

Criminalisation without condemnation

The Companies Consolidation Act 1908 provided for the prosecution of companies and company officers (Law Reform Commission, 2005: 3). This was part of a longer trajectory in which the Factories Acts in the nineteenth century had also criminalised corporate wrongdoing (Carson, 1974; Greer and Nicolson, 2003; Norrie, 2001). Subsequent Companies Acts continued to enforce corporate obligations using criminal sanctions. In fact, the Companies Acts 1963–90 specified 280 distinct criminal offences (McDowell, 1998: 9). These offences spanned a range of wrongs, from relative minor summary offences, such as failing to provide the articles of association to a member, punishable by a maximum fine of £25 in accordance with section 29(1) of the Companies Act 1963, to serious indictable offences, such as unlawfully dealing in securities, punishable by a maximum sentence of ten years imprisonment and a fine of £200,000 in accordance with section 111 of the Companies Act 1990.

The Companies Acts also contained a number of civil sanctions, such as the ability to strike a company off the register of companies. Excluding those sanctions which imposed individual personal liability for the debts of the company, arguably the most significant civil sanction was stipulated by section 184 of the Primary Act, which provided for the 'power of court to restrain certain persons from acting as directors of or managing companies'. It specified that if a director was convicted on indictment of an offence relating to the promotion, formation or management of a company, or any offence involving dishonesty, then the court, on the application of the Director of Public Prosecutions (DPP), could issue an order preventing the offender from acting as a director of a company. Therefore, this civil sanction could only be triggered by the criminal conviction of the accused, and then only on the application of the criminal prosecutor, and its breach was also a criminal offence, thereby demonstrating the primacy of the criminal law in the traditional period (O'Connell, 2009). Indeed, the influence and centrality of the criminal justice system to corporate enforcement was such that the DPP maintained the exclusive right to apply for a disqualification order on certain grounds right up to the enactment of the Company Law Enforcement Act 2001.

Criminal law was used to enforce corporate obligations but without much thought for enforcement. Prior to the Primary Act, companies could not be prosecuted on indictment in Ireland. In *State (Batchelor & Co. Ireland Ltd)* v. *O'Lennain* ([1957] I.R. 1), the Supreme Court held that the preliminaries to the indictment required by the Indictable Offences (Ireland) Act 1849 had to be carried out in the presence of the accused at the pre-trial hearing but that these could not be observed because the company itself could not appear in person. Murnaghan J. stated that the legislation could not be interpreted to allow for a representative to appear on behalf of the company because the jurisdiction of the District Court was to send the accused forward on bail, and bail, being a form of custody in itself, was not appropriate in the case of companies who could not, by their artificial nature, be held in custody. Though the Primary Act addressed this deficiency, the fact that companies could not be prosecuted on indictment in Ireland until the early 1960s is remarkable considering that such prosecutions had been explicitly permitted in England and Wales since the nineteenth century (section 2(1) of the Interpretation Act 1889).

Nevertheless, a lack of joined-up thinking regarding corporate enforcement persisted beyond the enactment of the Primary Act. For example, where no penalties were specified for particular indictable offences, then they were punishable by a maximum period of imprisonment of three years in accordance with section 240(1)(b) of the Companies Act 1990. However, for a suspect to be arrested without a warrant on suspicion of committing an offence, that offence had to be punishable by at least five years imprisonment, as stipulated by section 4 of the Criminal Justice Act 1984. This meant that company officers could not be arrested on the reasonable suspicion of committing the offence unless specific powers of arrest were specified for that offence in the Act. In addition, assimilating corporate wrongdoing into the criminal sphere meant that corporate wrongdoers had all the due process safeguards and subjective culpability requirements that generally attached to the criminal process (discussed further in Chapter 3). It also meant that the sanctions available to punish misbehaving company officers were the same for those who committed hard-core criminal offences. Given these issues, was the State really committed to prosecuting and imprisoning corporate offenders who were often regarded as pillars of the community, and for offences that were regarded as merely technically criminal rather than morally reprehensible? Was the State making a moral judgement about corporate deviancy? Or is it more likely that the State was simply drawing on the criminal law because it was a convenient enforcement mechanism that did not require any specialised knowledge or reflection on the nature of corporate activity? In the next paragraph, the sinking of the *Betelgeuse* is used as a case study to examine how Irish society traditionally thought about corporate harm.

On 7 January 1979, fifty people were killed when an oil tanker, the *Betelgeuse*, exploded while discharging fuel at an oil terminal at Whiddy Island in Bantry Bay, County Cork. Though these deaths, the highest number of people to be killed in a single incident in the history of the State, are officially recorded by the Marine accident statistics as 'shipping casualties', corporate irresponsibility was a key factor in the loss of life (McCullagh, 1995: 413). The Costello Inquiry (Report of tribunal into disaster at Whiddy Island, 1980) concluded that Gulf Oil, the owners of the oil terminal, had failed in numerous ways to maintain adequate safety measures to prevent or minimise emergencies. It had downgraded its fire-fighting systems, failed to train its staff or provide proper rescue facilities, failed to reassess its procedures with any regularity, and failed to observe its existing safety policies, like providing a fire-fighting ship to immediately assist in the event of an emergency. The Inquiry (322) concluded that had even some of these deficiencies been remedied then 'the lives of both the jetty crew and of those on board the ship would have been saved'. It also noted that the company which owned the *Betelgeuse*, Total, had failed to install basic safety technology that was standard on most ships at the time, and had failed to maintain the ship properly. Though the deaths of fifty innocent people attracted significant media coverage, the explosion was called a 'disaster', an 'accident' and a 'tragedy', terms which suggested a fait acompli for which no one could be held responsible, rather than an avoidable incident caused by companies who had taken unnecessary risks with peoples' lives while operating in an insufficiently regulated environment (*Irish Times*, 8 January 1978; 1; 9 January 1978; 6). Prosecutions were not taken and there were no demands at this point for a statutory offence to specifically address corporate manslaughter.

By contrast, companies had been indicted for corporate manslaughter in England as early as 1927 (*R* v. *Cory Brothers and Company Ltd* [1927] 1 K.B. 810) and put on trial for same in the 1960s (*R.* v. *Northern Strip Mining Construction Co.* (*The Times*, 2, 4 and 5 February 1965). Further prosecutions were taken later in the century, for example, against P&O Ferries (*R.* v. *P&O European Ferries (Dover) Ltd* (1991) 93 Cr. App. R. 72), when an inquiry found that the ship's crew and '[a]ll concerned in management, from the members of the Board of Directors down to the junior superintendents, were guilty of fault … [and] infected with the disease of sloppiness' (Department of Transport, 1987: 14). In total, 192 passengers were killed when one of its 'roll-on roll-off' ferries capsized in 1987 as a result of the failure to close its bow doors when setting sail. Though this prosecution was ultimately unsuccessful, the concept of corporate manslaughter was officially recognised in law. Unlike Ireland, it was addressed head-on by the criminal justice system and the concept of corporate manslaughter had a 'cultural recognition' and 'a clear place in popular vocabulary' (Wells, 2001: 106).

The Irish inertia in addressing corporate and white-collar crime may also be located within the broader apathy towards crime more generally. Though it is extremely difficult to measure crime precisely and reduce crime trends to a general statement, it may tentatively be suggested that Ireland experienced relatively low levels of crime from the early to mid-twentieth century. If the Irish prison population can be taken as an indication of the level of serious crime committed in Ireland, then it is of note that the number of convicts committed to prison after the establishment of the Irish Free State declined significantly. Nearly 120 prisoners were committed to prison per 1000 indictable crimes in the late 1920s but this had dropped to below 20 per 1000 by the early

1970s (Kilcommins *et al.*, 2004: 56). The prison population and crime rate were so low in the 1950s that prisons in Cork and Sligo were closed and the number of Gardaí was reduced (60–2). Though the level of crime rose in the 1960s and peaked in 1983, it would again generally continue to either plateau or decline for the rest of the century (109). The relatively low levels of crime meant that crime was not a significant issue which regularly concerned the public or animated political debates. The public demand for information on combating crime was so low that the government failed to publish any annual reports on crime until 1950 (65–6).

The low levels of public concern about crime continued well into the twentieth century. An examination of opinion polls conducted by Irish newspapers in the run-up to general elections in the 1980s and early 1990s revealed that 'the problem of crime was a low priority for voters. The over-riding concern was unemployment, usually followed closely by anxiety about how to get by in difficult economic circumstances' (136). Ireland, simply put, was a nation 'not obsessed by crime' (Adler, 1983). There was little political will to adopt a strong law-and-order agenda and even when concern was expressed regarding crime, the concern was limited to the type of conventional crimes attributed to members of the travelling community and street thugs, rather than wrongs perpetrated by companies and company officers (Kilcommins *et al.*, 2004: 66–7). Corporate activity generally maintained exclusively positive connotations.

Conclusion

As shown in the introduction to this chapter, it is quite difficult to capture all threads in a century of legal and socio-economic history. Of necessity, capturing the particular character of this period involved some generalisation and some omissions. Having made this qualification, this chapter has shown that Ireland moved from a closed, protected, agrarian state to one that advocated something closer to free-market, industrial capitalism. Agriculture was favoured above industry and foreign corporate activity was initially viewed with suspicion, as a threat to the sovereignty of the State. However, it was later seen to be a positive force that could stimulate economic recovery. Nevertheless, despite this shift in sentiment towards corporate activity, the State remained relatively consistent in its apathy towards corporate deviancy. Corporate wrongdoing was not a significant priority in a State which experienced relatively low levels of corporate activity and low levels of crime. In the midst of perpetual economic stagnation, the average member of the public was more concerned about the creation of employment, not whether or how corporate deviancy was being addressed.

This way of thinking supported the routine marginalisation of corporate issues within the legal system and had a profound impact upon the generative structure of company law. Regular company law review was non-existent, corporate governance mechanisms were weak, high-profile instances of corporate wrongdoing were not adequately addressed and, perhaps most significantly, appropriate reflection was not given to the best method of enforcing company law. Consequently, criminal liability was used to underpin the enforcement of the Companies Acts, almost by default, without the appropriate reflection as to whether it was suited to this process. Though instances of corporate deviancy were often regarded merely as technical breaches of law, they were incorporated into a criminal justice system developed to address morally reprehensible misbehaviours, and this posed particular difficulties. It not only had an impact on the definition of crime but also affected the substance and effectiveness of the law on corporate and white-collar criminality itself, and had implications for its enforcement. We turn our attention to these issues in Chapters 3 and 4.

3

Conventional crime methods

Introduction

The previous chapter showed that political apathy in the field of corporate and white-collar crime informed the generative structure of company law in twentieth-century Ireland. Addressing corporate deviancy was not a significant priority in a closed, agrarian State with relatively low levels of corporate activity. This way of thinking resulted in the use of criminal law sanctions to address corporate wrongdoing, without adequate reflection as to whether those sanctions were the most appropriate enforcement tools in the corporate setting. This chapter shows that conventional methods were adhered to in the application of criminal law. This 'general part' legitimised the criminal law as 'not merely an institutionalised system of coercion but, rather, a system which is structured around certain principles of justice or morality' (Lacey, 2007: 187). Punitive ends were legitimately pursued when fair and just means were employed. The respect for conventional criminal justice methods meant that the criminal justice system generally respected due process provisions like subjective culpability, the rule of law, the presumption of innocence and proportionate sentencing.

Sketching the contours of these methods requires mapping a vast terrain that exceeds the scope of this monograph. Therefore, depth has occasionally been sacrificed for breadth. This chapter only seeks to discuss a modest range of due process safeguards because these are considered to be representative of the conventional criminal justice system more generally. This is not to say that the conventional criminal justice system was uniformly and exclusively structured to reflect only these methods and values. The general principles could be manipulated, contradictory, and were often contingent on a variety of social and political factors (Norrie, 2001). It is acknowledged that when the criminal law was applied to corporate misconduct, the traditional framework occasionally departed from the conventional conceptions of subjective culpability and due process. As such, the principles, imperatives and rationales underpinning traditional criminal law were 'ideal rather than invariable features of criminal justice, but they set norms against which departures can be observed' (Zedner, 2004: 305). Moreover, in sketching these contours and allowing for some exceptions, the focus was not on the technical detail of rights and procedures, but on their overtones and what they revealed about the operational consequences of the conventional criminal justice model. Finally, this chapter is limited in its analysis to the laws relating to the apprehension, trial, and sentencing of offenders, not their enforcement in practice. This partial picture of the criminal process is supplemented in Chapter 4 by an analysis of the routine patterns of policing and prosecuting corporate and white-collar crime that could not be accommodated here.

Culpability

Culpability or 'fault' may be understood as a hierarchy of requirements with intention at the apex, followed by recklessness and then by negligence (Ashworth, 2009: 136). In *R.* v. *Woollin* ([1999] A.C. 82), intention was inferred where the prohibited consequences were a virtual certainty, rather than a natural and probable consequence, of the behaviour of the accused. While a number of departures have been accepted in specific situations, this case was also followed in Ireland in *DPP* v. *Douglas and Hayes* ([1985] I.L.R.M. 25), though there was some continuing uncertainty as to the exact parameters of the Irish test (LRC, 2008: para. 2.06). In attempting to nail down the legislative use of terminology like knowingly and wilfully, phrases frequently used in the Companies Acts, Ashworth (2009: 182–3) suggested that the standard for determining that an accused has knowledge is no less demanding than that of intention, though 'knowledge relates to circumstances forming part of the definition of the crime, and intention relates to the consequences specified in the definition of crime'. The Irish courts confirmed in *People (DPP)* v. *McGrath; Cagney* ([2008] 2 I.R. 111) that recklessness was also determined subjectively in terms of the accused's actual awareness of a risk that prohibited consequences will occur. By contrast, liability for negligence was imposed on the basis that a reasonable person would have foreseen the possibility of breaching the duty of care in potentially dangerous contexts; he or she could and should have been more careful (Williams, 1961: 100).

Subjective culpability, as reflected in both intention and reckless requirements, assumed its place at the top of the hierarchy because it expressed respect for the principle of individual autonomy by imposing liability for deliberate choices, and for the rule of law by protecting citizens from abuses of state power (Norrie, 2001: 11). Notwithstanding the distinctions between the various forms of culpability, it was clear that subjective culpability requirements were at the core of modern criminal liability. For this reason, subjective culpability was lauded by Denham J. as the 'silken thread in the fabric of the legal system ensuring a just process' (*PG* v. *Ireland, Attorney General and Another* [2005] I.E.S.C. 47). The Irish Companies Acts also emphasised this requirement.

Under the Companies Consolidation Act 1908, culpability was a significant precondition to criminal liability for company officers. In a wide variety of offences, where, for example, company officers had failed to add a statement to the memorandum specifying the unlimited liability of directors (s. 60(3)), or failed to publish (i.e. paint or affix) the name of the company (s. 63), or failed to allow a creditor or member to inspect the register of mortgages (s. 101(2)), it had to be shown that the officers acted knowingly, or both knowingly and wilfully. Though English company law did not develop ways of attributing *mens rea* to companies until the 1940s (Wells, 2001: 93–9), the 1908 Act did specify particular offences where criminal liability was imposed on both companies and company officers. Again, however, it also had to be shown that the officer acted intentionally as a precondition to criminal liability. These offences included: the failure to keep a register of members detailing certain information (s. 25); the failure to update the register annually with a summary (s. 26); the failure to provide the register for inspection (s. 30); altering the company share capital without reflecting this in the memorandum (s. 44); the failure to substitute a minute reflecting a reduction of share capital for the previous value in the memorandum (s. 52); the failure to hold a special resolution to make the liability of directors in limited companies unlimited (s. 61); the failure to publish the name of the limited company (s. 63); the failure to hold an AGM (s. 64); the failure to send a list of directors to the Registrar (s. 75); the failure to send the details of any mortgages or charges that require registration to the Registrar (s. 99); and the failure to allow debenture holders to inspect trust deeds (s. 102). This list gives the reader a flavour of the variety of offences in the 1908 Act. In each instance, the legislature stated that the wrongdoing had to be committed knowingly and wilfully by the company officers.

For the most part, subsequent Companies Acts also continued to emphasise culpability as a vital precondition to criminal liability for company law offences. In defining the meaning of 'officer in default' for the purposes of criminal liability under the Primary Act, section 383 stipulated that this 'means any officer of the company who knowingly and wilfully authorises or permits the default, refusal or contravention mentioned in the provision'. Therefore, in every offence in the Companies Acts that sought to pin criminal liability to company officers 'in default' of their obligations, there was a blanket subjective culpability requirement, unless otherwise stated in that particular offence. Specific offences not employing the 'officer in default' construction also required the accused to act culpably as a precondition to criminal liability. For example, section 147(6) of the Primary Act provided that a director was liable for the failure to keep proper books of account where he had caused the company to default on its obligations 'by his own wilful act'. While the 1990 Act imposed more stringent accounting provisions (s. 202(4)), criminal liability continued to attach to the company director when he or she wilfully caused the default by the company.

The emphasis on addressing culpable wrongdoing in the offence of failing to keep proper books of account is not an aberration in the Primary Act. For example, the penalties for the impersonation of a shareholder were only applicable where the impersonation was committed falsely and deceitfully (s. 90). Company officers must have been acting under false pretences or must have had intent to defraud the creditors of a company in order to be convicted of defrauding a company that goes into liquidation (s. 295). If any of the provisions of Part XI (relating to companies incorporated outside the State but who established a place or business within the State) were breached then the company and every officer or agent of the company was liable to a fine only if they had knowingly and wilfully authorised or permitted the default (s. 358).

Section 112(3) provided that if the company failed to register charges pre-existing the Act within six months of its enactment then the company and every officer of the company, or other person who was knowingly a party to the default, was guilty of an offence. The offence of altering/falsifying the company documents was only committed if the officer acted with 'intent to defraud' which implied that the test was subjective. Meanwhile, the 1990 Act, which repealed and replaced the offence of altering/falsifying company documents, stipulated that anyone who fraudulently altered the company books, or was party to this alteration, was guilty of a criminal offence (s. 243(2)). As noted earlier, with regard to the offence of fraudulent trading, acting fraudulently required the mental element of intention. The accused must have knowingly committed some deceit or falsehood. Furnishing false information was also a criminal offence but only where the company officer had been found subjectively culpable on the basis that he or she knowingly or recklessly did so (s. 242(1)). It was a criminal offence for a company officer to authorise or permit the breach of section 31 relating to a prohibition on directors' loans, unless it fell within a specific statutory exception but only where the accused acted knowingly or where he had reasonable grounds to believe that the company was contravening the Act (s. 40). It was also a criminal offence for officers to knowingly or recklessly make a false or misleading statement to the company auditor (s. 197).

This respect for subjective culpability requirements was also reflected in the serious criminal offences in the Act. For example, in the provisions specifying criminal liability for fraudulent trading under section 297, it was stated that only those controllers of a company who knowingly conducted the business of a company with intent to defraud creditors for any fraudulent or dishonest purpose were guilty of the offence. While the UK Court of Appeal held in *R* v.

Grantham ([1984] 2 ALL E.R. 166) that the intention of the accused in fraudulent trading cases could be determined objectively, Charleton, McDermott and Bolger have argued that proof of knowing involvement in this offence required a subjective test as to the state of mind of the accused (i.e. this particular accused, and not a hypothetical reasonable man), to have acted with knowledge of the fraud (1999: 915). Even if the circumstances of the case suggested that the accused did know of the fraud, the issue is whether, in fact, he actually did know. Courtney (2012: 943) agreed that the Irish courts might not follow the English jurisprudence on this issue given the specific wording of the offence.

All of the evidence considered so far shows that white-collar crime offences in the Companies Acts from the twentieth century emphasised subjective culpability as a precondition to criminal liability. This was evinced by the blanket subjective culpability requirement in section 383 of the Primary Act; in those offences often thought of as only technically criminal, such as those offences relating to the keeping of company accounts, and also in specific 'hardcore' offences carrying serious penalties, like fraudulent trading. While the specifics of the offences may have changed over the twentieth century and become more demanding in some ways, the commitment to the values underpinning this system have remained consistent over the traditional period of governance in the Irish State. There was clearly a strong commitment to subjective culpability as a precondition to criminal liability in the Companies Acts. This is not to say, however, that strict liability was not also present. Not only does strict liability have a long history, emerging to penalise breaches of the Factory Acts and the distribution of adulterated food and drink (Greer and Nicholson, 2003; Norrie, 2001; Sayre, 1933), its prevalence was often greater than conceded (Blake and Ashworth, 1996). In a dualist system which addressed both conventional and regulatory crime, it is considered unremarkable that certain crimes are enforced on the basis of strict liability (Hanly, 2006: 91–3; McIntyre and McMullan, 2005: 62–9). This view is supported by the jurisprudence of the superior courts. In *Shannon Regional Fisheries Board* v. *Cavan County Council* ([1996] 3 I.R. 267), and *Maguire* v. *Shannon Regional Fisheries Board* ([1994] 2 I.L.R.M. 253), it was held that *mens rea* was not required and the offence of causing deleterious matter to fall into any waters could be committed intentionally, recklessly, negligently or accidentally. Similarly, in *M'Adam* v. *Dublin United Tramways Company Ltd* ([1929] I.R. 327), Sullivan P. (334) held that the offence of overloading a tram was one of strict liability because the prohibited acts 'are not in any real sense criminal, but in the public interest, they are prohibited under a penalty'.

Unsurprisingly then, there were also a number of offences in the Company Acts which did not explicitly require *mens rea*. Strict liability offences were justified on the basis that because company officers derived the benefits of corporate organisation (such as corporate personality and limited liability), then they were also to be made criminally responsible in ways that prevented companies being used as vehicles for fraud (Charleton, McDermott and Bolger, 1999: 926). In the 1908 Act, for example, the offences not specifying culpability were particularly apparent in the circumstances where liquidators failed to notify the Registrar of the completed dissolution of a company (s. 172(3)) or where directors successfully applied to have the dissolution of the company declared void but failed to file the order with the Registrar within seven days (s. 223(2)). The absence of culpability requirements was also apparent in subsequent Companies Acts. Nevertheless, what is significant about all such offences was that 'invariably … their liability is provided for on a specific basis or subject to a specific defence' (Charleton, McDermott and Bolger, 1999: 926).

For example, while it was noted that section 147(6) of the Primary Act specified that the failure to keep proper books of account had to be committed wilfully, the offence could also be committed if the company officer 'fails to take all reasonable steps to secure compliance by the company', a construction also adopted when the offence was updated in 1990 (s. 202(10)). Nevertheless, the commitment to due process, fairness and culpable conduct was evident in a statutory defence and a mitigation of punishment. The company officer could not be subject to imprisonment for this crime unless he acted wilfully. He could also avail himself of the defence that he had reasonable grounds to believe, and did believe, that a competent and reliable person was charged with the duty of keeping the company books in order and could do so. Furthermore, the defence was framed subjectively in terms of what the director actually believed, though the belief must be a reasonable one and the court could require evidence of this from the accused (Charleton, McDermott and Bolger, 1999: 928). Similarly, the falsification of company books, as specified by section 243(1) of the Companies Act 1990, could also be committed on a strict liability basis where the books were destroyed or mutilated. Nevertheless, in these circumstances, 'it is a defence to show that the accused had no intention to defeat the law' and this 'implies a subjective test' (Charleton, McDermott and Bolger, 1999: 930). Therefore, even those circumstances involving strict liability offences, which on their face appeared to deviate from modern criminal justice methods, still emphasised the subjective culpability of the accused through the use of a defence, thereby retaining moral blameworthiness as a significant issue.

There were also other offences which did not specify a culpability requirement but it is not immediately apparent that they were all strict liability offences. In statutory offences not specifying any form of culpability, there is a presumption that *mens rea* is required. For example, in *DPP* v. *Byrne* (CC, 24 January 2002 (Lynch J.)), a case involving a prosecution for insider dealing, the legislature did not specify that *mens rea* had to be proven but it was held that for an offence to have been committed, the defendant must have known that he was dealing in shares and that he intended to make an improper profit from this dealing. The penalties were too severe (ten years imprisonment and a fine of €253,947.61) for the offence to be one of strict liability. As noted by Horan (2011: 1116), the case 'illustrates the onerous obligation on the prosecution to prove *mens rea* in a prosecution for insider dealing'. Members of the legislature also subsequently noted that this construction made it 'virtually impossible currently to prove insider trading' (Rabbitt, Dáil Deb 13 Oct 1994, vol. 445, col. 2022). Nevertheless, the traditional commitment to subjective culpability requirements was clear, even when onerous for the prosecution, because even where no specific culpability requirement was specified, the accused was entitled to presume 'that knowledge of the wrongfulness of the criminal act (*mens rea*) is an essential ingredient in any determination of guilt' (Vaughan and Kilcommins, 2008: 106).

In summary, the criminal offences stipulated in the Companies Acts throughout the twentieth century evidenced a strong tendency to favour a subjective culpability requirement. This stemmed from the constraint that criminal law addressed morally reprehensible conduct. In this respect, it fulfilled the retributive function of the criminal law, which holds that man is a responsible moral agent who deserves to be punished for wrongdoing. It espoused respect for traditional criminal justice values because it served as an important limitation on utilitarianism, which in its pure form would find wrongdoers criminally liable on any basis that was most likely to deter offenders and prevent crime (Packer, 1968: 67). Without culpability, the criminal law 'ceases to be a guide to the well-intentioned and a restriction on the restraining power of the state' (68). Of course, in saying this, company law offences also had a strict liability component. The Irish legal system addressing corporate and white-collar criminality was dualist in nature but traditional criminal law accommodated this departure because it also had a strict liability exception. Modern criminal law employed a graduated scale of culpability proportionate to the seriousness of the offence. The more serious the offence, the stronger the culpability requirement, and the same was true of company law in its modern construction.

Due process

The Irish Constitution is a significant source of due process safeguards for the accused. Through judicial interpretation, the Constitution has safeguarded vulnerable individuals from the power of the State, protected the integrity of the criminal justice system and championed the due process model of criminal justice. The values it espouses have penetrated and infused the pre-trial, trial, and post-trial stages of the criminal justice process. Of course, the Constitution was not the only source of due process rights for the accused. These due process values were an imbedded part of the system more generally and showed themselves in the construction of legislation, in court judgments and in the ethos of the traditional era (Vaughan and Kilcommins, 2008: 97–119). This section analyses the rights of the accused and illustrates the traditional commitment to due process values.

At the pre-trial stage of criminal proceedings, the rules governing the investigation, detention and arrest of the accused by authorities were identified and strictly limited according to constitutional values of fairness and justice. The constitutional right to liberty was protected under Article 40.4.1. Suspects who voluntarily answered questions when not under arrest had to be told of their right to leave the Garda station (*People (DPP)* v. *Lynch* [1982] I.R. 64). Summary arrest powers were only exercisable when there were reasonable grounds and suspects had to be told the reasons and legal basis for their arrest (*People (A.G.)* v. *White* [1947] I.R. 247; *Re O'Laighleis* [1960] I.R. 93). Though the Gardaí had wide powers to search and question suspects under common law, suspects did not have to answer these questions (*DPP (Statford)* v. *Fagan* [1994] 2 I.L.R.M. 349). However, some statutory powers did exist and suspects had to be informed of the nature and description of the statutory power being invoked (*DPP* v. *Rooney* [1990] 2 I.R. 7). Such powers could not be used as a substitute for arrest and a suspect had to be taken into custody if incriminating evidence was found on their person (*O'Callaghan* v. *Ireland* [1994] 1 I.R.555; People *(DPP)* v. *Boylan* [1991] 1 I.R. 555). Various other provisions and procedures also protected the accused in custody. These included the Criminal Justice (Treatment of Persons in Custody in Garda Síochána Stations) Regulations 1987; the Criminal Justice Act 1984 (Electronic Recording of Interviews) Regulations 1997, and the so-called 'Judges Rules' (a series of guidelines informing police conduct accepted in *People (A.G.)* v. *Cummins* ([1972] 1 I.R. 312). They ensured that suspects were not intimidated or ill treated while in custody, and ensured that any evidence, confessions, or samples obtained were not the product of coercion. In general, these initiatives were designed to protect suspects from themselves, from the abuse of Garda power and protected the integrity of the criminal justice system more generally.

The ability to enter property was sharply limited by the constitutional inviolability of the dwelling under Article 40.5. Dwellings could not be entered except in accordance with law and a warrant was generally required. Gardaí could presume that they had permission to enter a business premises, though the owner-occupier could withdraw this permission at any time (*Minister for Justice* v. *Wang Zhu Jie* [1991] I.L.R.M. 823). Search warrants were only authorised when the Gardaí proved to an independent official (usually a peace commissioner or judge) that there were reasonable grounds that the warrants were necessary (*Simple Exports Ltd* v. *Revenue Commissioners* [2000] 2 I.R. 243; *Byrne* v. *Grey* [1998] I.R. 31; *DPP* v. *Yamanoha* [1994] 1 I.R. 565). Technical defects in the warrant could render it void, especially where evidence collected was a conscious and deliberate breach of constitutional rights, but not where the defects were very minor (*People (A.G.)* v. *O'Brien* [1965] I.R. 142; *People (DPP)* v. *Edgeworth* [2001] 2 I.R. 131; *People (DPP)* v. *Balfe* [1998] 4 I.R. 50). This also suggested a process that was weighted against arbitrary state power and in favour of the accused. Those accused of crimes, including corporate crimes, also had the right not to have the defence prejudiced by pre-trial adverse publicity (*Zoe Developments Ltd* v. *DPP* (HC, 3 March 1999 (Geoghegan J.)). As noted by Horan (2011: 320), 'If a company can incur bias in the minds of the public, which ... is a concern for corporations, it can certainly incur bias in the minds of a jury.' Furthermore, the right to privacy, which was already protected under tort and criminal law, was recognised as an unenumerated constitutional right in *Kennedy* v. *Ireland* ([1987] I.R. 587). As a general rule, any evidence obtained by a breach of constitutional rights was inadmissible unless there were extraordinary excusing circumstances justifying their inclusion, and illegally obtained evidence could also be excluded at the discretion of the trial judge.

The right to silence was also recognised as an unenumerated constitutional right under Article 38.1 by Costello J. in *Heaney and McGuiness* v. *Ireland* ([1994] 3 I.R. 593). Suspects can refuse to answer any question put to them in the course of a criminal investigation. The right of reasonable access to a solicitor was originally recognised as a common law right but was subsequently accorded constitutional status in 1990 (*People (DPP)* v. *Healy* [1990] 2 I.R. 73). Lawyer–client communications were also privileged and could not have been used at trial even where their disclosure would have revealed the commission of the crime. As reasoned by Bruce L.J. in *Pearce* v. *Pearce* ((1846) 1 De. G. and Sm. 12), making an accused fearful of discussing all matters with his counsel would be too high a price to pay for a conviction. Bail was generally not refused except on specific grounds which had to be supported by evidence (*People (A.G.)* v. *O'Callaghan* [1966] I.R. 501).

At trial, the accused had the right to be presumed innocent. As stated by Murray J. in *PO'C* v. *Director of Public Prosecutions* ([2000] 3 I.R. 87: 103), the presumption meant 'that he or she was entitled to the status of a person innocent of criminal charges until such has been proven in a trial conducted in accordance with law'. The burden remained on the prosecution and the standard of proof required was beyond reasonable doubt (*Murphy* v. *GM* [2001] 4 I.R. 113). If the jury thought that there was any reasonable chance that the defendant had not committed the offence then he had to be released. Its existence was justified by 'the social and legal consequences of being convicted of a crime, in which context the principle constitutes a measure of protection against error in the process, and a counterweight to the immense power and resources of the State compared to the position of the defendant' (Ashworth, 2006: 83). This rule was so fundamental to the criminal process that it was considered the 'golden thread' running through the criminal law (*Woolmington* v. *DPP* ([1935] A.C. 462). Though not absolute in nature, the presumption was safeguarded by both Article 6.2 of the European Convention on Human Rights (ECHR) and the Irish Constitution (*O'Leary* v. *The Attorney General* [1993] 1 I.R. 102).

Article 38.1 provides that all persons must be tried in due course of law. Hogan and Whyte (2003: 1121) have observed that this is a 'fine-mesh catch-all notion' which covers the accused in numerous contexts. The provision prohibited retrospective criminalisation (*State (Walsh)* v. *Lennon* [1942] I.R. 112; *Enright* v. *Ireland* [2003] 2 I.R. 321), vague criminal laws (*King* v. *Attorney General* [1981] I.R. 233), double jeopardy (*Attorney General (O'Maonaigh)* v. *Fitzgerald* [1964] I.R. 458; *People (DPP)* v. *O'Shea* [1982] I.R. 384) and offences not known in law as crimes (*Attorney General* v. *Cunningham* [1932] I.R. 28). The accused had the right to know the charges against him (*State (Howard)* v. *Donnelly* [1966] I.R. 51; Article 6(3)(a), ECHR), to have enough time to properly prepare his defence (*The State (Howard)* v. *Donnelly* [1966] I.R. 51; *Re Haughey* [1971] I.R. 217; *Leonard* v. *Garavan* (HC, 30 April 2002 (McKenchie J.); Article 6(3)(b), ECHR), to a speedy trial (*State (O'Connell)* v. *Judge Fawsitt* [1986] I.L.R.M. 639; *Re Singer* 97 I.L.T.R. 130; *DPP* v. *Byrne* [1994] 2 I.R. 236), to have his case heard in a properly constituted court and in public (*Shelly* v. *District Justice Mahon* [1990] 1 I.R. 36; Article 34.1 of Bunreacht na hÉireann; *People (DPP)* v. *Ginley* (3 Frewen 251)), and to trial by jury for indictable offences (Article 38.5 of Bunreacht na hÉireann; *People (DPP)* v. *O'Shea* [1982] I.R. 384).

The accused also had the right to invoke the privilege against self-incrimination at trial. In *Re National Irish Bank* ([1999] 1 I.R. 145), the question was whether the obligation to answer questions or provide documents to inspectors, appointed to investigate companies under Part II of the 1990 Act, were breaches of the privilege against self-incrimination. The Supreme Court held that the statutory obligation to answer questions was not, in itself, unconstitutional. However, any answers were inadmissible in subsequent criminal proceedings because this would breach the privilege against self-incrimination and undermine the due process model of criminal justice. The accused also had the right not to give evidence at trial (Criminal Justice (Evidence) Act 1924, s. 1). Evidence could be excluded at the discretion of the trial judge where it was determined to be more prejudicial than probative, that is, that the evidence hurt the accused's case more than it helped to achieve a just outcome (Vaughan and Kilcommins, 2008: 110–11). Hearsay evidence was excluded in all but exceptional circumstances (*Cullen* v. *Clarke* [1963] I.R. 368; *Eastern Health Board* v. *MK* [1999] 2 I.R. 99). The accused had the right to cross-examine his accuser under Article 38.1 (*Re Haughey* [1971] I.R. 217). Evidence of the accused's previous bad character also could not be admitted in case the jury might convict him for other wrongs (*King* v. *Director of Public Prosecutions*

(24 October 1978 (McWilliam J.)), finding him 'to be *a* "bad man" rather than *the* "bad man" [emphasis in original]' (Vaughan and Kilcommins, 2008: 113).

Unconstitutionally obtained evidence, including confessions extracted through the breach of constitutional rights, was inadmissible at trial unless extraordinary circumstances dictated otherwise (Hogan and Whyte, 2003: 1101). The courts could also exclude a confession even if it was not obtained unconstitutionally but where they still thought it was unfair or unjust to admit it (*DPP* v. *Shaw* [1982] I.R. 1). The jury, rather than the legislature, determined his or her guilt. In accordance with the Seventh Protocol to the European Convention on Human Rights, the accused could also appeal his conviction to a higher court.

The various rights and procedural protections at all phases of the criminal justice process reflected a commitment to due process. Though these due process rights and protections were often forged in a conventional crime context, they also applied in the regulatory context. For example, the right to trial by jury was also reflected in the judicial treatment of penalties for failure to produce documentation, appear before an inspector, or answer his questions as stipulated in the provisions for company investigations. Section 10(5) of the 1990 Act provided that failure to do so would render that person liable to punishment 'in like manner as if he had been guilty of contempt of court'. In *Desmond* v. *Glacken* (No. 2) ((1993) 3 I.R. 67), O'Hanlon J. in the High Court held that this provision was unconstitutional because it deprived the accused of his right to trial by jury for a major charge. The Supreme Court upheld this decision on appeal and Findlay C.J. stated that the imposition of severe penalties were appropriate only to the commission of major criminal offences, not regulatory offences. Summary conviction would not be permissible in such serious cases but rather the guilt of the accused would have to be determined by jury at trial.

The rules on exclusionary evidence have also been upheld in the regulatory context in the case of *Competition Authority* v. *Irish Dental Association* ([2006] 1 I.L.R.M. 383). In this case, the plaintiff obtained a civil warrant that authorised the entry, search, seizure and retention of documents on the premises of the defendant, whose business was stated to be that of selling, supplying or distributing motor vehicles. The defendant was actually a body representing practising dentists so the warrant was invalid. McKechnie J. excluded the evidence obtained as a result of the warrant on the grounds that it constituted a deliberate violation of the defendant's constitutional rights and that no extraordinary excusing circumstances existed such as to justify its inclusion. These cases confirm that exclusionary rules apply in regulatory contexts outside of the ordinary realm of criminal law. More generally, unless rights were specifically excluded, then due process rules also applied to those suspected of corporate and white-collar crime offences.

Though the situation is far from clear, it is arguable that the Irish courts have granted companies the constitutional right to due process as a reflection of the commitment to fairness and justice in the modern criminal sphere. In a number of cases where companies have submissions based on their constitutional rights to the rule against double jeopardy (*Register of Companies* v. *Judge David Anderson and System Partners Ltd* ([2005] 1 I.R. 21)), trial by jury (*Att.-Gen.* v. *Southern Industrial Trust Ltd* ((1957) 94 I.L.T.R. 161)), and the privilege against self-incrimination (*Re National Irish Bank* [1999] 1 I.R. 145), the courts have considered the cases on their merits without explicitly accepting or denying that companies have constitutional rights or considering their status as artificial persons. The courts do not appear to have considered the instances when companies may be entitled to other due process provisions, such as whether companies are entitled to the presumption of innocence. What is significant, however, is that the courts have never explicitly denied that companies are entitled to constitutional rights. O'Neill (2007: 122–3) has suggested that companies appear to be able to claim constitutional rights where the right is designed 'to uphold institutional or structural values which are crucial to the integrity of the criminal justice system'. If companies were not entitled to basic constitutional due process rights then they would be compromised at all phases of the criminal process and this would affect the legitimacy of the criminal justice system more generally. The courts seem to have extended due process safeguards to companies in criminal matters and this extension affirms the traditional respect for fairness and the fundamental principles of justice.

In conclusion, the criminal justice system instituted a system of procedural rules that have been collected together into a 'due process model' of criminal justice. These rights were fully realised in the twentieth century by the enactment of Bunreacht na hÉireann and through its interpretation by an active Irish judiciary. The system operated under an equality of arms framework, whereby the State limited its power and granted special rights to accused persons to protect them from abuses of power and unfair criminal processes. In doing so, it prioritised the protection of the individual from the awesome power of the State and stood strong against the adoption of a wholly utilitarian stance, by espousing and enshrining values that transcend the goal of crime prevention. These self-imposed limitations operated to prevent the justice system from operating instrumentally, at maximum velocity, in recognition that the protection of the individual and the integrity of the system were more important values. The presumption of innocence, the standard of proof to beyond all reasonable doubt, requiring the prosecution to discharge the burden of proof, and the right of access to a lawyer, all stood as barriers to easy conviction and represented 'powerful curbs on unwise, sweeping use of the criminal sanction' (Packer, 1968: 139). The due process model was an 'obstacle course';

one in which 'each of its successive stages is designed to present formidable impediments to carrying the accused any further along in the process' (163). These limitations, stemming from the values, sentiments and beliefs of the traditional period, shaped the formal letter of law to such an extent that legal rules insist on the prevention and elimination of mistakes where possible, and also attempt to address the system's own abuses through the exclusion of illegal evidence and through the appeals process. Furthermore, this was aided by a 'mood of scepticism' about the criminal sanction which made officials open to suggestions that the system itself can be a source of injustice (163–73).

Sentencing imperatives: the dominance of proportionality

The Irish courts have explicitly adopted proportionality as the dominant principle informing their sentencing policy. Walsh J. in *People (AG)* v. *O'Driscoll* ((1972) 1 Frewen 351) stated that it was 'the duty of the courts to pass appropriate sentences in each case having regard to the particular circumstances of that case – not only in regard to the particular crime but in regard to the particular criminal'. The Irish judiciary subsequently asserted that proportionate punishment is a constitutional right (*State (Healy)* v. *O'Donoghue* ([1976] I.R. 325: 353; *People (DPP)* v. *C(W)* ([1994] 1 I.L.R.M. 321). In all circumstances, the courts emphasised that punishment was individuated and personalised to the particular case at hand (*People (DPP)* v. *Cormack* ([2000] 4 I.R. 356). Denham J. stated in *People (DPP)* v. *Sheedy* ([2000] 2 I.R.184: 192) that the practice of constructing a proportionate sentence required the courts to implement a two-part test, such that 'sentences were to be proportionate to the crime and also to the personal circumstances of the applicant'. The court first considered the range of penalties for the offence, where this particular offence lay on the spectrum of wrongdoing for the offence and determined what sentence was appropriate to the particular act of the offender. Then the court applied the mitigating and aggravating factors and adjusted the sentence up or down to reflect the particular circumstance of the accused (*People (DPP)* v. *Kelly* [2005] 1 I.L.R.M. 19; *People (DPP)* v. *Sheedy* [2000] 2 I.R.184; *People (DPP)* v. *Dillon* (CCA, 17 December 2003 (McCracken J.)). The gravity of the offence was determined according to the harm caused by the offender and how culpable he or she was for the wrongdoing, even where the offence was one of strict liability (O'Malley, 2006: 92). Offences were considered particularly reprehensible or 'aggravated' if they were premeditated, if they were excessively violent or involved a weapon, if they were committed by criminal gangs, if victims' homes were invaded or if motivated by the victims' race or religion. The most significant mitigating factors were arguably the good character of the accused and the absence of previous convictions (92). These principles applied to all offenders.

Nevertheless, McGrath (2012) has questioned whether white-collar offenders were less likely to receive custodial sentences than ordinary offenders. The organisational structure of the company, its internal lines of decision making and accountability, the geographical scope of its operations and the nature, volume and complexity of transactions it conducts, all gave rise to ambiguities such that responsibility could become diffused and fragmented throughout the organisation (Jackall, 1988; Wolgast, 1992). This can make it difficult to prove culpable wrongdoing or premeditation. In additional, though white-collar crimes can have serious consequences, they were rarely considered to be as harmful as more conventional crimes. Consequently, these offences may not have commanded the same level of condemnation in sentencing. Moreover, white-collar criminals were unlikely to trigger the usual aggravating factors. White-collar offences, unlike homicides and rapes, are rarely violent. The tools of industry are spreadsheets and meetings, not guns and knives. Victims' homes are not invaded and neither ethnicity nor creed are likely to be the inspiration for wrongdoing. Corporate collectives are not considered criminal gangs, but rather effective forms of large-scale business administration. Therefore, these aggravating factors, often associated with conventional offences, seem unlikely to apply to corporate wrongdoing.

Meanwhile, the particular circumstances of white-collar offenders are such that they are likely to benefit from well-recognised mitigating factors, like the absence of previous convictions. Given the difficulties in detecting white-collar crimes, particularly when companies are reluctant to report fraud from within their ranks (Gallagher, 1999), corporate wrongdoing is likely to be 'filtered' out of the criminal justice system (O'Donnell, 1998: 33). Indeed, surveys have shown that people from the poorest sections of the community are much more likely to face criminal prosecution than those from the least deprived communities. Bacik *et al.* (1998: 25) note that '73% of District Court defendants are from the most economically deprived areas. In fact, one might be forgiven for suggesting on the basis of the data that the Dublin District Court system appears to be there *for* people from deprived areas' (emphasis in original). The courts are also likely to be lenient to offenders without criminal records because it is suggested that their wrongdoing is an aberration and that such offenders are unlikely to commit future crimes (*People (DPP)* v. *Lynch* (CCA, 29 May 1995, *ex tempore*)). However, some research suggests that white-collar criminals are likely to reoffend (Weisberg, Waring and Leeper Piquero, 2008).

Nevertheless, owing to the absence of previous convictions, white-collar criminals may have benefited from 'a well-recognised mitigating factor' (O'Malley, 2006: 141), and one to which the judiciary attach 'very considerable weight' (*People (DPP)* v. *Kelly* [2005] 1 I.L.R.M. 19: 33). It was also thought that first-time offenders should not receive custodial sentences because they would find the experience even tougher than seasoned criminals (O'Malley, 2006: 141–2), though recent empirical research has suggested that white-collar criminals fare no worse than others and, in some respects, adapt to prison life better than ordinary criminals (Stadler *et al.*, 2013). Furthermore, while cooperation with the authorities, pleading guilty, and showing remorse are all mitigating factors, the offender is not punished for non-cooperation with the authorities or for mounting a vigorous defence at trial, features which often mark companies and company officers who are prosecuted (Mann, 1985; Rottman and Tormey, 1986).

Company officers are also more likely to be of good character, as evinced by a steady employment record, good family background, and a history of charitable work (*R.* v. *Howells* [1999] 1 W.L.R. 307; O'Malley, 2006: 140). It might be argued that these features are more easily evidenced by the middle classes who are often raised in intact families and have more secure employment opportunities, greater access to education and colleagues in positions of power and influence (O'Mahony, 1998, 56–7). In addition, there is some evidence that courts believe that 'respectable' corporate offenders are more adversely affected by imprisonment than ordinary offenders, particularly where they are at risk of losing their jobs, pension rights, social standing, and where it could cause the dissolution of family relationships (Ashworth and Player, 1998; Mann, Wheeler and Sarat, 1979–80). Indeed, Bacik *et al.* (1998: 26) have shown that defendants from deprived areas were 49 per cent more likely to receive a custodial sentence in the District Court than those from the least deprived areas once age, gender and other variables were taken into account. In addition, O'Mahony's analysis of the inmates in Mountjoy Prison revealed that most were poorly educated, had chronically unemployed parents, came from broken homes or large families, and had to compete for scarce material and emotional resources. He concluded that inmates 'tend to be young, urban under-educated males from the lower socio-economic classes and the so-called underclass, who have been convicted predominantly for relatively petty crimes against property without violence. Very few offenders are imprisoned for white collar crime' (O'Mahony, 1998: 54).

Company officers may also be in a better position to pay compensation to victims of their wrongdoing. In the past, the Irish courts were willing to give wrongdoers lighter punishments when this occurred, even though it overtly privileged offenders with greater resources over those with more modest means (*People (DPP)* v. *McCabe* [2005] I.E.C.C.A. 90; *People (DPP)* v. *McLaughlin* [2005] I.E.C.C.A. 91). In a corporate fraud case involving Patrick Gallagher of Merchant Banking in Northern Ireland, sentencing was deferred to allow Mr Gallagher raise funds to compensate his victims. It was only when he failed to do so that he was sentenced to two years' imprisonment (*Irish Times*, 2 October 1990: 13). In *Re McIlhagga* (SC, 29 July 1971), O'Dalaigh J. in the Supreme

Court ruled that imprisonment for failing to compensate victims did not discriminate in favour of wealthy offenders. The court was particularly keen to make the point that the payment was restitution and not a fine. Nevertheless, the central issue remains that those with greater resources are better equipped to avoid prison through financial means. Even though never explicitly reasoned as such, it may represent tacit agreement with Posner (1979–80) that large financial penalties are more effective than custodial sentences when dealing with wealthy offenders. Meanwhile, O'Malley (2006: 103) notes that the courts do not necessarily consider social disadvantage as a factor in mitigation because 'matters such as poverty, lack of education, addiction and financial pressure are by no means universally accepted by the public as valid mitigating factors'. He also notes (117) that the courts are obliged to consider factors in mitigation 'in every case in which a court has a discretionary sentencing power'. This means that the courts cannot disregard mitigating factors on the basis that they are more likely to exist by the nature of the wrongdoing, say, in corporate and white-collar crime cases.

The evidence considered so far suggests that sentencing is generally informed by the principle of proportionality. However, Irish sentencing is unstructured. It is also informed by other rationales such as rehabilitation, individual and general deterrence, just deserts and incapacitation, albeit irregularly and even then to varying degrees. For example, the courts are inclined to temper proportionality with rehabilitative ideals by ensuring that offenders are not adversely affected by punishment such that they are likely to be less able to subsequently pursue an honest life (*People (AG)* v. *O'Driscoll* (1972) 1 Frewen 351: 359, Walsh J.). Therefore, with the exception of very serious wrongdoing, the courts are naturally reluctant to subject any offender to prison because this could inhibit his or her ability to find subsequent employment and make it even more difficult to reintegrate him or her into society. White-collar criminals are prime candidates for rehabilitation. They are typically well-educated members of the middle class with positive prospects who, more often than not, have had access to higher education (McCullagh, 2002; O'Mahony, 1998). Consequently, as they are unlikely to reoffend and do not need be contained or incapacitated for the benefit of society, it is understandable that the judiciary may be reluctant to incarcerate corporate wrongdoers or deny them the benefit of probation. On a subconscious level, by virtue of shared social values and background, it may also be that judges are more likely to identify with these wrongdoers who commit 'respectable' offences, than with conventional criminal offenders who snatch handbags or deal drugs. The latter offences are likely to be outside the ordinary experiences of the judiciary (Mann, Wheeler and Sarat, 1979–80: 500). As surmised by Foucault, the process of punishment is designed to apply equally in theory but is practised against the poor. He recognised (1991b: 276):

> that in principle it applies to all citizens, but that it is addressed principally to the most numerous and least enlightened classes; that in the courts society as a whole does not judge one of its members, but that a social category with an interest in order judges another that is dedicated to disorder: 'Visit the places where people are judged, imprisoned or executed ... One thing will strike you everywhere; everywhere you see two quite distinct classes of men, one of which always meets on the seats of accusers and judges, the other on the benches of the accused' ... Law and justice do not hesitate to proclaim their necessary class dissymmetry.

The evidence has shown that the traditional approach was committed to ensuring proportionality in sentencing offenders. Those convicted of criminal offences had the constitutional right to proportionate punishment which was tailored both to the particular circumstances of the offender and the particular circumstances of the offence. This right evinced the modern commitment to fairness and justice in punishment and it applied to all offenders convicted of 'ordinary' crimes and white-collar crimes alike. However, it was submitted that this system of proportionate punishment tended to privilege white-collar criminals. Owing to their personal circumstances and the nature of their crimes, they were more likely to avail themselves of mitigating factors and avoid any aggravating factors, and may, therefore, have been less likely to receive severe punishments. In particular, it was shown that white-collar criminals are more likely to be of good character and often do not have previous convictions. They are unlikely to use weapons, invade homes or be members of criminal gangs. They have more to lose than ordinary criminals and can integrate back into society with ease. For these reasons, the rules on sentencing, though ostentatiously orientated to each individual's circumstances, were actually systemically biased and resulted in lighter penalties for white-collar criminals.

Conclusion

This chapter has analysed various criminal law rules under three headings: subjective culpability, due process and proportionality in sentencing. These features were representative of the conventional criminal justice system because they limited the power of government to provide for the investigation, apprehension, prosecution and punishment of corporate suspects. Their common rationale was assumed and unarticulated but overtly anti-utilitarian: that justice was personalised and individuated, that the security and the privacy of the individual should not be invaded, that the individual was an end in himself and not a means to an end. These values were enshrined in culpability requirements which addressed the moral reprehensibility of the wrongdoer, in due process values developed under an equality of arms framework, in proportionate sentences which were tailored both to the particular circumstances of the crime and the offender, and in the adversarial system of criminal justice more generally. The principles of subjective culpability, due process and proportionality in sentencing, all had a significant impact on the way in which cases of white-collar crimes were prosecuted. The burden of proof was on the prosecution to prove that a suspect acted knowingly or willingly to commit the crime and to satisfy the court or jury of this beyond any reasonable doubt. These were very difficult tasks in complex corporate cases. Furthermore, the adversarial nature of the system and the availability of significant due process constitutional protections for persons suspected of corporate wrongdoing, allowed companies and company officers to challenge the imposition of sanctions against them in regulatory contexts, like those relating to company investigations. Even when offenders were successfully convicted of white-collar crimes, the Irish system of structuring proportionality in sentencing meant that white-collar offenders were far more likely to benefit from the mitigating sentencing factors than suffer from the aggravating ones. Therefore, they were far less likely to receive a custodial sentence than conventional wrongdoers from deprived backgrounds.

This chapter emphasised that the approach to corporate crime in the twentieth century was informed by conventional criminal law methods but also acknowledged that regulatory impulses competed with due process values. The regulatory and conventional crime models coexisted side by side. The regulatory model also respected the individual but to a lesser extent than that of the conventional crime model. The conventional crime model repressed criminal conduct but without the same pressing emphasis on instrumentalism that was evident in the regulatory model. Both models sought efficient outcomes but seemed to turn on whether efficiency was its animating value. In fact, the coexistence of each model was often so peaceful that they could not really be considered as entirely separate models of criminal justice. Instead, they enjoyed a symbiotic relationship in which the due process model denied its affair with instrumentalism but needed it to secure accountability on occasion, while regulatory criminal law, also, to some degree, had to respect due process and fairness for legitimacy.

Building and structuring these models as distinct concepts with subcategorisations was artificial but it facilitated our understanding of the particular contours of the traditional corporate criminal justice system. More importantly, it allowed us to understand the values underpinning and reinforcing the system. It was shown that corporate criminal law was informed by both conventional and regulatory impulses but it was primarily informed by the moral, symbolic and expressive limb of the criminal law. This probably occurred because of its incorporation into the criminal justice sphere generally, without specialised attention to the application of criminal law to the corporate context. Given the difficulties with subjective culpability requirements, strong due process safeguards and proportionate punishment, the conventional criminal justice architecture may not have been the most effective way of dealing with corporate wrongdoing. However, this cannot be determined by an analysis of legal mechanisms in abstraction from the reality of enforcement. Therefore, Chapter 4 analyses the enforcement of the conventional system of criminal law in practice, thereby completing our examination of the 'logic of action' addressing corporate wrongdoing in the twentieth century.

4

Policing, prosecution and punishment

Introduction

In Chapter 3 it was shown that the rules of evidence addressing the investigation and prosecution of white-collar crimes developed under an equality of arms framework to protect individuals from arbitrary state power. By design, these rules were weighted in favour of those accused of crimes so that they were less likely to be convicted if prosecuted and unlikely to receive too harsh a punishment if they were convicted. This chapter goes beyond the examination of the legal principles and explores how the system coped with the detection, investigation, and prosecution of corporate and white-collar crimes in practice. It analyses the activities of the various agencies responsible for the detection and prosecution of crime to show how the persistent under-policing of the corporate sector endured for so long. Though enforcement was supplemented by some regulatory agencies such as the Companies Registration Office (CRO), operating under the aegis of the Minister for Industry and Commerce (hereafter the Minister) and his or her department, it is shown that corporate and white-collar crimes were often addressed by the same police and prosecutors who addressed conventional crimes, even though they lacked the necessary resources and expertise to detect and investigate complex cases of corporate wrongdoing.

This chapter also emphasises that the failure to enforce company law was not merely the consequence of applying a conventional crime model to address corporate wrongdoing. It was a reflection of the broader inertia in corporate affairs in Ireland. The State was not committed to prosecuting 'respectable' company officers for 'merely technical' wrongs because corporate deviancy was not considered as morally reprehensible as conventional crime. In this sense, the failure to prosecute corporate offenders may be understood in the same context as the marginalisation of corporate deviancy from the definition of crime by the courts. In both contexts, a 'real crime' perspective animated the public conception of criminality. Both phenomena are manifestations of the logic of action arising from the broader social and political inertia in corporate affairs.

A culture of non-compliance and non-enforcement

Record keeping on conventional crime deteriorated in Ireland in the twentieth century (Kilcommins *et al.*, 2004: vii). In a context where company law was rarely reviewed or updated, it is unsurprising that information on corporate enforcement is also minimal. The State did not establish a committee to investigate corporate compliance and enforcement until the end of the twentieth century, though the Cox Report in 1958 did peripherally consider the issue. Despite the absence of any visible engagement with evidence or statistics on compliance, it asserted (18) that the 'great majority of companies in the State are honestly conducted and managed', though, 'There is undoubtedly a tendency, especially in the case of private companies, to disregard or to be careless about the obligations which the law imposes as to the making of annual returns or even as to the keeping of books of account.' It stated (20) that these infractions were often not taken seriously because: 'In most cases in which prosecutions for offences under the Companies Acts are brought, there is a tendency to regard the offences as being trivial or technical.' It also acknowledged (53) that there were some isolated high profile instances of corporate fraud which involved 'a complete disregard of the requirements of the Companies Acts'.

Nevertheless, the subsequent practice of corporate enforcement did not significantly change. Forty years after the publication of the Cox Report, the Working Group on Company Law Compliance and Enforcement stated (McDowell, 1998: paras 2.4–2.5) that Ireland was 'characterised by a culture of non-compliance ... Those who are tempted to make serious breaches of company law have little reason to fear detection or prosecution. As far as enforcement is concerned, the sound of the enforcers' footsteps on the beat is simply never heard.' Though it also did not engage in any visible compilation or breakdown of crime statistics, it concluded (para. 2.10) that, 'the great majority of the hundreds of summary offences provided for in the Acts have never been the subject of any criminal proceedings, and there has only been a handful of occasions on which the indictable offences have been prosecuted'. The following sections analyse the activities of the various agencies responsible for the detection and prosecution of crime and attempt to show how the persistent under-policing of the corporate sector, as illustrated by both the Cox and McDowell Reports, relates to the broader inertia and logic of action discussed in previous chapters.

Conventional criminal law machinery

The Irish Police Force (An Garda Síochána or 'Gardaí') and the Office of the Director of Public Prosecutions (DPP), formerly the Attorney General, monopolised most of the responsibility for addressing corporate and white-collar crime in Ireland, particularly serious crimes like fraudulent trading and offences relating to insolvency (McDowell, 1998). The DPP exercised the exclusive right to prosecute indictable crime (tried before a judge and jury) though it concurrently shared the ability to prosecute summary company law offences (tried before a judge without a jury). However, the composition, education and training of the Gardaí suggest that they were not ideally placed to detect and investigate sophisticated forms of corporate wrongdoing. In the early days of the State, An Garda Síochána was largely composed of members from a military or a farming background. As observed by McNiffe (1997: 39, 47), almost two-thirds of all Garda recruits between 1922 and 1952 had been in the Irish Republican Army (IRA) and approximately half of the recruits in this period were either farmers or labourers. He also noted (51) that most recruits had received only primary school education. This was supplemented by some very basic legal training on admission to the force. One recruit from this period recalled being told that the law was based on the Ten Commandments and that if he could remember this then he would not go far wrong (Ua Maoileoin, 1989: 96).

The primary duties of the Gardaí in this period were enforcing licensing laws, detecting illicit distillation, detecting agrarian crime, and detecting ordinary crimes against person and property, particularly larceny (Interdepartmental Inquiry, 1951). The Gardaí were also 'an indispensible cog in the wheel of government administration' (McNiffe, 1989: 109). A study conducted in the 1950s suggested that the Gardaí outside Dublin spent approximately 40 per cent of their time performing administrative duties, including the collection of agricultural statistics, the distribution of old age pension books and the enforcement of legislation ensuring that children attended primary school (Allen, 1999: 142–4; Interdepartmental Inquiry, 1951). It would seem that policing the corporate sector was not a significant priority for the force. The Gardaí also lived among the people they policed and their presence was a reminder both of the existence of the law and the willingness to enforce it. Their presence in the community meant that they were usually aware of the potential opportunities for criminality in their district and, as a result of their knowledge, were often able to identify those prone to breaking the law (Leahy, 1996). The immediacy of the law was heightened when the Gardaí walked the beat. Nevertheless, though information on Garda activity in this period is minimal, the Gardaí did not start publishing reports on its activities until 1950 (Kilcommins *et al.*, 2004: 66), it seems likely that this model of policing was not suited to the corporate context because soldiers and farmers, rather than accountants and lawyers, were investigating technical breaches of the Companies Acts.

A specialist subgroup, the Garda Fraud Squad, was subsequently established to police less conventional, more complicated forms of crime. Even then, fraud was still relatively unsophisticated. For example, the public was put on alert that secretaries were being blackmailed into ordering more carbon paper than they needed, behaviour that would not have demanded much in the way of a diabolical criminal mind (*Irish Times*, 13 September 1969: 9). An examination of newspapers from this period suggested that the Fraud Squad was mainly concerned with cheque fraud, embezzlement and conmen absconding with funds for bogus investments (*Irish Times*, 1 November 1973: 17; 7 August 1976: 12; 4 June 1986: 6; 7 October 1987: 8; 19 December 1987: 10). However, the Fraud Squad did not seem to have any specific remit or area of specialisation so it seemed to be called upon in any situation outside the expertise of the average Garda member. It investigated substandard deliveries to building sites, planning irregularities, the substitution of disposable napkins for prescription incontinence sheets (a Government minister promised prosecutions), video piracy, the refusal to renew membership with a local GAA sports club, the theft of ransom money for the racing horse 'Shergar', and the leaking of State examination papers (*Irish Times*, 11 July 1980: 1; 16 April 1981: 1; 3 May 1982: 6; 31 May 1982: 21; 15 October 1982: 1; 11 November 1983: 1; 26 June 1985: 1). The Fraud Squad also investigated various forms of social welfare fraud, raising the question of whether the State was more concerned with punishing the poor rather than elite wrongdoers (*Irish Times*, 18 February 1983: 6; 6 August 1984: 6; 12 September 1986: 8; 16 September 1986: 8; 25 March 1988: 10).

In the early 1970s, the Squad reported that it was struggling to tackle financial frauds due to the growth in banking and credit transactions (*Irish Times*, 12 August 1971: 12). Problems intensified further when its existing caseload, with which it was already struggling, grew further because of a '1976 bank strike when cheque forgeries became rampant and criminals at large became aware for the first time of the lesser risks involved in paperwork crime' (*Irish Times*, 25 September 1990: 13). Nevertheless, the Squad remained severely under-resourced throughout this period. In 1971, the nationwide force consisted of seventeen men (*Irish Times*, 12 August 1971: 12). By 1990, the Squad was operating with fewer than thirty officers working a shift system that left as few as five officers on duty at any given time (*Irish Times*, 25 September 1990: 13).

In addition to poor staffing levels, the Garda policy on promotion undermined the effectiveness of the Squad. Garda policy dictated that promoted officers were moved out of the branch in which they were working. So when Squad officers were promoted, they were moved into non-fraud roles, divesting the Squad of acquired expertise. Conversely, when Gardaí were promoted to senior roles in the Fraud Squad, they came from non-fraud backgrounds and lacked the required skills to investigate white-collar crimes. This policy demoralised the Squad because members were reassigned if they were too good at their jobs and because promotion to senior posts in the Squad was rarely from within their own ranks (*Irish Times*, 25 September 1990: 13).

Furthermore, as more Irish people began to avail themselves of higher education, Garda recruits with degrees in business and accounting felt little desire to specialise in fraud because they could build careers with more ease elsewhere in the force (*Irish Times*, 23 February 1990: 9). This also contributed to the failure to develop expertise within the Squad. In addition, the Minister for Justice acknowledged that the Squad did not retain any full-time accountancy or legal staff to help them analyse and interpret company accounts and papers (Burke, Dáil Deb. 5 February 1991, vol. 404, col. 1480). It was later also suggested that the Squad was reluctant to consult outside accountants and auditors for help, believing that it was unprofessional to ask civilians to aid them in law enforcement (*Irish Times*, 11 April 1995: 13). If this was the case and considering their general lack of resources, it is questionable to what extent the Gardaí were capable of doing their job, especially when it is considered that economic crimes are generally far more complicated than street crimes, involve intricate accounting practices, double books, enormous amounts of paperwork, and the fact that prosecutors often need to have specialised skills to interpret data and must dedicate large amounts of time to the entire process (Braithwaite, 1984: 324; Wilson and Matz, 1977: 651).

In addition, the effectiveness of the Squad was limited by its operational approach to investigations. It seems that it investigated cases only when it received complaints. One officer acknowledged that companies tend not to report frauds from within their own ranks so it may be that most cases were never even investigated (Gallagher, 1999: 263). Furthermore, Carney observed that the Squad seemed to take a deferential approach to suspects accused of fraud because it 'sees its suspects by appointment rather than dawn raid and it may be that if he or she doesn't confess in remorse at this genteel confrontation which the suspect has prepared for, they have not the resources to go further and build a case through documents' (*Irish Times*, 31 August 1990: 10). He pointed out that this approach, when combined with the lack of forensic accountancy skills, effectively rendered successful prosecution impossible because 'The capacity to build a case through documents without a suspect's co-operation should be a fraud squad's basic skill. The courts have not seen any evidence that such a skill exists in Ireland.'

In part, the failure of the Gardaí to address significant issues of corporate wrongdoing persisted because they were simply unaware that the law had been breached. While lawyers and accountants presumably would have advised their clients to comply with the law, the State did not rely on them as a source of crime detection. Lawyers, accountants and auditors were under no obligation to report the suspected commission of indictable offences to the authorities. Furthermore, professional bodies were not required to report that a disciplinary tribunal had determined that one of their members had failed to maintain accurate records of a liquidation or receivership, nor were they required to report that they suspected one of their members had committed an indictable offence (McDowell, 1998). Consequently, the State failed to capitalise on those closest to potential wrongdoing and it was rarely even aware that a criminal offence had been committed. Company officers who sought professional advice would also have been advised that if they broke the law, they would probably go unpunished (Appleby, 2005: 267).

By contrast, in cases of compulsory liquidations, liquidators were obliged, in accordance with section 299 of the Companies Act 1963, to report their suspicions that a company officer had committed a criminal offence, and to assist with any prosecution arising from this report. In theory, this was an effective way of ensuring that corporate wrongdoing – most of which is often only discovered when a company is wound up – was reported to the authorities. In reality, however, this provision was traditionally of little effect. Most companies in Ireland were not wound up when they ceased to trade (McDowell, 1998, para. 2.5). Therefore, most wrongdoing was not discovered or reported. Furthermore, even when companies were wound up and offences were reported to the Office of the DPP, it simply passed on the report to the Garda Fraud Squad for investigation, a body that had neither the resources nor the skills to conduct an effective investigation into complicated company law provisions (McDowell, 1998: para. 2.14). In addition, if the liquidator had provided a damning report of the activities of the company and its directors, this would not of itself have provided any admissible evidence for the prosecution (McDowell, 1998: para. 2.11). Furthermore, it seems that the officers of the Central Bank refused to cooperate with the Gardaí in their investigations, because of the oath of secrecy specified in section 31 of the Central Bank Act 1942 (Law Reform Commission, 1992: 333). This statutory impediment persisted until it was finally repealed by section 16 of the Central Bank Act 1989.

All this suggests that the DPP and the Gardaí were often unaware that white-collar crimes were being committed. However, it must also be pointed out that even when high-profile cases of corporate wrongdoing were discovered, prosecutions rarely followed. In the case of *Re Aluminium Fabricators* ([1984] I.L.R.M. 399), the directors of the company were not prosecuted when they kept double books to divert company funds into their own private bank accounts in the Isle of Man. In *Re Contract Packaging Ltd* (HC, 16 January 1992 (Flood J.)), the directors were not prosecuted when they siphoned off in excess of £384,000 of company money for their personal use and defrauded the Revenue Commissioners. In *Re Kelly's Carpetdrome Ltd* (HC, 1 July 1983 (Costello J.)), the directors were not prosecuted when they defrauded the Revenue Commissioners of €2 million. In an effort to withhold evidence from the liquidator, they burned down the business premises which stored company files, put out other files for waste collection by the local authority, and threatened the bookkeeper with a gun so that he would not give evidence at the trial.

The liquidator concluded that company assets had been illegally transferred to another company to defraud the Revenue Commissioners but the directors were civilly sanctioned, not criminally prosecuted, for this misconduct. In *Re Hunting Lodges* ([1985] I.L.R.M. 75), the directors sold the main asset of the company, a pub called 'Durty Nelly's', but the company did not receive the full sale price. The directors had transferred £160,000 of the proceeds to bank accounts with false names to deprive the Revenue Commissioners of stamp duty on the full consideration of the sale price. Though these cases unearthed instances of deliberate corporate fraud, liquidators took civil proceedings under section 297(1) of the Companies Act 1963, even though the directors could have been criminally prosecuted for fraudulent trading under section 297(3) of the same Act.

Arguably, one of the most significant corporate frauds in the Irish State in the twentieth century involved Merchant Banking, a company in the Gallagher Group which failed in the early 1980s, owing debts of tens of millions of pounds (Carswell, 2006: 24). The liquidator's investigation concluded that Merchant Banking had seriously breached several pieces of legislation, including the Companies Acts, the Central Bank Acts and the Larceny Acts. In particular, the bank had failed to hold annual general meetings, had falsely recorded transactions, made false returns to the Central Bank, obtained and managed its assets fraudulently, and had failed to maintain independent legal counsel in accordance with its banking licence (Carswell, 2006: *Irish Times*, 23 February 1990: 9; 15 May 1984: 1). Merchant Banking had not maintained its independence from other companies in the Group because 80 per cent of its assets were provided as loans to finance Gallagher's other companies (Carswell, 2006: 24). The bank had also issued loans as gifts to members of the Gallagher family. It seems that the bank had never expected repayment on these loans, many of which were so old on winding up that the liquidator could not collect on them because they were statute barred (34). These transgressions were facilitated by a weak and ineffective Central Bank. It had expressed concerns about the running of the bank since 1973 but did not send in inspectors to investigate it (*Irish Times*, 3 March 1990: 8; 15 March 1990: 5). When it ordered the Bank to reduce its borrowings to the Gallagher Group in 1977, this was ignored and the activities of the Bank and the Group actually became even more intertwined (Carswell, 2006: 32).

Though the Gardaí subsequently investigated these allegations, they lacked the resources and skills to deal effectively with cases of white-collar crime. It took several fraud squad officers working full-time on the case six years to complete their investigation and for a report to be sent to the DPP (*Irish Times*, 7 December 1989: 14). Even then, they had not been able to compile sufficient evidence to ground a successful prosecution so the State decided not to prosecute the case (*Irish Times*, 25 May 1990: 1). By contrast, the British authorities dealt much more decisively with Merchant Banking's activities in

Northern Ireland. This wrongdoing was strikingly similar to that perpetrated in the South because it also involved using bank funds to finance companies in the Gallagher Group, the provision of loans without any expectation of repayment, and the filing of misleading reports with the Bank of England (Carswell, 2006: 37–9).

By contrast to the approach in the Republic, however, the British conducted a two-year investigation that provided sufficient evidence to prompt Patrick Gallagher, the Chairman of the Gallagher Group, to plead guilty to five offences. He was not treated deferentially. He was arrested and initially denied bail (*Irish Times*, 31 March 1988, 1; 2 April 1988: 6). He was subsequently sentenced to two years imprisonment, despite the payment of significant compensation on his behalf (*Irish Times*, 2 October 1990: 13). Even though Merchant Banking had a significantly smaller operation in Northern Ireland than in the Republic, the investigation was taken more seriously in the United Kingdom and Patrick Gallagher was serving time there while all that happened in Ireland was that the liquidator considered a civil suit.

The evidence detailed in this chapter certainly suggests that the Garda Fraud Squad was hampered by the absence of an obligation to report offences to it, but perhaps even more so by a lack of resources and expertise to deal with wrongdoing once discovered. Though it is difficult to know precisely how many cases were processed by the Fraud Squad in this period, it is known that it was investigating thirty-nine cases in 1991 (Burke, Dáil Deb. 5 February 1991, vol. 404, col. 1480). Owing to inadequate records, it is not clear how many of these cases were referred to the DPP for prosecution, how many were actually prosecuted, or how many resulted in a conviction. However, Carney has suggested that 'major allegations of serious fraud ... seem to have gone no farther than the submission of a file to the office of the Director of Public Prosecutions' (*Irish Times*, 31 August 1990: 10). Unsurprisingly then, the McDowell Group (1998: para. 2.5) reported that 'Enforcement of non-registration type offences is very rare and wholly unpredictable. Most statutory offences have never been the subject of prosecutions, and those which have been prosecuted have resulted in only a handful of convictions.'

Nevertheless, the DPP has not claimed ownership for any part in the lack of prosecutions or convictions. In the first instance, it stated 'that any decision of the DPP not to commence criminal proceedings for breaches of the Companies Acts is due entirely to the quality of the evidential material available at the time of decision' (McDowell, 1998: para. 4.28). This seems to place blame back on the doorstep of the Gardaí which conducted these investigations and collected evidence for the DPP. In the second instance, the DPP also suggests that its efforts at law enforcement had been thwarted by rules of evidence which were weighted too heavily in favour of the accused. In particular, suspects were under no obligation to answer the questions posed by the Gardaí. In order for a prosecution to have any chance of success under the existing laws, the suspect had to cooperate with the investigation or reveal the nature of his fraud (*Irish Times*, 16 March 1991: 13). On his retirement, having served for twenty-five years as DPP, Barnes (2002: 97–8) reiterated that:

> The area of criminal activity now most urgently in need of law reform is that of fraud … Until now we have sought to counter such activities under legislation conceived in a very different era. The main statute dealing with most of these matters remains the Larceny Act 1916, the draftsmen whereof were unlikely to have any conception of the electronic world in which we live and through which those with fraudulent intent and a modest proficiency in automated procedures can roam with impunity. We have been deeply frustrated on many occasions over the past twenty four years at our inability to prosecute many cases of obvious fraud, very often because there was no criminal offence to match the particular fraudulent activity.

In summation, the detection, investigation and prosecution of corporate and white-collar crimes were colonised by machinery more suited to addressing conventional crime. The composition, education and training of early Garda recruits suggest that they lacked the necessary skills to deal competently with sophisticated corporate wrongdoing. The model of policing whereby Gardaí lived among their community and walked the beat was also unsuited to this exercise. Though the standard of education and training for subsequent recruits substantially improved, the Gardaí remained under-resourced and it appears that they lacked the necessary skills and specialised in-house professional advice necessary to adequately address corporate wrongdoing. Their model of policing was deferential to suspected wrongdoers and officers were often demoralised by Garda policies. The Gardaí were often unaware that the law had been breached and rarely gained experience of dealing with the kinds of offences often only discovered on the winding up of companies. Even when liquidations occurred and files were submitted to the DPP, cases were rarely prosecuted despite the fact that they represented significant corporate wrongdoing in the Irish State. Such cases involved fraudulent trading, the manipulation of company records, and the illegal misappropriation of corporate property for personal use. These cases may be taken to reflect the regulatory failure of the modern period, a failure which may be attributed to the inadequacies of conventional policing agencies that lacked the resources, expertise and powers to investigate the wrongdoing effectively, or treated the wrongdoing without any sense of exigency.

Specialised corporate enforcement machinery

In the eighteenth and nineteenth century, policing was private, local and principally concerned with the regulation of trade, commerce and the markets.

Policing was not restricted to theft or offences against the person, but also extended to the regulation of weights and measures, and early forms of health and safety law, consumer protection and environmental protection (Braithwaite, 2005: 13–14; 2000: 225). Braithwaite (2008: 13–14) noted that it was only in the nineteenth century, when the centralised State monopoly on policing was established, that the system became preoccupied with conventional crime offences:

> Uniformed paramilitary police, preoccupied with the punitive regulation of the poor to the almost total exclusion of any interest in the constitution of the markets and the just regulation of commerce, became one of the most universal of globalized regulatory models. So what happened to business regulation? From the mid-nineteenth century, factories inspectorates, mines inspectorates, liquor licensing boards, weights and measurements inspectorates, health and sanitation, food inspectors and countless others were created to begin to fill the vacuum left by constables now concentrating only on crime. Business regulation became variegated into many different specialist regulatory branches.

Braithwaite suggests that regulatory bodies rather than conventional crime police increasingly addressed corporate wrongdoing from about the nineteenth century onwards. Furthermore, Appleby (2010: 178–9) has shown that numerous regulatory bodies have been created to deal with corporate wrongdoing since the foundation of the State, many of which had the power to prosecute corporate and white-collar crimes on a summary basis. All of this could suggest that specialised regulatory agencies were responsible for the policing of corporate and white-collar crime. This would seem to contradict the argument made in this chapter that conventional police and prosecutors were primarily charged with policing and prosecuting corporate and white-collar crimes in Ireland in the twentieth century.

However, it is submitted that Braithwaite oversimplifies the position and Appleby overstates it. It is true that a number of agencies were created at the end of the eighteenth century, and in the nineteenth and early twentieth century, and that they continued to play key roles in regulating the corporate and financial sector thereafter. For example, the Dublin Stock Exchange was created by the Stock Exchange (Dublin) Act 1799 and subsequently joined forces with the Cork Stock Exchange, later merging also with the Stock Exchange of London (Thomas, 1986). It became its own entity upon the enactment of the Stock Exchange Act 1995. The CRO was established by the Joint Stock Companies Acts 1844 (although it was then known as the Registrar of Joint Stock Companies). Similarly, the Central Bank, established in accordance with the Central Bank Act 1942, had existed in a more limited form as a Currency Commission since the Currency Act 1927.

Nevertheless, these agencies performed mostly administrative functions. The Irish Stock Exchange controlled the admission of public limited companies to the exchange through its listing rules (White, 2011: 144). While the Irish Central Bank performed a variety of functions, it was principally concerned with the prudential supervision of financial institutions and monetary policy (O'Grady Walshe, 1991: 93, 95–6). Even then, it had a limited role in monetary policy due to the fixed parity of Irish currency with British sterling until 1979 (97–8). Its regulatory function also arrived late in the day because 'the Central Bank's supervisory role began with the Central Bank Act 1971, which gave it the task of licencing and supervising banks' (99). Prior to that, licences were issued by the Revenue Commissioners 'whose main concern was to ensure the correct tax status of any interest institutions' (DKM Consultants, 1984: 39). When the Central Bank did eventually acquire more significant powers in 1971, enhanced in 1989, it performed its regulatory functions by selectively issuing licences to respectable operators, suspending or revoking them when necessary and by inspecting financial institutions and their reports. Similarly, the CRO was also largely concerned with administrative matters. Its main role was to process the registration of companies, maintain records of statutorily required information on companies and enforce these corporate filing obligations (Cahill, 2008: 545). Parties were required to file a number of documents with the CRO, including the company memorandum and articles of association, the annual returns, the company accounts, any changes to information already registered, liquidators' reports and company charges. The CRO championed the values of transparency and disclosure in corporate enterprise by making these documents available for public inspection so that people could make more informed decisions about their dealings and investments with companies.

Crucially, however, these bodies were not significantly concerned with prosecuting corporate or financial crime until late in the twentieth century, if at all. Section 385 of the Primary Act empowered the Minister and the Attorney General (subsequently the DPP) to prosecute the summary offences in the Companies Acts. The enforcement role of the Irish Stock Exchange was extremely limited. In accordance with section 115(1) of the Companies Act 1990, if the Irish Stock Exchange suspected that the offence of insider dealing was taking place, it reported the matter to the DPP. Moreover, it did not have the power to prosecute offences specified in the Stock Exchange Act 1995 because section 70 of that Act provided that these offences were prosecuted by the DPP or the Central Bank. The role of the CRO was also limited. It was only with section 16 of the Companies (Amendment) Act 1982 that the CRO was empowered to prosecute summary offences in the Companies Acts. Even then, this power was restricted to a small number of filing offences. Though its prosecutorial ambit subsequently grew slightly, it could only prosecute a small fraction of the hundreds of offences in the Companies Acts so it continued to perform a largely administrative role (Cahill, 2008: 545–9; McDowell, 1998: para. 2.9).

Similarly, the Central Bank was not able to prosecute summary offences until it was empowered to do so by section 59 of the Central Bank Act 1971. For most of the twentieth century, it was clearly envisaged that the conventional police force would continue to play a major role in prosecuting breaches of financial services legislation. For example, section 55(3) of the Central Bank Act 1942 specifically provided that failing to supply information to the Gardaí on forged bank notes was a criminal offence, suggesting that these kinds of offences were being addressed by the ordinary police. Furthermore, the offence was prosecutable by the Attorney General. Indeed, the Attorney General, and later the DPP, continued to exercise exclusive jurisdiction for prosecuting all indictable crime (and still does). This shows that the conventional crime police and prosecutors dominated the enforcement of corporate and financial crime laws.

This is not to suggest that other agencies did not regulate or prosecute certain forms of corporate wrongdoing. However, they existed on a much smaller scale and did not employ a streamlined, pyramidal approach to enforcement, a modern development discussed further in Part II. It is also suggested that they played a largely administrative or peripheral role compared to the conventional crime police and prosecutors. For example, many of the bodies specified by Appleby, such as the Bacon Marketing Board, while possessing the power of summary prosecution since the 1930s, played a peripheral role, at best, in corporate enforcement more generally. In accordance with the Pigs and Bacon Act 1935, the Bacon Marketing Board largely dealt with administrative matters, like the registration and licensing of curers and butchers; the slaughter of pigs; the grading, production, sale and exportation of bacon; the administration of veterinary examinations and the regulation of bacon prices. All of this suggests that the conventional crime police and prosecutors were principally responsible for the enforcement of corporate and financial laws, not regulatory agencies. In the remainder of this section, it will be shown that some regulatory agencies, particularly the department overseen by the Minister, addressed corporate wrongdoing, but that their role was largely ancillary or supportive of the Gardaí and the DPP who continued to dominate the policing and prosecution of corporate crime in the twentieth century. To the extent that these agencies and the Minister did enforce the law, it is shown that prosecutions were rare, fines were low, and offenders rarely received criminal records.

The Minister was expected to perform an active role in enforcing the Companies Acts and was empowered under section 385 of the Companies Act 1963 to prosecute all summary offences. In assuming this responsibility, the Minister (Lynch, Dáil Deb. 14 November 1962, vol. 197, col. 1190) recognised that 'there would, of course, be little point in imposing obligations on companies and their officers unless suitable provisions were made for the prosecution of offenders … [T]o the extent which our resources permit, steps will be taken to ensure that the requirements of the law are complied with, and that offenders are punished'. Though record-keeping on the prosecution of company offences is poor, the annual Companies Reports prepared by the Minister show, despite his tough rhetoric on enforcement, that corporate wrongdoing was not a significant priority. The next paragraph analyses these reports from 1963 onwards, the same year that the Primary Act was enacted, when the Minister vowed that a new era of enforcement would begin. Though this information is often fragmented and vague, the available information is presented in tables where it is reported consistently for a period of years, in an attempt to specify trends which capture the Irish approach to corporate wrongdoing.

The Companies Report 1963 (1964: 9) stated that 'during 1963, the institution of legal proceedings was necessary to secure submission of a number of legal returns. To secure compliance with other sections of the Act, proceedings were necessary in a few cases.' It did not identify the number of prosecutions or convictions secured by the State. In 1964, one case was prosecuted for the improper use of the word 'limited'. The case was unsuccessful and was dismissed (1965: 9). In 1965, sixty cases were instituted for the failure to file annual returns and ten were initiated for failing to file notice of situation of registered office and /or the particulars of directors and secretaries. Only two cases were heard that year and the Probation Act, which allows offenders to escape criminal records, was applied in both cases (1966: 9). Between 1966 and 1971, the State prosecuted: the failure to file notice of situation of registered office and/or the particulars of directors and secretaries; the failure to file notice of change of registered office; and the failure to file annual returns. Data on the enforcement of these offences is compiled in Table 4.1. This shows that though 708 cases were reported or 'on hands' for prosecution in 1966, only 361 of these resulted in the imposition of a fine. In addition, the Probation Act was applied forty-nine times. Although the number of cases fluctuated over the next five years, fines were rarely imposed: only 29 per cent of cases in 1967 (47 out of 162 cases), 28 per cent in 1968 (41 out of 146 cases), 25 per cent in 1969 (20 out of 79 cases), 15 per cent in 1970 (22 out of 148 cases), and 18 per cent in 1971 (47 out of 262 cases). The Probation Act also continued to be applied. In 1971, the Probation Act was applied 19 times when only 47 cases resulted in a fine. This suggests that even when companies did break the law, and were convicted, they were rarely fined and often left the court without a criminal record.

The Companies Reports do not record many details on the enforcement of the Companies Acts between 1972 and 1980. No data are recorded on the number of convictions, the application of the Probation Act, the number of cases withdrawn, and so on. However, as depicted in Table 4.2, it is shown that 236 prosecutions were taken for the failure to provide annual returns in 1972, resulting in total fines of £2,445 (1973: 11), before rising to 781 prosecutions in 1980, with fines imposed totalling £2,482 (1981: 11). There was a significant

Table 4.1 Prosecutions under the Companies Act (1966–71)

Year	Number of cases on hand since previous year and reported this year	Number in which fines imposed	Probation Act applied
1966	708	361	49
1967	162	47	8
1968	146	41	6
1969	79	20	1
1970	148	22	0
1971	262	47	19

Sources: Companies Reports (1967–72)

Table 4.2 Failure to provide annual returns (1972–80)

Year	Prosecutions	Fines imposed (£)
1972	236	2,445
1973	103	1,373
1974	295	3,441
1975	301	6,979
1976	176	1,983
1977	237	5,252
1978	528	2,269
1979	633	3,145
1980	781	2,482

Sources: Companies Reports (1972–81)

increase in the number of prosecutions, and therefore presumably convictions also, but the total value of the fines remained relatively constant, which suggests that the average fine imposed was reduced. For example, the total amount of fines resulting from 236 prosecutions in 1972 was £2,445, which means that the average fine per prosecution in this period was £10.36. By 1980, the average fine per prosecution was £3.18. Small fines became smaller. The reports do not indicate why this occurred.

Slightly more detailed information is provided on the prosecutions for failure to file annual returns for the next three years, as shown in Table 4.3. In 1981, 897 cases were referred for prosecution. These resulted in 262 prosecutions. The total value of the fines imposed was £9,500 (1982: 11). In 1982, 192 of the 920 cases referred were prosecuted and the value of the fines imposed that year totalled £7,420 (1983: 11). In 1983, 224 of the 932 cases referred were prosecuted and the value of the fines imposed that year totalled £15,730 (1984: 11). If any trend can be revealed from this information, it is that only a fraction

Table 4.3 Failure to provide annual returns (1981–83)

Year	Referred for prosecution	Prosecutions	Fines imposed (£)
1981	897	262	9,500
1982	920	192	7,420
1983	932	224	15,730

**Sources:* Companies Reports (1982–84)

Table 4.4 Prosecutions, convictions and fines for breaching the Companies Acts (1984–85)

Year	Convictions	Fines imposed (£)
1984	293	50,845
1985	8	2,025

Sources: Companies Reports (1985–86)

of the cases which could potentially have been prosecuted were actually prosecuted, with low fines being imposed.

In 1984, the Minister ceased to provide information in the same manner as presented in 1983. The reports do not record the total number of offences prosecuted, the specific offences prosecuted, the number of prosecutions per offence, the number of convictions per offence, details on the application of the Probation Act and number of cases withdrawn. Two figures were, however, provided: the total number of convictions and the total amount of the fines imposed. From these figures, it is known that in 1984 fines totalling £50,845 were imposed as a result of 293 convictions that year (1985: 11). In 1985, £2,025 was imposed as a result of eight convictions (1986: 10).

The Companies Reports in the late 1980s did not record details on convictions or fines. Instead, they provided details on the total number of prosecutions for breaches of the Companies Acts. From this data, collated in Table 4.5, it is known that no prosecutions were initiated in 1986 or 1987, and that only eight prosecutions were taken in 1988 (1993: 11). However, the number of prosecutions did jump in 1989 to 334, peaking in 1990 with 960 prosecutions taken that year, before falling to 29 prosecutions in 1991.

It is difficult to explain this sharp peak and fall with certainty. No clues are provided in the Companies Reports for the extraordinary rise and sharp fall in prosecutions in this period. However, the rise in prosecutions did follow the EC Fourth Directive which required the annual accounts of public and private accounts be annexed to the annual returns to the CRO. Prior to this, private companies had not been required to supply this information. The Directive was implemented by the Companies Act 1986, though small

Table 4.5 Prosecutions for breaching the Companies Acts (1986–91)

Year	Prosecutions
1986	0
1987	0
1988	8
1989	334
1990	960
1991	29

Sources: Companies Reports (1987–92)

and medium-sized private companies were exempted from this obligation. A prominent Irish businessman, Fergal Quinn, complained that his largest corporate competitors were forming smaller subsidiaries and exploiting legal loopholes to exempt them from filing full annual accounts. He decided to publish his accounts in full to shame his competitors to do the same (*Irish Times*, 1 February 1989: 17). The resulting declaration by the Minister that it would prosecute all companies who failed to file full annual accounts was greeted with scepticism by the *Irish Times* (16 February 1989: 11) because 'this is not the first time the Department has said this; and information is as sparse as ever … The old secretiveness still prevails.' This in turn provoked a letter to the editor by a registration agent for the CRO who stated that greater calls for enforcement failed to consider that the office is so 'seriously understaffed and underequipped' that it is not 'available to check and file the bundles of documents stacked on the floor' (*Irish Times*, 23 February 1989: 11). This significant media attention on this issue may correlate with the spike in prosecutions at that time.

The decline in prosecutions was met by a temporary resurgence in subsequent years. Though the data was reported across an eighteen-month period instead of the usual twelve months, thereby frustrating direct year-on-year tabulated comparisons, the Minister reported that 1,963 companies were prosecuted for the failure to file returns between 1 of January 1992 and 30 June 1993, 'a ten year high' (1993: 8, 23). The maximum penalty for failure to file returns under the Acts at this point was £1,000 and the fines imposed totalled £0.501 million, a staggering sum compared to past levels: £2,445 in 1972, £1,983 in 1976, £2,482 in 1980, £2,025 in 1985 (1973: 11; 1977: 11; 1981: 11; 1986: 10). Prosecutions subsequently continued but there was a marked preference for prosecuting companies rather than company officers during this period, as shown in Table 4.6. In 1994, 1,979 companies were prosecuted, as compared to 103 prosecutions against company directors (1995: 29). Similarly, in 1995, 626 companies were prosecuted but only 116 prosecutions were taken against company directors (1996: 17). Company directors were not prosecuted for failing to file annual returns in 1996 but eighteen were convicted of that offence in

Table 4.6 Prosecutions for failure to provide returns (1994–98)

	Prosecutions against companies for failure to provide returns			Prosecutions against directors for failure to provide returns		
Year	**Number of prosecutions**	**Number of convictions**	**Fines imposed (£)**	**Number of prosecutions**	**Number of convictions**	**Fines imposed (£)**
1994	1,979	1,418	2,024,550	103	43	11,700
1995	626	546	684,950	116	55	37,675
1996	43	26	16,475	0	18	8,630
1997	0	0	0	107	30	52,460
1998	0	0	0	0	0	0

Sources: Companies Reports (1995–99)

respect of cases carried over from 1995. It also seems that the State had a much better chance of securing convictions against companies than their officers, perhaps because the State had the burden of proving that officers in default had acted knowingly and wilfully as a precondition to criminal liability, as specified in section 383 of the Companies Act 1963. This 'created a very high evidential burden for the prosecution that necessitated proof of a defendant's subjective state of mind' (Courtney, 2012: 1768). This high evidential hurdle was not required to secure convictions against companies. The reports show that while 87 per cent of cases (546 out of 626) against companies resulted in convictions in 1995, only 45 per cent of cases (55 out of 116) in 1995 were successful against company directors, and only 28 per cent of cases against directors (30 out of 107) resulted in convictions in 1997 (1996: 17; 1998: 16).

Nevertheless, even as enforcement increased in the early and mid-1990s, compliance with the obligation to file annual returns under the Companies Acts declined, as shown in Table 4.7. Though 69 per cent of companies eventually complied with their obligation in 1991, this fell to 42 per cent in 1994, and declined further to 36 per cent in 1997. The number of companies filing 'on time' was even lower. The number of 'live' or active companies that filed on time dropped from 16 per cent in 1994 to 13 per cent in 1997 (1998: 16). The Minister admitted that 'the overall compliance rate cannot be regarded as satisfactory' (1995: 13). The emphasis on a more active sanctioning approach had failed to secure better corporate compliance with the law. The number of prosecutions against both companies and company directors subsequently ceased entirely. No companies or company directors were prosecuted in 1998 (1999: 45).

The McDowell Report explained that the Minister had difficulty enforcing the law because his Department was inadequately resourced. It determined that the Minister allocated the equivalent of only eight full-time staff members

Table 4.7 Compliance rates for filing annual returns (1991–97)

Year due	Returns due	Returns filed	Compliance rate
1991	78,508	53,845	69%
1992	93,102	55,816	60%
1993	107,652	55,435	51%
1994	121,600	51,062	42%
1995	127,279	42,662	34%
1996	112,668	38,632	34%
1997	136,245	49,242	36%

Sources: Companies Reports (1992–98)

of the Department to its Company Law Administration Section, two members of which were concerned with the regulation of credit unions and other societies (1998, para. 2.18). The remaining six members were fully absorbed with civil company investigations and performing the wide range of administrative tasks allocated to the Minister. The Report stated (1998: paras 2.21–2.22):

> As regards Departmental resources for the investigation and prosecution of breaches of the Companies Acts the Group was satisfied that other commitments of the Department left the manpower equivalent of about one half of one full-time staff member of the Department to discharge this vital function. In the UK, such functions are discharged by many hundreds of full-time public servants. Put shortly, demands on manpower meant that there are currently no Departmental resources allocated for the enforcement of the law. In these circumstances, the Group came to the conclusion that day to day investigation and prosecution of breaches of company law (other than Companies Registration Office offences) is close to non-existent and that ... there is no realistic prospect that the Department's function of enforcement, as envisaged by the Acts, will be discharged.

Considering that the Minister was charged with a significant role in enforcing company law, but that it had not allocated the equivalent of even one full-time staff member to discharge this function, it is unsurprising that compliance with the Companies Acts was traditionally so low. Similarly, the internal allocation of the CRO, which operated under the aegis of the Minister, also suggests that the detection of white-collar crimes was a low priority. The CRO employed 112 staff in 1998 but only eight of these were allocated to the enforcement of company law, an increase from four members of staff in 1997 (para. 2.39). The remaining members of staff were allocated to performing the CRO's administrative duties.

A number of broad conclusions relating both to the architecture of enforcement and the practice of enforcement may be drawn from the material discussed here. While specialist agencies have undoubtedly played a role in regulating particular parts of the corporate and financial sector, they played a limited role in enforcing the law in practice. As observed by Bannon (2006: 6), 'while there were a number of different agencies with some responsibility for the enforcement of company law, it was a priority for none. Moreover, within those agencies, there was an insufficiency of resources assigned to the task.' Only a handful of the hundreds of offences in the Acts were prosecuted and only the failure to file annual returns was prosecuted with any regularity. The low levels of prosecutions appeared to be matched by lower levels of convictions and even lower levels of fines. Unsurprisingly, it was observed that 'the experience of the Department and of the CRO is that it has been the practice of the courts to impose low fines for company law offences' (Company Law Review Group, 2001: 151). O'Malley (2006: 415–16) notes that while legislators may set high maximum fines for a number of reasons, and while many considerations may come into play, generally, the courts impose penalties proportionate to the perceived gravity of the wrongdoing committed. Therefore, the low penalties suggest that corporate wrongdoing and breaches of the Companies Acts were viewed as trivial or merely technical breaches of the law. It would also appear, from the data available, that the Probation Act was often applied in favour of corporate defendants. Though the data in the Reports can be inconsistent and is often vague, itself illustrative of the ambivalent attitude to corporate enforcement, the evidence shows that the enforcement of company law, which was underpinned by hundreds of criminal sanctions, was almost non-existent.

Conclusion

In conclusion, the detection, investigation and prosecution of corporate crime was often colonised by machinery more suited to addressing conventional crime. The Gardaí lacked the necessary resources, training and in-house expertise to competently deal with sophisticated corporate wrongdoing. Owing to the traditional failure to wind up companies, and the failure to capitalise on information reporting mechanisms, the Gardaí were often unaware that the law had been breached and never gained experience in dealing with the kinds of offences often only discovered on the winding up of companies. Even when liquidations occurred and files were submitted to the DPP, cases were rarely prosecuted, despite the fact that they represented significant corporate wrongdoing in the Irish State. On the rare occasions when files were sent to the DPP for prosecution, cases were not treated with any sense of urgency. Prosecutors also suggested that they were hamstrung by criminal law rules and rules of evidence which were weighted too heavily in favour of the accused. The conventional crime machinery was assisted by the CRO and the Minister but they played a peripheral and administrative role and were so severely under-resourced as to be largely ineffective. Consequently, the prosecution of registration-type offences was also erratic and rare. Convictions were also uncommon, fines were low, and the Probation Act was often applied in favour of corporate defendants.

Friedman (1975: 108) has observed that 'a law which goes against the grain, culturally speaking, will be hard to enforce and probably ineffective'. In Ireland, the failure to enforce corporate laws should be understood as a reflection of social and political apathy in corporate affairs, detailed previously. Ireland was not concerned with corporate wrongdoing because it was a rural State with minimal corporate activity and low crime rates. Irish citizens were more concerned with finding employment than with crime. Corporate activity was associated with positive concepts, such as prosperity, economic security and progress. Furthermore, politicians were not concerned with the intricacies of corporate regulation, a legislative issue which they generally found boring and irrelevant. It may also be the case that the prosecution of respectable pillars of the community for technical wrongs went 'against the grain' and had little social or political support in practice. Consequently, corporate enforcement was not resourced or supported and Ireland overlooked the prosecution of corporate and white-collar crimes in a way it would never have done with more conventional crime. The breakdown of the rule of law was evidenced by 'a failure of congruence between the rules as announced and their actual administration' (Fuller, 1964: 39). However, the sheer scale of non-enforcement and non-compliance with company law was so extensive that it threatened the State's economic viability and its reputation as an attractive place in which to do business. It was not protecting legitimate businesses that complied with the law from those that operated to defraud the market. Ireland was not protecting the public from fraud and corporate irresponsibility. It was not protecting the interests of employees, traders and suppliers that needed Irish businesses to remain viable and the State was not protecting its own tax revenues. The failure to enforce law could not last. A new architecture of enforcement was required.

Summary of Part I

Part I of this monograph involved a doctrinal, historical, and institutional analysis of the Irish approach to corporate deviancy in the twentieth century. This was necessary to illustrate how the newly emerging architecture of corporate enforcement is a striking departure from that previously employed. It was shown that the traditional approach was informed by the socio-economic climate in Ireland. Ireland had an agrarian economy which stagnated for most of the twentieth century. It employed inward-looking economic policies that did not sufficiently promote Ireland as an attractive place in which to do business. The State was concerned with self-sufficiency, was politically deferential to the agricultural sector, romanticised rural Ireland, and was influenced by an anti-business church which tied Catholicism to rural life and anti-materialism. The combination of these factors caused Ireland's economic health to suffer, already high levels of emigration to rise, and low levels of corporate activity to persist. Consequently, the State was not concerned with issues of corporate and white-collar crime or governance and this affected the content of company law. Company law was not reviewed with any regularity and the laws that existed did not operate to adequately protect stakeholders from the deviant behaviour of company officers. As a result of Ireland's lack of experience in corporate affairs, it did not have the requisite knowledge to structure its own company law framework and often transplanted English company legislation into the Irish Statute Book, without appropriate reflection as to whether or not such legislation was suitable in the Irish context. More vocal members of the legislature complained that company law was not politically stimulating, reflecting the lack of political interest in corporate affairs that characterised the Irish approach to corporate deviancy in the twentieth century.

Though some civil sanctions existed, company law enforcement was overwhelmingly underpinned by criminal sanctions in Ireland with 280 offences in the Companies Acts 1963–90. It was argued that corporate misconduct was assimilated into the conventional crime sphere because this was more convenient than designing a specialised system of corporate enforcement dedicated to achieving high levels of corporate compliance. Designing such a system would have required an interest in issues of commercial regulation which was not apparent, a knowledge of corporate governance that the State did not have, and a familiarity with corporate activity that was simply beyond its experience. It is therefore understandable that the State was unable to engage in discourse about whether the criminal justice system, which was orientated to tackle morally reprehensible 'street crime', would be effective in policing the corporate sector.

Moreover, assimilating corporate wrongdoing into the conventional criminal justice system also meant that company law offences were constructed in light of Ireland's liberal legal tradition. Persons accused of committing white-collar crimes were provided with full due process safeguards and could often only be convicted on the basis that they were subjectively culpable for wrongdoing. These mechanisms provided the accused with significant protections against conviction. The burden of proof was on the prosecution to prove beyond a reasonable doubt that the accused acted knowingly or willingly to break the law. This was particularly difficult in complex corporate matters because the organisational structure of the company; its internal lines of decision making and accountability; the geographical scope of its operations; and the nature, volume, and complexity of transactions it conducted, all gave rise to ambiguities such that responsibility could become diffuse and knowledge fragmented throughout the organisation. Furthermore, companies and company officers were typically more likely than conventional offenders to have the resources to exploit due process safeguards and advance legal arguments to avoid criminal liability. Therefore, the application of conventional due process and subjective culpability requirements created significant barriers to the prosecution of corporate wrongdoing in Ireland.

Even when offenders were successfully convicted of white-collar crimes, the Irish system of structuring proportionate sentences also privileged white-collar offenders. Corporate and white-collar crimes were often viewed as less harmful than conventional crimes. Those accused of wrongdoing were also far more likely to benefit from the mitigating sentencing factors than suffer from the aggravating ones. This was because instances of commercial wrongdoing, by their nature, rarely involved violence. White-collar offenders were also unlikely to use weapons or invade victims' homes, or have been motivated by race or religion. They were unlikely to have previous criminal convictions and were often of good character, as evidenced by a stable employment record and good family background. The courts may also have been influenced by the fact that company officers often had a greater stake in conforming to social norms, which may have justified less severe punishments. It could be considered, for example, that white-collar offenders had more to lose than the average offender, such as where an adverse finding against them negatively affected their otherwise strong prospects for future employment. White-collar offenders were also more likely to have the resources to compensate victims and seek the leniency of the court. Consequently, company officers from middle-class backgrounds were far less likely to receive a custodial sentence than conventional wrongdoers from deprived backgrounds.

Not only did the traditional approach to corporate deviancy affect the content of company law, it also affected the way the courts defined crime. Crimes were defined in terms of traditional criminal procedures like arrest and imprisonment, the role of the State as prosecutor, the presence of culpability requirements, criminal law as strictly punitive in purpose, the vocabulary used in the construction of the offence and the severity of the sanctions. These features were often associated with conventional criminal offences such as homicides, sexual offences and violent assaults. Consequently, this approach did not fully reflect the duality of the approach to corporate wrongdoing. Regulatory criminal law did not always use traditional criminal law procedures and often did not provide for custodial sentences. It was sometimes enforced by regulatory agencies operating at arm's length from the State, rather than by the DPP on behalf of the State. Furthermore, it was sometimes enforced on the basis of strict liability to deter rather than punish wrongdoing. Regulatory crimes generally did not share the characteristics more associated with conventional criminal law, or fit within its paradigm, and were often thought to be less criminal in character. As a result, corporate wrongdoing was often marginalised from the legal definition of crime. This marginalisation was facilitated by the public perception that corporate and white-collar crimes were not truly immoral and that regulatory crimes were not 'real' crimes. Corporate and white-collar crimes often lacked readily identifiable victims and this made them seem invisible. They traditionally lacked the sensationalism of conventional crimes and therefore did not dominate the media in the same way, a factor which also contributed to their seeming invisibility. Furthermore, the public perception of the criminal continued to be informed by this classic form. He was the drug dealer, the rapist, or the murderer who hid down a dark alley, but not your neighbour, the company director, who drove a nice car and wore a suit to work. The social construction of crimes and criminals was understandable given Ireland's traditional unfamiliarity with corporate activity, and the lack of urgency which the political establishment has treated the phenomenon of corporate and white-collar crimes.

Institutional responses to corporate enforcement (as reflected by the choices of the Gardaí, the DPP and the courts) also mirrored the apathy shown by the political establishment and society more generally. Corporate non-compliance with the law was widespread, yet prosecutions rarely took place and convictions were rarely achieved. In part, this may have been because corporate offenders were accorded a high level of due process protections, but it is more likely a consequence of addressing corporate deviancy through conventional criminal law machinery that was ill-suited to this purpose. The Gardaí were, for the most part, charged with the detection, investigation and summary prosecution of company law offences. However, they lacked the necessary resources and training to deal with complex cases of corporate and white-collar crime. The DPP was responsible for the prosecution of indictable offences but it was also ill-equipped to prosecute such cases, not least because it required an overstretched police force to conduct investigations and prepare the evidence for prosecution, but also because it was hamstrung by outdated laws. The CRO, operating under the aegis of the Minister, assisted the Garda and the DPP in the detection and prosecution of corporate wrongdoing. However, both the CRO and the Minister were so under-resourced that effective enforcement was impossible. Even when corporate offenders were successfully convicted, they were usually subject to very small fines, reflecting the sentiment that corporate deviancy was not sufficiently serious as to demand severe penalties.

As a result of Ireland's history as a rural state with minimal corporate activity, addressing corporate and white-collar crimes was not treated as a significant priority. These crimes were addressed by conventional crime rules and procedures, and were, for the most part, investigated and prosecuted by conventional policing agencies. The conventional criminal justice model was unsuitable for use in the corporate context. Company offences were less likely to be thought of as 'truly criminal', less likely to be prosecuted and less likely to result in convictions. On the rare occasions that offenders were convicted, they typically received small financial penalties and were unlikely to receive custodial sentences. All levels – social, political, policing, prosecutorial and judicial – were infected by inertia in corporate affairs, which can be located in Ireland's historical context as a developing economy in the twentieth century. Part II provides a critical analysis of the new logic of action that has informed the contemporary approach to corporate wrongdoing since the 1990s. This logic is the fresh understanding that corporate wrongdoing can severely affect the security of the State and it is the actual structural changes in law implemented to satisfy the increased social and political appetite for corporate accountability. This approach to corporate wrongdoing is a striking departure from that which had previously prevailed.

Part II

THE CONTEMPORARY ARCHITECTURE OF ENFORCEMENT

5

From apathy to activism: causal factors stimulating change

Introduction

Part I showed that the State was not concerned with issues of corporate and white-collar crime because it had a largely agrarian economy with low levels of corporate activity. Increased corporate activity was a way of providing employment. It had positive connotations so there was little social or political recognition of the potentially negative effects of inadequate corporate regulation. This chapter analyses the causal factors that led to the recognition that corporate misconduct could threaten the security of the State. This awareness was facilitated by a number of factors which had also increased the level of corporate activity in Ireland. In particular, globalisation and the European common market provided easier access to a higher number of customers and created significant opportunities for business. Advances in communication, transport and e-commerce meant that companies could operate transnationally and the financial market became global. At the same time, Ireland grasped the nettle and seized the opportunity to develop from an agrarian to a more commercially orientated society. It lowered the rate of corporation tax, introduced facilitative 'light-touch' company law rules, and aggressively marketed Ireland as an attractive place in which to do business internationally.

It is shown that these policies, and the rise of an entrepreneurial ethos, resulted in much higher levels of industrialisation, incorporation and corporate activity towards the end of the twentieth century. Ireland's spectacular economic success, the so-called 'Celtic Tiger', boosted living standards, and reversed settled patterns of emigration and agrarianism. However, as ever more workers became white collar, more high-profile corporate scandals emerged and the corporate corruption of politics became more apparent. These factors were compounded by major international scandals in the corporate and financial community, some of which had close Irish connections. It became clear that these events could cause people to lose their jobs, their life savings and their personal security. The tipping point came in 2008 when corporate irresponsibility in the Irish banking sector exposed Ireland and Europe to an unprecedented level of economic harm. The economy declined, unemployment rose, global confidence in the Irish financial community plummeted and indebtedness soared. At this point, new sentiments crystallised and both politicians and the public alike showed a more determined resolve to address corporate wrongdoing.

These causal factors were very diverse. They had their own origins and momentums and moved at different paces. Some, such as the corporate corruption of politics, were local. Others, such as the collapse of Enron and WorldCom, were international. Globalisation and Europeanisation were dilatory factors that impacted on Ireland over a significant period of time. Changing sentiments about corporate wrongdoing involved a gradual process that gained momentum with each subsequent emerging scandal. Change was slow, halting and sometimes inconsistent. By contrast to these slow burners, the banking crisis burned brightly, crystallising the existing resolve to deal with corporate wrongdoing. These causal forces were very different but they all made the State more aware of the dangers of corporate wrongdoing and stimulated the new appetite for corporate accountability. This chapter takes a diagnostic rather than a descriptive approach to chart these generative forces of change which influenced Ireland to reappraise its understanding of harm and re-evaluate its corporate enforcement architecture.

Enterprise inducing factors

Europeanisation and globalisation

A significant factor in Ireland's economic success was its membership of the European Community since 1973. It also had a significant effect on the structure and content of Irish company law, which was now informed by treaties, regulations from the Council of Ministers, Council directives and ECJ case law. Article 100 of the Rome Treaty specifically provided for the harmonisation of company law in all member states that constituted the common market. Article 54(3) required community institutions to provide similar safeguards for company shareholders, creditors and others in member states. Numerous European directives were also introduced to regulate corporate activities resulting in 'the *ad hoc* and piecemeal reform of Irish company law' (Courtney, 2012: 43). Nevertheless, European initiatives generally improved the quality of Irish company law and were to be regarded as welcome developments in securing greater corporate transparency and accountability. For example, until the Fourth Council Directive (No. 78/660 O.J. L 222/11 (1978)) on company law, private companies were not required to file annual accounts with the Registrar of Companies or make them available for public inspection. Given that most companies in Ireland were private companies, rather than public companies, the Irish corporate disclosure requirements prior to European intervention were more illusory than real. Similarly, Ireland did not regulate insider dealing until the Companies Act 1990. It did so only at this point because 'the coordination of regulatory measures in this area in the EU generally made such legislation here inevitable' (Keane, 2007: 501).

Many of the positive European initiatives which improved Irish company law were adopted not out of choice but obligation. If the Irish legislature did not implement the directives, then the Commission was entitled to take proceedings against the member state for this failure. Furthermore, European Council regulations were 'directly effective' meaning that they applied automatically and did not require any domestic measures to become legally binding in Ireland. The European imperative to harmonise company law was not lost on members of the Irish legislature, who recognised 'a spate of new company law, almost all of it inspired or required by developments in the European Community ... how much of this legislation would have emerged ... if we did not have the stimulus needed to change our laws or, indeed, the requirement to change our laws. Certainly our pre-EC history showed us as having neither much initiative nor any sense of urgency in the area' (Manning, Seanád Deb 20 May 1987, vol. 116, col. 318–19).

The argument so far is that Irish company law had been undergoing a period of 'Europeanisation' since the 1970s (Olsen, 2002; Vink, 2003). Irish regulatory intervention existed 'under the spur of European Union reforms, and even then reform was reluctant and often slow' (OECD, 2001: 16). Closer European integration also required that Ireland respect the free movement of goods, services, capital and people. In particular, the creation of the European Internal Market presented unique opportunities for Ireland and substantially helped to improve Ireland's economic fortunes. Companies could base themselves in one country and sell to anywhere in Europe, with reduced trade barriers, accessing 250 million potential clients. This chapter shows that Ireland used these rules and its access to the European market to attract a significant amount of foreign direct investment from American companies under the conditions of globalisation.

Globalisation has been a significant agent of change such that people and societies are more connected than ever before, through international agreements and trade, electronic forms of communication and advanced transport systems (Giddens, 2009: 109). Though a complex web of processes, the erosion of economic borders is seen as particularly crucial because globalisation 'refers to those processes which tend to create and consolidate a unified world economy' (Twining, 2000: 4), and because corporations, financial markets and regulation all operate transnationally (Braithwaite and Drahos, 2000). One of the most significant calls in Ireland to abandon protectionism and join the global economy came from the Secretary of the Department of Finance. Whitaker (1958: 13–14) argued that developing goods for a small home market had restricted the growth of big business in Ireland so he called for new industries to be developed that could compete in export markets. Whitaker's report (217–18) reflected the emerging understanding that the State needed to develop industry in order to create a more balanced economy, and that foreign industrialists could bring the necessary skills and techniques to do so. Consequently, from about the late 1950s onwards, Ireland initiated 'a radical turnaround in policy focused on the attraction of foreign-owned export-oriented manufacturing industries with the objective of fast-tracking economic development' (Forfas, 2002: 34). *The Way Forward: National Economic Plan* (1982: 7) recognised that Ireland faced a 'grave and historic test', but was 'prepared to accept that our national income depends on our ability to produce and sell goods and services which are competitive in price and quality with those of other nations ... We must earn our living by our ability to sell enough abroad to pay for all the goods we want to import for production, processing or consumption.'

Ireland actively sought to attract foreign business inwards and passed and implemented the laws and policies it thought necessary to do so. It enacted the Finance Act 1980 which lowered the rate of corporation tax from 50 per cent to 10 per cent for profits earned by corporations in manufacturing and manufacturing-related activities (Blue, 2000: 445). Section 71 of the Finance Act 1999 taxed company profits at 12.5 per cent from 2003 onwards. Nevertheless, it still remained substantially lower than that of the USA (35 per cent) or those of its European neighbours, like the UK (30 per cent), France (33.33 per cent) or Germany (26.38 per cent) (IDA Ireland, 2004: 8). Ireland then established its Irish Financial Services Centre (IFSC) in the 1980s and it also took advantage of the low corporation tax rate (Blue, 2000: 458). Moreover, Ireland was quick to advertise its flexible regime in the regulation of the financial services sector. At an IDA event in London in 1990, Minister for Finance, Albert Reynolds, stated that the regulation of financial services in Ireland was performed with 'commendable flexibility and without detailed rule books' (Reddan, 2008: 71). In advertisements posted internationally in papers such as the *New York Times*, it emphasised its reputation as a State 'noted for its favourable government attitudes towards business' (Mac Sharry and White, 2000: 257–8). The OECD (2001: 27) reported, 'By the end of 1997, Ireland was one of the less regulated OECD countries in terms of barriers to entry and entrepreneurship, market openness, and labour markets.'

In addition to its low corporate tax rate and flexible light-touch legal regulations, Ireland promoted its people to the corporate world (but particularly the American audience) as the highly educated 'young Europeans' (Mac Sharry and White, 2000: 257–8). It also emphasised how its common law system and native English speakers were particularly advantageous for US-based companies. Moreover, Ireland's newly digitised telecommunications infrastructure was one of the most modern in Europe in the late 1980s and it realised it was in the perfect position to exploit the borderless world economy created by technological advances in communication (Reddan, 2008: 74). Ireland shrewdly promoted itself as an international centre for financial services when the financial services industry was separating its front office – which dealt with clients – from its back office, which dealt with clearing house operations and other administrative matters. Traditionally, these two offices were located close to each other but as telecommunications developed these offices could communicate with each other without being in close proximity. This meant that the back offices did not need to be near the trading floors of London or New York and could be relocated to cheaper locations like Dublin. In addition to facilitating communications between front and back offices, Ireland told executives that this technology and Ireland's ideal geographical location between the US and Asian time zones, would allow them to ring Tokyo in the morning and New York in the afternoon (74).

The evidence considered so far shows that Ireland actively marketed itself as an attractive place for foreign businesses. An important part of this approach was to embrace free trade in a way that could not have been imagined in previous decades. By the 1990s, Ireland's ratio of trade to GDP rose by 50 per cent and was second only to Luxembourg in terms of trade openness (Smith, 2005: 64). In 2003, the World Trade Organization (2003: 21) ranked Ireland nineteenth in the world in terms of merchandise trade (the amount of imports or exports which affects the level of state resources and excludes goods which merely pass through an economic territory). According to the National Competitiveness Council (2003: 67), Ireland was the most open to trade among a number of countries it surveyed in 2003, outperforming the UK, Germany, the USA, Korea and Japan, among others. The seeds of change sown in Whitaker's plans for development and expansion were now being realised. Foreign investment poured in. As observed by Mac Sharry and White (2000: 376), 'Foreign owned firms now dominate the industrial base, and their arrival since the early sixties has helped open up the Irish economy. Today, the foreign sector accounts for half the total employment in manufacturing industry, over three-quarters of industrial exports, and two-thirds of the output of the manufacturing sector.'

Ireland was particularly successful in attracting US companies. It had not only managed to attract some of the leading financial service providers to the IFSC but had also enticed other major players such as Pfizer, GSK, Intel and General Electric from the pharmaceutical and electronic industries, among others. In fact, the OECD (2001: 73) shows that Ireland was receiving substantially more in foreign direct investment from the USA than from the entire EU by the 1990s. As a result of this inward flow of money from direct foreign investment, the level of unemployment fell. In 1988, 1.1 million people were unemployed – more than in 1926 (Mac Sharry and White, 2000: 376). However, total unemployment fell from 15.2 per cent in 1989 to 5.8 per cent by 1999 (OECD, 2001: 20). Emigration was replaced by immigration with net immigration reaching 38,000 between 1996 and 1998 (Mac Sharry and White, 2000: 120). Government debt fell and living standards were boosted considerably (OECD, 2001: 29). Government debt fell from 116 per cent of GDP in 1987 to 55 per cent of GDP by 1998 (Mac Sharry and White, 2000: 119), and Ireland was reported to be the fourth richest country in the world in 2003 (OECD, 2003: 12–13). McWilliams (2005: 94) has argued that Ireland achieved this spectacular success by virtue of the ability to take a chameleon-like approach and appear 'Ameropean', 'tying ourselves politically to Brussels' orbit while not merely retaining but actively encouraging a rather promiscuous relationship with the US'.

Ireland's efforts at international self-promotion and its embrace of free-market capitalism were well rewarded. Reddan (2008: 7) reported that Ireland was 'the fourth largest European funds centre; the eighth largest global banking centre; the fourth largest reinsurance centre; and the leading European cross-border centre for life insurance'. Ireland went from being a State where international banks were going to 'pull down the shutters' to being the place where they established their headquarters (*Irish Times*, 10 February 1987: 17). In 1988, *The Economist* (16 January 1988: 1) described Ireland as being 'the poorest of the rich', personifying the Irish economy on its cover with an image of a woman begging on O'Connell Bridge in Dublin. Less than a decade later, it described Ireland as 'Europe's shining light' (21 May 1997: 16). Ireland transformed 'from Celtic pauper to Celtic tiger' in what must have seemed like a miraculously short time period (Mac Sharry and White, 2000: 356). This economic success was attributable in no small way to closer international economic integration. Consequently, Ireland was crowned one of the most globalised countries in the world (Kearney, 2004: 54), a 'showpiece of globalisation' (O'Hearn, 2000: 73), and a 'Celtic tiger in a global jungle' (Quinn, 1997).

The commercialisation of Irish society

Ireland was keen to develop its corporate base. The State opened its borders, joined the EEC and embraced competition. Though Europeanisation and globalisation provided the conditions for economic advancement, it was Ireland's budding entrepreneurial spirit that made it seize these opportunities. It lowered its rate of corporate tax and introduced a light-touch regulatory regime. It emphasised the advantages of its common law system, its educated workforce, its geographical location and the technological infrastructures available to businesses. Irish society was no longer content to define itself in terms of an anti-materialist rural identity, or in opposition to the British. Society realised that it needed a new identity because the old one could neither be sustained nor sustain its people (Whitaker, 1958: 5). It knew it could only achieve this if it were transformed from an agricultural society to one driven by commercialism, entrepreneurship and professionalism. The purpose of this section is to analyse how this change in ethos also created a new dynamic in how people perceived of corporate wrongdoing and reacted to it.

Policy makers realised their current economic problems could not be solved by the continuation of existing policies supporting and relying so heavily on the agricultural sector. However, it would not be enough to abandon restrictive policies and rebalance the economy to encourage more industry because, as Whitaker (1958: 7) noted, 'The nerve centre of the whole forward movement may lie, not in finance, but in entrepreneurial capacity.' He argued (7, 20) that this could only be achieved by 'raising the general level of education', 'the practical encouragement of initiative and enterprise' and 'a greater will to work'. In making these suggestions, Whitaker urged the State to develop an entrepreneurial spirit in Irish society. The Whitaker Report was implemented by Lemass's administration in the programmes for economic expansion (Lemass, 1959; 1964). Under his leadership, protectionism was abandoned, the Control of Manufactures Acts from the 1930s were repealed, and grants were given to foreign firms to establish in Ireland.

Lemass's government also made significant efforts to boost trade and open up the Irish economy. It signed the General Agreement on Tariffs and Trade (GATT) in 1960 to reduce worldwide tariffs, applied to join the EEC in 1961 (then unsuccessfully), and signed the Anglo-Irish Free Trade Agreement in 1965. These pro-industry policies were continued by subsequent political administrations. The determination to develop the financial services sector, for example, was evident in the address of An Taoiseach, Charles Haughey, to the IFSC Committee in 1987. He told its members: 'I've called you here together not to ask you if we are going to have an international financial centre – but to tell you we are going to have one. I expect to have your cooperation in making it a success' (Reddan, 2008: 34).

The political determination to develop an entrepreneurial spirit was also evident in the 1980s when the government started negotiating agreements with employers and trade unions to keep wages low in exchange for low taxes, a process known as 'social partnership'. The idea was to make Ireland more attractive to business by ensuring an inexpensive supply of labour, fewer 'lost' days and relative stability through fewer industrial actions and strikes. More jobs and taxes would pay for the tax cuts for employees (Hardiman, 2002; O'Donnell and O'Reardon, 2000). These agreements were reached when the partners realised that 'fighting over shares of a declining income was fruitless' (OECD, 2001: 25). This acknowledgement also facilitated social acquiescence to severe cuts in government expenditure. Such measures were necessary, it was argued, to reduce government debt, to retake control of the public finances, and to achieve economic stability (Mac Sharry and White, 2000; Honohan, 1999). Without these fiscal corrections, foreign investment 'would [have] gone elsewhere and the Tiger would not have roared' (O'Grada, 2002: 6). Furthermore, efforts were also made in the 1980s to develop indigenous industry, as evinced by 'the decision to increase resources allocated to indigenous industry from 40 to 50 per cent [and] the selective allocation of grants to firms with the greatest potential of export growth' (Smith, 2005: 85–6). All of this suggested that the political climate had changed to become pro-business, that various parts of society were working together to promote growth, and that Whitaker's suggestions on trade liberalisation were being implemented.

Another important part of Whitaker's strategy, which Lemass and his successors also enthusiastically advanced, was the promotion and improvement of education in Ireland. Education 'has been treated as a key priority by Irish governments since the 1960s' (Smith, 2005: 74). Class sizes in primary schools were reduced to improve the teacher–student ratios, small schools with only one or two teachers were closed to improve facilities more generally and greater efforts were made to transport students to school for free to compensate for these closures (Lee, 1989: 361). Following on from reports on investment in education compiled by the Minister for Education and the OECD (1965; 1966), the State also established comprehensive schools where a wider range of subjects were taught, provided funding to build more secondary schools and introduced free education at secondary level. The numbers attending secondary school increased from 104,000 in 1966 to 144,000 in 1969 as more children from families of modest means embraced educational opportunities (Lee, 1989: 362). Improvements were also made at tertiary level in the 1960s. The State established regional colleges to 'educate for trade and industry over a broad spectrum of occupations, ranging from craft to professional level, notably engineering and science but also commercial, linguistic and other specialties' (Kennedy, Seanad Deb 10 July 1992, vol. 133, col. 1818). Though attendance at university was dominated by the middle classes, with only 2 per cent of children from working class backgrounds attending in 1967, this was ameliorated by a more generous system of State scholarships (Nevin, 1967–68). The number of scholarships provided to students increased from 1,119 in 1968 to 6,168 in 1975, so that approximately one quarter of all students received some State support (Rottman *et al.*, 1982; Lee, 1989: 362). In the 1970s, national institutes for higher education were established in Limerick and Dublin (later known as the University of Limerick and Dublin City University). These efforts at improving access to education evinced a new desire to develop Ireland into a more commercially driven society with a new emphasis on professionalism. They marked the beginning of the movement away from agrarianism to entrepreneurship.

The educational reforms and policies initiated in the 1960s had a significant impact on the level of educated and skilled persons available to enterprise in Ireland. The retention rate of students at secondary level rose from 20 per cent to 81 per cent between 1960 and 2002 (IDA Ireland, 2004: 4). Six times as many students attended university in 1994 than in 1964 (Smith, 2005: 75). The National Competitiveness Council (2003: 74) recorded that Ireland had twice as many science and engineering graduates as the OECD average in the year 2000, per 1,000 of the population aged 20–34. It noted (2011: 112, 121) that by 2007, 44 per cent of all persons aged 25–34 in Ireland had a third-level qualification, 5 per cent above the OECD average. Almost one million people were in full time education in 2011 (IDA Ireland, 2011: 9). The availability of such a highly educated workforce has been credited as one of the most important factors for Ireland's success in attracting foreign direct investment in the highly skilled pharmaceutical and electronic sectors (Tansey, 1998: 105). Indeed, a survey by Forfas (2002: 34) has shown that more than half of foreign-owned enterprises ranked the appropriately skilled workforce in Ireland as its best advantage over other jurisdictions. Similarly, a survey of international business people conducted by the OECD (1996: 16) showed that Ireland was ranked second in Europe for the availability of skilled labour and first for the relevance of its education to the needs of business.

Not only have educational reforms been essential in creating skilled labour to attract business into Ireland, they may also have facilitated the acceptance of capitalism, materialism and international economic integration. Previously, it was noted that the Catholic Church wielded significant power to affect policy in Ireland for much of the twentieth century. It tended to define Ireland in terms of a rural identity and advanced isolationist and anti-materialist policies. These philosophies tended to inhibit the development of business in the State. As noted by Lee (1989: 362), however, educational reforms in the 1960s and 1970s 'began to shift the balance of power in the administration of education between the traditional hegemonic Catholic Church and the State'. An increasingly educated workforce was now emerging with more skills to question and challenge the rigid lines of authority that had previously been advanced by the Church. Such changes may have made it easier to accept economic openness and industrialisation in Ireland. It seems that Irish people did not resist industrialisation or materialism in any substantial way but instead became good capitalist consumers. For example, when fashion house Hermès started selling its handbags in Dublin, bags which apparently sell for thousands of euros, a long queue of people formed to buy them. One woman was said to have gushed that the arrival of these handbags was 'great for the country' (*Irish Times*, 21 May 2005: C1).

These efforts succeeded in reorienting society towards commercialism, industry and professionalism, and away from reliance on agriculture. In the 1970s, one in four people were working in agriculture but this had dropped to one in twelve by the end of the 1990s (Mac Sharry and White, 2005: 153). The small farmer working class shrank and most people in Ireland now identified themselves as belonging to the middle class in what McWilliams (2005: 15) has called 'the Wonder Bra effect', whereby society is lifted up and into the middle. Summarising the composition of the work force during the Celtic Tiger, he noted (23): 'Manufacturing is on the way out. Only 16% of us make anything anymore. Less than one in twenty works the land. One in ten works in construction …The rest of us, which is just under three in every five, toil away at the water cooler in office jobs … We are all white-collar.'

Reflecting on these developments, it was evident that Irish society underwent some profound changes as it moved towards the end of the twentieth century. Ireland had traditionally been a rural inward-looking state. It had an 'economy based on low wage agriculture and basic manufacturing, and exported large amounts of labour to other countries in the form of emigration' (OECD, 2001: 16). However, Ireland abandoned protectionism, embraced competition, lowered corporate tax, championed facilitative corporate and financial regulations, and aggressively marketed Ireland as an attractive place in which to do business. It also facilitated easier access to education thereby creating a pool of highly educated and skilled workers which appealed to industry and convinced them to establish their businesses in the State. Consequently, Ireland experienced greater levels of industrialisation and of incorporation. Between 1956 and 2005, the number of private companies in Ireland rose from 7,388 to 138,215 and the number of public companies rose from 372 to 1,103 (Cox, 1958: para. 41; DETE, 2006: 16). 'Ireland Inc.' was a tremendous success. However, increased corporate activity was a dangerous phenomenon in a State with lax laws and little cultural recognition of the harms that companies could cause to society. The next section investigates the correlation between the increased corporate activity in the State and the growing social and political awareness of corporate harm. It is shown that the celebration of enterprise elided with a recognition that 'suite crime' could threaten the security of the State in ways that are at least as serious as 'street crime'.

Awareness inducing factors

Ireland embraced the opportunities presented by its membership of Europe and by increased globalisation. Companies became a more prominent form of business organisation in Ireland and more and more workers became white-collar. However, as a result, there were more opportunities to commit white-collar crimes. High profile domestic corporate scandals emerged in the 1990s and these were compounded by high profile international corporate scandals, some of which had strong Irish connections. These scandals made the public more aware that corporate and white-collar criminality can cause serious harm and stimulated an increased demand for corporate accountability in law.

Domestic scandals

In the 1990s, 'a series of scandals shook confidence in sectors of the Irish business world' (Keogh, 2005: 390). When the state-owned company, Siúicre Éireann (subsequently known as Greencore), was being privatised, allegations emerged that the managing director, Chris Comerford, and three other executives, had used the company's funds to purchase a subsidiary of the company which they then sold back to the State at a profit (Byrne, 2012: 104). In accordance with the Companies Act 1990, High Court Inspectors investigated and concluded that 'Mr Comerford was given and corruptly accepted monies' and was 'an unfit person to be a director of a company in the State' (Foley and Barry, 1992: 211–13). The Minister for Industry and Commerce, Des O'Malley, hoped that prosecutions would follow but they did not (*Irish Times*, 4 March 1992: 7). As noted by Byrne (2012: 105), 'The only consequences were to the public purse and the private pocket of the citizen.'

Just weeks after the Greencore scandal, it emerged that the semi-state telecommunications company, Telecom Éireann, had bought land linked to the well-connected Irish businessmen, Dermot Desmond (the government-appointed Chairman of a State-owned airport authority, Aer Rianta) and Michael Smurfit (the government-appointed Chairman of Telecom), for £9.4 million, despite being valued at £6 million by the State Valuations Office (Byrne, 2012: 105–6). Both men contested their involvement with companies that had bought and sold the site. As with the Greencore affair, a High Court inspector investigated the matter in accordance with the Companies Acts. Collins and O'Shea (2000: 35) noted that the 'allegations of corruption appeared to gain currency when the Taoiseach requested the Chairman [of Telecom] to "stand aside" pending the investigations'. The Taoiseach also described Mr Desmond's decision to resign as Chairman of Aer Rianta as 'sad but inevitable' (*Irish Times*, 4 October 1991: 1). In the end, the Inspector exonerated Mr Smurfit, concluding that even though he had invested in a company selling the site, he was not aware of its dealings in relation to the sale of this land (Glacken, 1993: 119). He also concluded, however, that Mr Desmond was the 'true beneficial owner' of some of the companies involved in the selling of the site and was 'financially interested in them' (1993: 78–9). The Inspector also found that proper procedures on the valuation of the land had not been followed. Byrne (2012: 106–7) notes that prior to the Telecom scandal, the term 'golden circle' had 'denoted sunflowers and airline business travellers clubs' but was subsequently used with regularity 'to describe the belief that an elite had access to insider information which was making them very rich'. Both the

Greencore and Telecom scandals, she observes, 'served to illustrate the layered connections between business and politics at this time' (107).

Allegations also emerged that the prominent meat processing company, Goodman's International, was defrauding not only the Revenue Commissioners in Ireland but had also defrauded a scheme of subsidies paid by the EEC by falsifying documents, reclassifying meat using bogus stamps and falsifying both the quality and weight of the meat (McCullagh, 1996: 72). The Dáil established a Tribunal of Inquiry to investigate the company and the Minister for Agriculture, Michael O'Kennedy, vowed that 'nobody, and I mean nobody, will be exempt in any way from the rigours of the law' (Dáil Deb 15 May 1991: vol. 408, col 1213). Though it failed to reach clear conclusions on many other allegations of wrongdoing (Byrne, 2012: 111), the Tribunal of Inquiry (Hamilton, 1994: 335–6) did conclude that Goodman's had a deliberate policy of tax evasion which had been concealed by its senior management. Even this finding did not lead to criminal prosecutions. As noted by Byrne (2012: 112), 'the timing of the 1993 tax amnesty was fortuitous for the Goodman group and also prevented the prosecution of those behind the tax scam'. Goodman's reached a tax settlement with the Revenue Commissioners the following year. Ultimately, two low-level Goodman's executives were the only ones prosecuted for customs-related frauds, though they did not instigate or financially benefit from the frauds (Byrne, 2012: 114). Instead, 'Ultimately, the state was at a loss of €83 million. The state did not bring those responsible for these crimes to justice or try to get the public's money back' (125).

McCullagh (1996: 72–3) is right to observe that the failure to prosecute the instigators and beneficiaries of the frauds perpetrated by the Goodman Group evince continued inertia in addressing corporate wrongdoing. However, it was also a significant catalyst that prompted commentators to contrast the scale of the wrongdoing in Goodman's with the majority of small larcenies that are regularly prosecuted in the State, forcing the public to ask itself the question: 'Is there not something radically wrong with the values enshrined in our criminal law system that focuses so much attention on the anti-social acts of society's deprived and such little on the far more grievous anti-social acts of people from the privileged section of society' (*Irish Times*, 7 February 1996: 12). It would appear that the increased awareness of corporate and white-collar crime issues was beginning to elide with the old inertia and lack of urgency with which corporate wrongdoing was treated.

More extraordinary revelations emerged in late 1998 and early 1999. Investigative journalists, Lee and Bird (1998), revealed that the State-owned National Irish Bank had been facilitating and encouraging tax evasion through the use of offshore investments. Deputy Quinn called the wrongdoing 'an obscenity against the taxpayer' and called for the investigative powers in the Companies Acts to be invoked (98). The Financial Editor of the *Irish Times*, noting the political pledge to introduce tougher laws, stated that 'perhaps the Government is finally realising just how deeply the public feel about the issue' of financial crime (99). The press, once again, were tapping into the changing moral sentiments about elite wrongdoing. More sensational revelations were revealed only a few weeks later. Bird and Lee had also discovered that National Irish Bank was knowingly overcharging its customers, focusing particularly on those clients it thought to be troublesome or overly demanding. Within an hour of the national news bulletin revealing this, the government had called an emergency meeting of the Cabinet, 'an unprecedented response to a news exposé' (135). The government called upon the Central Bank, the Gardaí, the Attorney General and the Director of Consumer Affairs to advise them and to investigate the scandal. Deference to financial and corporate elites was dissipating. The media demanded accountability, stating (*Irish Times*, 26 March 1998: 17), 'Theft and fraud on a considerable scale appear to have been perpetrated. These cannot be other than matters for the Gardaí and for the prosecution authorities.' The Central Bank was criticised for being 'the dog that did not bark' (*Irish Times*, 9 October 1998: 14; Lee and Bird, 1998: 152). Public perceptions of respectable wrongdoers were changing and now people wanted those responsible to be held accountable, stating (*Irish Times*, 4 April 1998: 15), 'news of the proposed updating of legislation to tackle white collar crime is welcome. This has been promised often in the past, but in the current climate there is no excuse for the Government not reforming the law in this area.'

The public was reeling from the high profile corporate and financial scandals that had emerged but more was still to come. In 1999, the Comptroller and Auditor General reported that the Irish banks had facilitated the large-scale evasion of deposit interest retention tax (DIRT). The tax did not apply to migrants who had money on deposit in Irish banks, so the banks conspired with Irish residents to help them take advantage of these tax-free and supervision-free accounts by providing a foreign address. It was maintained that the State knew of the evasion but had refused to deal effectively with it. The Committee of Public Accounts confirmed the conclusions of the Comptroller and Auditor General that 'the problem of DIRT evasion was an industry-wide phenomenon' (Parliamentary Inquiry, 1999: 68) and that the banks 'had knowingly facilitated the practice' (Parliamentary Inquiry, 2001: 4). The wrongdoing was so extensive that by 2001, 3,675 bogus non-resident account holders had voluntarily paid back €227 million on 8,380 accounts (Keogh, 2005: 429). The Committee (2001: 6) was also highly critical of the responses of the State and its regulatory agencies to this blatant wrongdoing, describing them as 'incoherent, spasmodic and ad hoc'.

In addition, the change in Ireland's economic context resulting in a booming construction industry saw an increased scrutiny of workplace fatalities. Kilcommins *et al.* (2004: 54) stated, 'it is a sobering fact that Irish citizens are more likely to be wounded or killed at work, sometimes because their employer has broken the law, than they are to be attacked and harmed by a stranger'. Responding to the public sense that corporations must be held accountable for their actions, the Corporate Manslaughter Bill 2001 was proposed 'against the background of increasing public concern at the rate of fatalities arising from industrial accidents and of public frustration at the difficulties involved in holding corporate bodies liable in criminal law' (Explanatory Memorandum, 2001: 1). Though the bill lapsed, the Law Reform Commission subsequently researched the issue and also recommended that a criminal offence with severe penalties be created to address this wrong, stating emphatically that 'where a corporate entity is responsible for a death, there is a clear need for an expression of public condemnation' (LRC, 2005: para. 1.15). These proposals received momentum when they formed the basis of the Corporate Manslaughter Bill 2007, necessitated 'by the fact that so many workers continue to be killed and injured in the workplace' (Explanatory Memorandum, 2007: 1). Though this bill also lapsed, the State had belatedly recognised that workplace deaths were a significant problem that could not be ignored, at least signifying that the issue was on the agenda.

This section has argued that the turn of the twentieth century was a time of considerable corporate and financial scandal. Though once again there was a continuing failure to properly address and punish corporate wrongdoing, this approach was being questioned and journalists were asking why the State treated 'respectable' wrongdoers so differently from 'ordinary' criminals. The deeply engrained deference to corporate and financial elites was starting to dissipate and corporate wrongdoing was garnering more public attention. The increased prominence of corporate wrongdoing in the press and public conscience can be understood as a product of the changed economic context in Ireland. Ireland had developed a vibrant business culture in which there were more white-collar business entrepreneurs and more opportunities to commit white-collar crimes. Significantly, however, the changed economic context not only created more opportunities for corporate wrongdoing but also for political wrongdoing. The next section shows that the corporate corruption of politics was a significant feature of Irish society at the end of the twentieth century.

Political institutional structure

Ireland's economy developed spectacularly in a remarkably short period of time. In many senses, it developed too quickly for Irish political institutions. Irish politics was originally designed to be local and the public approached members of the national Parliament to solve local or personal problems. Under this system, known as 'clientelism' or 'brokerage', politicians worked to resolve electors' issues in the hope that it would help them to get re-elected (Collins and O'Shea, 2000: 12). This was often a way for working-class citizens to access power and they may not have had their problems successfully addressed without it (Gallagher and Komito, 1996). Of course, there have been some instances of business people seeking preferential political treatment since the foundation of the State, but very little thought was given to the need to maintain distance between politicians and big business because big business, as we understand it today, rarely existed. This started to change with the emergence of self-made entrepreneurs in the 1960s and particularly in the 1990s as free trade advanced and reduced State intervention in the market became more evident (Byrne, 2012: 212–14).

Nevertheless, though the Irish economy and society became more complex, Irish politics was still rooted in parochialism, localism and clientelism. Businessmen reckoned that senior politicians should also respond personally to their commercial problems because 'it was, and still is, perfectly fine in Ireland for a rich man to lift the phone to a minister and expect to get things done' (*Irish Times*, 26 March 2011: B3). Though politicians did not encourage big business in the decades following independence, they subsequently became embedded in it. Some senior politicians socialised with prominent businessmen, drank with them and played golf with them (*Irish Times*, 10 January 2011: 1). They held large fundraisers at prominent social events such as the 'Galway Races' where businessmen were allowed to buy access to the Taoiseach and other powerful politicians, presumably with a view to influencing policy (*Irish Times*, 13 April 2011: 14). Businessmen funded the personal lifestyles of senior politicians and in return were given the inside track on securing government contracts and other favours. There was also a complete lack of separation between regulators and big business. The remainder of this section analyses how a culture of corruption and cronyism became more pervasive whereby 'it became completely clear that the public interest was literally being sold out to an inner circle of businessmen' (O'Toole, 2010: 31).

In the late 1990s, the McCracken Tribunal of Public Inquiry investigated a number of allegations of corruption concluding that the Minister for Transport, Energy and Communication, Michael Lowry, had received substantial amounts of money in his personal capacity and the Dunnes Group had also paid £395,000 to refurbish Mr Lowry's home (McCracken, 1997: 68–70). It also determined that Ben Dunne from this Group had made four payments to An Taoiseach Charles Haughey, amounting to £1.1 million through his accountant, Des Traynor. He had also made a personal payment directly to Mr Haughey in the amount of £210,000. Though there was no evidence that political favours had been performed for these payments, the Tribunal concluded that it was inappropriate for such senior members of government to be personally supported by prominent businessmen, asserting (73), 'The possibility that political or financial favours could be sought in return for such gifts, or even being given without being sought, is very high, and if such gifts are permissible, they would inevitably lead in some cases to bribery and corruption.' It also revealed that the Dáil Deputies and the businessmen involved in these matters had maintained secret bank accounts to evade tax in Ansbacher Cayman Ltd, a bank in the Cayman Islands managed from within Guinness and Mahon Bank, one of the largest merchant banks in Ireland at the time (70–1).

It appeared that the Central Bank had known about the illicit overseas accounts since 1976 (Ross, 2009: 73). Moreover, an investigator at the Central Bank discovered that a member of its board, Ken O'Reilly-Hyland, was implicated in illicit activity. He had received a loan of £416,000 from Guinness and Mahon Bank had used the £230,000 in his illicit Caymans account as collateral (Byrne, 2012: 156). The allegation that a senior regulator used the institution he regulated to commit crime should have shaken the Central Bank to its core and provoked strong unambiguous censure. However, the official response was to doctor the inspector's report, replacing the word 'evasion' with 'avoidance' thereby turning criminal action into immoral but legal action (Ross, 2012: 74). Therefore, it seems that regulators within the Central Bank had also got too close to the institutions they were supposed to be regulating, sharing the same intimacy that politicians and business people shared. It was subsequently revealed that senior bankers also socialised with the regulators who policed them and this became such an ingrained tradition that 'dinner with the watchdogs was part of the job' (1). A practice had also developed of Governors from the Central Bank joining the boards of the banks they had regulated on their retirement (*Irish Times*, 14 October 2008: 12). Ross observed that not only was there a 'well-oiled door between regulator and regulated' but that 'the relationship between the regulator and the regulated was so close that there were instances of AIB and Bank of Ireland directors sitting simultaneously on the board of the Central Bank' (71). What this points to is that the web of money and power that enmeshed politics and business had also caught the regulators.

The Moriarty Tribunal, established in 1997, also investigated the Ansbacher deposits. Reflecting on the period spanning the late seventies to the early nineties, it concluded (Moriarty, 2006: 547) that this 'was a dismal period in the interface between politics and business'. This interference manifested itself in the sale of Irish passports to Lebanese nationals, the systemic denial of taxes to the State, and the making of enormous payments to politicians. In a systematic analysis of the former Taoiseach's accounts, the Tribunal noted that Haughey received funds of over £9 million between 1979 and 1996, despite earning relatively modest amounts of money. In attempting to show the discrepancy between Haughey's income and expenditure, it was noted (545–7) that Mr Haughey had access to a sum of money that was 117 times his average gross annual income and would be the equivalent in today's terms to the Taoiseach receiving €45 million. The Tribunal (544) could not have been more damning in its criticism that the 'secretive nature of the payments from senior members of the business community, their very incidence and scale, particularly during difficult economic times nationally, and when Governments led by Mr Haughey were championing austerity, can only be said to have devalued the quality of a modern democracy'.

In a subsequent report, the Moriarty Tribunal also concluded that Ben Dunne, had used his influence with Michael Lowry in 1995 to try to make the government pay more rent for property he was leasing to a State company. It concluded (Moriarty, 2011: Volume 1, 419) that these 'unwarranted rent increases ... would have improperly enriched Mr Dunne ... and thereby burdened public funds ... What was contemplated ... was profoundly corrupt, to a degree that was nothing short of breathtaking.' Byrne (2012: 163) notes that 'the strength of the judge's estimation of Lowry's conduct can be gauged from the fact that this was the only occasion through-out the 2,395 page, two-volume report, that the word corrupt was evoked to describe a political action'. The Tribunal also concluded that Lowry had influenced the decision to award the largest privately awarded contract in the history of the State, a mobile phone licence, to prominent Irish businessman, Denis O'Brien. In return, Lowry received support for a loan of £420,000 (British pounds) and payments of £147,000 and £300,000 in Irish and British pounds respectively (2011: Volume 2, 1058). O'Brien or his companies had also supported fourteen Fine Gael fundraising events and made £22,140 in party political donations (1064). One of O'Brien's companies also secretly made a £50,000 donation to Lowry's political party two months after it was awarded the licence but while the details of the licence were still being negotiated (2011: Volume 1, 455–9). The Moriarty Report concluded (Volume 2, 1059) that 'in the cynical and venial abuse of office, the brazen refusal to acknowledge the impropriety of his financial arrangements with Mr Denis O'Brien and Mr Ben Dunne, and by his contemptuous disregard for his taxation obligations, Mr Lowry ... has cast a further shadow over this country's public life.'

The Flood Tribunal was also established in 1997 and later became known as the Mahon Tribunal. It investigated the provision of corrupt payments to politicians for planning favours. It concluded that the Minister for Justice, Ray Burke, had rezoned land and awarded a broadcasting licence in exchange for corrupt personal payments. These payments were made 'to ensure that he would continue to act in the best interests of those who had paid him when performing his public duties as a member of Dublin County Council, and as a member of Dáil Eireann' (Flood, 2002: 138). It also concluded that Deputy Liam Lawlor and Dublin City Assistant Manager, George Redmond, had received corrupt payments from property developers to rezone land but it subsequently withdrew its findings against Redmond because it had withheld information relevant to his defence.

In 2008, the Tribunal also probed the financial affairs of the then sitting Taoiseach, Bertie Ahern, following an allegation that he had received a bribe from a property developer. It unearthed a number of bizarre irregularities including the fact that Ahern did not have a personal bank account while he was Minister for Finance in the early 1990s, preferring instead to deal in cash. The Tribunal investigated deposits totalling £452,800 to the accounts he used between 1988 and 1997, finding a number of lodgements made in GBP sterling which could not have come from his salary. Ahern's insistence that he always acted properly in the discharge of his duties was somewhat discredited in the Mahon Report. The Tribunal found that by writing letters to businessmen seeking party political donations, when those businessmen were promoting their interests with government, both Ahern (and then Taoiseach, Albert Reynolds) had acted in a way that 'was entirely inappropriate, and was an abuse of political power and government authority' (Mahon, 2013: 2471). The Tribunal did not go so far as to find Mr Ahern corrupt but the consistent message in the report is that they found him to be untruthful and uncooperative to the extent that they could not establish the source of the funds he received. However, the Tribunal did find that the former Dáil Deputy, Padraig Flynn, had acted in a corrupt manner (2013: 2458).

The evidence considered so far suggests that business and politics became too close in Ireland during the 1990s. As Ireland experienced the fruits of increased competition, industrialisation and light-touch regulation, moving from statist to market-orientated polices, Irish society learned that the invisible hand could also be a greased palm. As observed by O'Toole (2010: 25, 43), 'An atmosphere of insider intimacy in which cronyism thrived continued to hang over boomtime Ireland … It tilted relations between money and politics, business and the State away from the general public interest and towards the search for mutual benefits in which politicians got access to the money and business people got access to the politicians.' Such intimacy continues to this day. Transparency International Ireland reported (2012) that there were significant gaps in Ireland's regulations addressing corruption and that there was still a perception or understanding that political influence, appointments to public bodies and favours could be bought. However, public confidence in the integrity of business was not only shaken by domestic developments. Ireland had developed into a globalised economy which could also be harmed by crises in the international financial markets. The next section examines the role of global financial crises in shaping Ireland's perception and treatment of corporate wrongdoing. It also analyses how Ireland's more prominent role in international business resulted in it being implicated in a number of high profile international scandals and discusses how they re-enforced the resolve of the Irish State to increase standards of accountability among corporate actors.

Global scandals

A series of international corporate scandals also impacted on domestic sentiments regarding corporate accountability in Ireland. One of the most sensational was the sudden collapse of Enron in 2001. Prior to its insolvency, Enron traded in energy assets and was the seventh largest corporation in America with revenue of over $100 billion (Rhode and Paton, 2003). However, Enron was hiding its liabilities by pretending that its investments had been hedged against risk by third parties. In reality, however, Enron often had a significant financial stake in these third parties and was effectively hedging against itself (McBarnett, 2006). In October 2001, it restated its earnings to reveal that it had an additional debt of $544 million. It issued another restatement in November acknowledging that its income was actually $1.5 billion lower that it had previously reported. Rating agencies downgraded Enron's debt to 'junk bond' status later that month and the company filed for bankruptcy by the end of that week. The collapse had a devastating impact because 'more than 4,000 employees lost their jobs; thousands of investors also lost their life savings, as "$70 billion in wealth vanished." Confidence in Corporate America plunged' (Rhode and Paton, 2003: 625–6). The public 'awoke ... to realize that they no longer could trust corporate financial reports' (Bratton, 2004: 8).

In February 2002, it emerged that rogue trader John Rusnak had hidden losses of over $800 million while trading for American bank Allfirst (Creaton and O'Clery, 2002). Not long after, in June 2002, WorldCom acknowledged it was involved in a $4 billion accounting fraud, one of the biggest ever and eclipsing even Enron (*Irish Times*, 27 June 2002: 14). Élan, the twentieth largest pharmaceutical company in the world, had also been hiding losses. It classified the once-off sale of assets (product lines) as regular income, making it impossible for investors to see that this did not reflect sustainable earnings. When Élan restated that its earnings were hundreds of millions lower than previously indicated, its share price dropped from $65 in 2001 to less than $2 in 2002, with its total market capitalisation dropping from $20 billion to $600 million during this time (*The Wall Street Journal*, 30 January 2002: A1; Donnelly, 2008; Pierce, 2003). In 2003, the Italian company Parmalat was caught up in one of the most significant accounting frauds yet when '$4.9 billion in supposed company assets were revealed to be complete fiction' (Snider, 2008: 47). It claimed assets it did not have, recorded sales which did not exist, borrowed on imaginary assets, and hid debts where they would not be found. In total, it had hidden secret losses amounting to €17.38 billion over a decade and it collapsed with debts of €14 billion (44).

These scandals were international in nature. However, in an increasingly global financial system, the lack of confidence also spread to the European and Irish markets. The WorldCom crisis alone wiped €1.4 billion or 3 per cent off the value of the Irish stock market, the significance of which was not lost on the public when it appeared on the front page of Ireland's leading broadsheet (*Irish Times*, 27 June 2002: 1). Moreover, they had particular resonance in Ireland because many of the implicated companies had strong Irish connections. Élan was Ireland's largest company at the time, accounting for more than 25 per cent of the Irish Stock Exchange. Allfirst was a wholly owned subsidiary of Allied Irish Banks (AIB), one of Ireland's largest banks. It also emerged that Parmalat had a Dublin-based subsidiary which had dispensed bonds and processed currency transactions for its parent and was complicit in offences relating to false accounting. It also emerged that Enron had been working out of a number of subsidiaries in the IFSC (Reddan, 2008: 228). Even after these revelations, the IFSC continued to be mired in controversies for the failure to regulate business closely. When General Reinsurance and AIG arranged a sham transaction to boost AIG's reserves by $500 million, both the IFSC subsidiaries of General Reinsurance and AIG were implicated (*New York Times*, 1 April, 2005: C1; *Irish Independent*, 18 February 2010: 73). In addition, Sachen LB, the Dublin based subsidiary of the German Landesbank, was found to be 'juggling off-balance sheet sums worth 20 times the bank's entire capitalisation without adequate controls' (*Irish Times*, 27 August 2007: 18).

Ireland had competed internationally to attract some of the biggest players in the global financial markets, flaunting a relaxed regulatory regime but now this had come back to haunt it. This style of regulation was attracting negative attention in the international press, especially when the New York Times called the IFSC the 'wild west of European finance' (*New York Times*, 1 April 2005: C1). Within Ireland, the IFSC was described as a 'financial El Paso' without a sheriff and Irish regulators were blamed for 'facilitating the development of the International Financial Services Centre in Dublin as the destination of choice for second-tier financial institutions which want to undertake lucrative but highly risky activities in an unregulated environment' (*Irish Times*, 27 August 2007: 18). It was opined that 'when you consider the size of the Irish stock exchange, we are disproportionately represented in … global corporate disasters. Perhaps we should be asking ourselves if there might not be something amiss in the way we approach corporate governance here' (*Irish Times*, 1 July 2002: 16).

In conclusion, high profile international corporate scandals damaged global confidence in the market. In a very short space of time, scandals emerged in some of the world's largest and most profitable companies, such as Enron, WorldCom, AIB, Élan and Parmalat. When these frauds emerged, thousands of people lost their jobs and their savings. Investors lost confidence in the stock market because it was shown that they could not trust corporate financial records, either because the company was using apparently legal accounting mechanisms to hide its losses, or because the company was itself simply unaware that it was being defrauded by its employees. Furthermore, many of these scandals, though involving foreign companies or companies with international operations, gave rise to the inference that the Irish regulatory regime had facilitated the frauds. AIB and Élan were Irish companies and the frauds perpetrated by Enron and Parmalat seem to have been partially orchestrated by their subsidiaries in the IFSC in Dublin. Both the foreign and Irish press criticised Ireland as an unregulated space where companies could go to hide wrongful activities. Ireland Inc. had suffered a staggering blow to its reputation and the legislature vowed to introduce stricter laws which it would enforce.

The incomplete emergence of a regulatory impulse

The sustained period of significant corporate misconduct prompted increased political interest in corporate wrongdoing. When debating the Stock Exchange Bill 1994, which according to members of the legislature was the first substantial update in this field in almost 200 years, Deputy Kemmy stated: 'Many of the criminals involved in white collar crime simply laugh at the police and at the politicians because they believe we are only amateurs operating in an area where the professionals have been able to pull the wool over our eyes. We must tighten our laws and their application' (Dáil Deb 13 October 1994, vol. 445, col. 2027). The Minister for Justice, Máire Geoghegan-Quinn, launched the *Fianna Fail and Labour Programme for Partnership Government 1993–1997* and pledged to 'provide the resources to fight crime, including white-collar crime' (39). In a three-year strategic plan entitled *Tackling Crime* (1997), the Department of Justice stated that one of its objectives was to pursue a 'zero tolerance' approach to crime, including white-collar crime. In the *Action Programme in the Millennium* (1998), an outline of new objectives in key areas of public life for the next five years, the Irish government pledged that it would be 'tough on crime', adopting a 'zero tolerance policy' to all crime, again expressly including white-collar crime. The same year, the Minister for Justice, John O'Donoghue, emphasised, 'in the strongest possible terms that this Government is not soft on white collar crime' (Dáil Deb 26 November 1998, vol. 497, col. 839). The government also established numerous review groups analysing corporate compliance with law, the role of regulators in enforcing the law and the need to update company law in Ireland. The conclusions of the reports were damning. In 1998, the McDowell Group on corporate compliance and enforcement reported (para. 2.5) that 'Irish company law has been characterised by a culture of non-compliance' and 'those who are tempted to make serious breaches of company law have little reason to fear detection or prosecution'.

In 1999, the McDowell Group on financial regulation concluded that the regulation of financial services in Ireland was too fragmented and recommended that a single regulatory authority should be established with enhanced powers beyond those of the existing regulators. The Review Group on Auditing concluded (2000) that the auditing profession needed more regulatory oversight and recommended that an independent board should be established to regulate the profession, to ensure the proper accounting standards were being observed and to discipline wrongdoers for non-compliance. The Group also recommended that auditors and company directors would have to make an annual statement confirming that they were complying with their relevant legal obligations. In 2000, the Department of Public Enterprise published *Governance and Accountability in the Regulatory Process: Policy Proposals* and recommended (34) that regulators be given the power to enter and search premises and to compel regulatees to produce documentation for the purposes of inspection. In recognising that regulatory crimes can be immoral and cause significant harm, it also recommended (37) that an investigation be undertaken to examine 'whether the penalties attaching to offences under the regulatory legislation for each sector are in line with the scale of the wrong-doing'. Subsequently, the Company Law Review Group (CLRG), which had operated on a non-statutory basis since the 1990s, was established in accordance with section 67 of the Company Law Enforcement Act 2001. It reported at the end of 2001 and proposed 195 recommendations to simplify and update company law, to boost protections for shareholders and creditors, and to reframe corporate legislation to recognise that the private company was the standard corporate form in Ireland. These reports saw an increased scrutiny of corporate affairs at the turn of the twenty-first century following the revelation of significant corporate wrongdoing in the 1990s. They commenced an important public discourse on the culture of indifference to corporate regulation, the relationship of business to politics and the importance of regulation in society.

Previously, the Irish legislature had been fortunate in attracting huge amounts of foreign investment on the basis of a low-tax, light-regulatory-touch model, spiced with a cheap educated workforce and some additional grants and incentives. Regulatory rules existed but they were neither enforced nor was there any real expectation of enforcement. Now, however, in order to retain and continue to attract foreign direct investment, the State had to reassure business that the existing environment was sufficiently regulated to protect against corruption and fraud. Minister Quinn explained (Seanád Deb 26 June 2001, vol. 167, col. 719–20):

> It is a myth that foreign investors always look for a location with the least regulation. That is what we used to think. They know that good regulation provides them with protection if it means that decisions are open and transparent. They know that the absence of effective regulations leads to corruption and uncertainty … However, various incidents over the past decade have greatly undermined Ireland's reputation as a clean investment destination.

Prior to the 1990s, the old anti-corruption framework consisted of archaic legislation in the form of the Prevention of the Corruption Acts 1889–1916. However, in stark contrast to the period 'from 1924 to 1995 [when] there were no serious legislative attempts to combat corruption in Irish politics', the State had since engaged in a 'frenzy of legislative reform' (Higgins, 2012: 21). It introduced new laws targeting bribery, misconduct in public office and money laundering. It enhanced public access to government records via freedom of information requests but also enhanced the ability to seize the proceeds of corruption and boosted investigative powers to facilitate the detection of corruption. Other laws, like the Criminal Justice (Theft and Fraud) Act 2001 updated the offences on embezzlement and related areas to protect businesses from employees who might steal from them. Previously, such issues were so neglected that they were governed by legislation predating the foundation of the State, like the Larceny Act 1916. Insider dealing was criminalised by the Companies Act 1990. Prior to this, such conduct had not generally been considered immoral, but merely a consequence of being involved in the markets and having the desire to make money (Clarke, 1990: 162). However, in the late 1980s and 1990s, politicians complained that it 'is happening all the time ... on the Dublin Stock Exchange', calling it a 'highly immoral offence' (Ross, Seanád Deb 16 July 1987, vol. 116, col. 2549) and 'an evil disease that must be stamped out' (McCarthy, Seanád Deb 13 December 1990, vol. 127, col. 228). The transition from a society of only insiders (Stanley, 1992), to one which considered such misconduct to be a fraud on the market, reflected the stricter social attitudes to this kind of wrongdoing and the greater desire for transparency (Nelkin, 2007: 738). Similarly, stricter rules prohibiting market manipulation were introduced to reassure business by 'reinforcing market integrity and increasing investor confidence in the financial market' (Ahern, DJEI: 6 July 2005). This demonstrates that the State was attempting to assure members of the corporate and financial communities that these sectors are sufficiently regulated to protect them from the fraudulent actions of other internal market players.

Gathering these threads together, the State started to treat corporate wrongdoing much more seriously than previously. The government established review groups on corporate compliance and enforcement, on auditing and on financial regulation. Government policy documents started referencing the need to adopt a 'zero-tolerance' approach to white-collar crime. All of this suggests that the deeply ingrained deference to corporate and financial elites was dissipating. However, it is important to emphasise the incomplete nature of the governance shift in the 1990s because the expressed desire for greater corporate accountability was not always genuine or consistent. For example, when questioned on the specific measures the government had taken to achieve its 'zero-tolerance' stance on white-collar crime in policy documents, the

Minister for State at the Department of Justice admitted that it was focusing on drug-related crimes because it considered these more serious (Wallace, Dáil Deb 21 October 1997, col. 69). Similarly, the *Action Programme for the Millennium* (Department of an Taoiseach, 1998) pledged to tackle the causes of crime, including white-collar crime, by addressing 'economic deprivation, educational disadvantage and social exclusion'. Yet, as noted by Punch (2008: 103), corporate and white-collar crimes are typically perpetrated by the well-educated and privileged, and made possible because the corporate setting provides motive, opportunity and means. Therefore, the report was clearly speaking to conventional crimes not white-collar crimes which seem to have been referenced as an afterthought.

More rhetoric was evident when the Chief Executive of the Financial Regulator appeared to take a hard line on overcharging and other wrongdoing in the banking sector stating the 'failures uncovered ... by the investigations are completely unacceptable. We will not tolerate such practices within the financial services industry' (*Irish Times*, 8 December 2004: 18). However, the next year, this 'banking Rottweiler' once again championed light-touch regulation, opining that while financial service providers must behave properly, 'there is a need for letting business do business and letting us interfere as little as possible' (*Sunday Independent*, 13 November 2005: 3). Indeed, when the frauds at General Reinsurance and AIG were linked to the IFSC in Dublin, O'Brien (2006: 189) noted that the Financial Regulator was evasive and 'played for time' in its only public comment on the issue, stating: 'We find out the facts before we act. We're not a regulator that reaches for the gun and shoots people down before we know what the real situation is.' Remarkably, also later than same year, the then EU Commissioner for Internal Markets and former Irish Minister for Finance, Charlie McCreevy, was actually making a play for further 'regulatory liberalisation' to the Financial Regulator (191–2), stating: 'Don't try to protect everyone from every possible accident. Concentrate on the big things that really matter. And leave industry with the space to breathe and investors with the freedom to learn from their mistakes.' If sentiments were changing among politicians and regulators, it was not always obvious.

Furthermore, though high profile public tribunals revealed the criminal breaches of the law at some of Ireland's most prominent companies, the chronic corporate corruption of business in Ireland, and extensive regulatory failure, very few prosecutions were made as a result of these investigations. Following the Goodman's beef scandal, Deputy McDowell asked (O'Toole, 2010: 70): 'will any of these people hang their Armani jackets on the back of a cell door in Mountjoy [jail in Dublin]?' However, apart from two low-level employees at Goodmans, only the journalist who discovered the wrongdoing was subsequently prosecuted when she refused to reveal her sources to the tribunal of inquiry (Byrne, 2012: 128). Summarising the legal response to the investigations by the Tribunals, O'Toole stated (*Irish Times*, 26 March 2011: 3), 'In all, almost twenty years of investigations have resulted in a grand total of 112 weeks behind bars: 56 for the lobbyist Frank Dunlop, six for Liam Lawlor, 14 for Ray Burke and 36 for the former assistant Dublin city manager George Redmond whose conviction was subsequently quashed. Two years' jail for two decades of scams – for anyone thinking of enriching themselves corruptly, not bad odds.' This relative impunity merely reassured wrongdoers that they could act without sanction. Following the latest report of the Moriarty Tribunal, Lowry, O'Brien and Dunne all welcomed its referral to the DPP, safe in the knowledge they would never be prosecuted (*Irish Times*, 26 March 2011: 3). Certain commentators have defended these tribunals on a cost–benefit analysis, arguing that though they cost the State hundreds of millions in running costs, they have generated far more income through tax settlements with the Revenue Commissioners (Byrne, 2012: 181). Others have been right to emphasise the important symbolic value of the tribunals in publicly confronting high profile wrongdoing, investigations which 'shone light into dark and nasty corners where the interests of politicians and businessmen intersected' (*Irish Times*, 25 January 2005: 19). Nevertheless, the failure to successfully prosecute many of the wrongdoers diminished their true potential cathartic value. The tribunals were expressions of rhetoric without action.

Furthermore, the failure to pass and implement laws, despite the strong recommendations of both research groups and the pledges of politicians themselves, also indicated that the State was still not fully committed to effectively policing the corporate sphere. For example, the Corporate Manslaughter Bill 2007 lapsed and was not enacted in law, just like the Corporate Manslaughter Bill 2001 before it. This suggested that when it came to the crunch, the legislature was more concerned with using its time to pass laws on other matters. Similarly, following the DIRT scandal, the Review Group on Auditing recommended in 2000 that auditors should have to produce an annual statement confirming that the company being audited was complying with its relevant legal obligations. The scale of potential harm which subsequent auditing scandals in Enron and elsewhere caused should have confirmed the need to update corporate monitoring laws. However, the proposals on the directors and auditors compliance statement in the Companies (Auditing and Accounting) Act 2003 were never commenced by the Minister, even though the Irish proposals were actually much more moderate than the subsequent US reforms (Appleby, 2005: 261). Gathering these threads together, it seems that efforts to promote higher standards of corporate governance were highly contradictory. This was a period of talk, inquiry, investigation and consciousness-raising but often not of action or change. The need to address corporate wrongdoing was beginning to enter the consciousness of legislators and citizens alike but the efforts to act on these sentiments lacked commitment.

The tipping point

The tipping point arrived in 2008 when serious misconduct in Ireland's major banks was revealed and the State faced a severe economic crisis. The reports compiled by Honohan (2010) and Regling and Watson (2010) officially chronicled the misbehaviours that had already been widely reported in the press for some time. The reports detailed that banks had been lending money to property developers in an irresponsible manner with overvalued property as collateral, or on the basis of very fragile security. It was 'old-fashioned asset bubble in the form of a construction boom fuelled by cheap credit' (Kinsella, 2013: 561). The Irish banks in turn were receiving their capital from foreign banks rather than from depositors. In the absence of effective regulatory oversight, the Irish banks had not leveraged themselves properly or diversified sufficiently into other forms of lending. When the supply of property exceeded demand, property values declined, the international banks refused to lend more money to Ireland and the liabilities of Irish banks far exceeded their assets.

In September 2008, the Irish banks sought an emergency guarantee of their liabilities from the Irish government to allow them to borrow capital from the foreign markets. It approved a guarantee system four times its annual gross domestic product (Kinsella and O'Sullivan, 2013: 14). This drew enormous scrutiny of Irish banking operations and it then emerged that banks were not observing proper prudential regulatory requirements and regulators were not policing the financial sector effectively. The government guarantee and the revelation of serious irresponsibility in the banking sector caused the economy to go into freefall, unemployment to rise and the nationalisation or recapitalisation of Irish banks. The State was unlikely to be able to pay its debts and it was feared that the bankruptcy of the Irish State would destabilise the common currency of Europe (*Irish Times*, 6 March 2010: 16). When the true extent of the damage caused by the wrongdoing in the Irish banks was revealed in 2010, Ireland sought a bailout of approximately €85 billion from the EU and the IMF (Kinsella and O'Sullivan, 2013: 15). This exposed the capacity of corporate and financial crime to damage the security of the State and addressing it became an issue of strategic national importance. Sentiments crystallised and support for the rigorous regulation of both corporate and financial sectors was galvanised.

Politicians urged that the prosecution of white-collar crimes must take place and condemned these crimes in the strongest of language. The Minister for Justice in 2009, Dermot Ahern, emphasised that the law would 'bring to justice those who may have played hard and fast with the financial security of this country. We operate the rule of law. As far as I am concerned, that provides that, whether you have a balaclava, a sawn-off shotgun or a white collar and designer suit, the same rules apply' (*Irish Times*, 25 February 2009: 1). The Minister for Transport, Noel Dempsey, accused the bankers of 'economic treason', pledging that they would 'pay a price' (*Irish Times*, 24 February 2009: 1). Not to be outdone, an opposition spokesman, Leo Varadkar, thundered that bankers did more damage to the State than the IRA and should be treated like subversives (*Irish Times*, 29 October 2010: 10). In the past, the Irish public allowed the State to pick up the tab for corporate wrongdoing with a sort of quiet indifference (Kilcommins *et al.*, 2004: 131). This was no longer the case. For example, when the State assumed the debts of Anglo Irish Bank caused by the allegedly criminal activities of its senior management, hundreds of people took to the streets in protest (*Irish Times*, 19 May 2010: 7). One particularly irate protestor immobilised a concrete mixing truck at the entrance to the Dáil. The vehicle had the words 'Toxic Bank Anglo' painted on it (*Irish Times*, 30 September 2010: 9). When a newly appointed financial regulator promised stricter supervision of corporate and financial affairs, journalists reported, 'it was the kind of language taxpayers wanted to hear' (*Irish Times*, 9 April 2010: 13).

Politicians have since attempted to 'govern through crime' (Simon, 2007) by introducing new laws which crack down on corporate and white-collar crime and enhance the capacity of enforcers. The Companies (Amendment) Act 2009 was enacted with immediate effect to enhance the investigative powers of the Director of Corporate Enforcement and implements new disclosure rules on company loans to directors. The Companies (Miscellaneous Provisions) Act 2009 introduced tightened-up transitional accounting rules for companies moving to Ireland. The Criminal Justice (Money Laundering and Terrorist Financing Act) 2010 increased the capacity of the Central Bank to fight money laundering. The Central Bank Act 2010 gave the Central Bank more powers to supervise and monitor financial institutions. The Department of Justice held the first ever consultation seminar analysing white-collar crimes, releasing a White Paper that recognised that 'the harms caused by these activities are substantial and widespread' (2010: 57). The government then enacted the Criminal Justice Act 2011. This obliged suspects to answer questions, required banks to provide information relevant to investigations, and broke up detention periods so that suspects could be questioned on a number of different occasions while the Gardaí investigated their statements. The Minister for Justice, Alan Shatter, stated (*Irish Times*, 26 March 2011: 6): We must put an end to any hint of a culture that sees less culpability on the part of a white-collar thief when compared to a mugger on the street. Those who have, through greed, abused the responsibility and influence of their positions, in financial institutions or elsewhere, cannot be seen as the authors of victimless crimes.'

The Central Bank (Supervision and Enforcement) Act 2013 further increased the investigative and sanctioning powers of the Central Bank by specifying new information gathering powers, specifying rules to challenge legally privileged information, increasing penalties for administrative sanctions and protecting whistle-blowers. The Law Reform Commission also pledged, in its Fourth Programme of Law Reform (2013: 1–2), to 'examine criminal law enforcement mechanisms for corporate offences, including whether the range of existing corporate offences are sufficient, the range of sentences available on conviction for corporate offences and the use of deferred prosecution agreements. It will also examine civil law mechanisms, including the imposition of administrative sanctions.' These measures have been advanced in recognition of the seriousness of corporate wrongdoing and to remedy defects, both real and perceived, in the laws addressing corporate and white-collar crimes. As such, they represent genuine efforts on the part of the political establishment to grapple with issues that have long been ignored but which they are now committed to addressing. In addition, however, legislation was enacted because politicians want to be seen to be addressing the public's concerns. They want to show society that they are tough on financial and corporate crime because the public attitude to these forms of crime has also changed.

In conclusion, political apathy was replaced by demands for higher standards in the corporate and financial sectors. Public ignorance and indifference was replaced by indignation. People who broke corporate laws were not seen as respectable criminals any more (Cullen *et al.*, 2009). The beliefs held by the Irish people had changed. If corporate and white-collar crimes had been ignored in the past because they did not impact on people's everyday lives, this was no longer the case. People recognised that misconduct in commercial life had caused job losses, devalued pensions and ultimately threatened the economic security of the State. The need for a united 'civil ethic and political will' was championed, in recognition that 'financial misbehaviour threatens the entire system' (*Irish Independent*, 5 July 2010: 12). The public appetite to hold corporate wrongdoers to account was readily apparent.

Conclusion

Ireland's history as a closed agrarian state with minimal corporate activity and low levels of crime meant that it was not concerned with protecting itself from the potentially harmful effects of corporate activity. However, this began to change as it opened up its economy, embraced competition and joined the EEC. Ireland aggressively marketed itself as an attractive place for business, championing, in particular, its facilitative 'light-touch' company law rules, low corporate tax rates and young, educated workforce. This initiative was successful and Ireland experienced significantly higher levels of foreign investment, industrialisation, incorporation and corporate activity. Up to this point, developments boosting corporate accountability in Irish law had mostly been mandated by closer European integration or by imitating British legislation. Though early demands for higher standards of corporate accountability were made, they were half-hearted, rare and often unsustained. Unfortunately, however, more business and less regulation was a hazardous mix. Increasing levels of corporate activity, when combined with an environment that allowed 'business to do business', did not result in the close observance of law. Consequently, the 1990s was a time of both spectacular economic success and also corporate corruption and scandal.

Ireland was not alone in experiencing corporate scandal at this time. Companies with global operations were implicated in major accounting scandals at the turn of the twenty-first century. The spectacular collapses of Enron and WorldCom, compounded by the tremendous losses sustained by Parmalat, Allfirst, Élan, and later General Re and AIG dominated the world press. Investors lost confidence in the financial markets and the world economy slid further into the recession already caused by the 9/11 terrorist attacks. However, many of these international scandals had an Irish angle. The frauds at Enron, Parmalat, General Re and AIG had been orchestrated in part by their subsidiary companies at the IFSC in Dublin. Élan was an Irish company and Allfirst was a wholly owned subsidiary of an Irish bank. Ireland's efforts at attracting big business with a hands-off regulatory environment had backfired. The national and international press condemned Ireland as an unregulated territory, where bad companies could go to hide their criminal activities.

Though corporate and financial scandals were increasingly the subject of political and press coverage and condemnation, the response was rarely to be unequivocally resolved to address corporate wrongdoing thoroughly. Pledges to address corporate criminality as part of government policy were tokenistic and vague. The recommendations of review groups were acted on but not when fiercely opposed by business, as was the case with certain regulations on auditing. Draft legislation to address corporate killing was never enacted. When tighter laws and regulations were introduced, they were designed to protect businesses from the fraudulent activities of their employees or rival businesses, not to protect the public more generally. The financial regulator maintained that the light-touch environment, which was at least partially responsible for some spectacular corporate losses, was good for business. For the most part, the State did not seek to prosecute the wrongdoing unearthed by the public tribunals of inquiry.

Reflecting on these trends, it is evident that the response to corporate wrongdoing was not uniformly consistent in securing increased corporate accountability in law, despite changing sentiments on corporate crime. However, these sentiments crystallised further following irresponsible and allegedly criminal behaviour in the Irish banking sector. In order to prevent the implosion of its entire financial network, the State guaranteed bank debt, turned private liabilities into sovereign debt and indebted taxpayers in the amount of approximately €85 billion. The Irish economy slipped back into recession, levels of unemployment rose, the value of pensions depreciated and many were left saddled with huge debts from negative equity as a result of deflated property prices. Politicians could not blame the lack of corporate accountability on some cultural sentiment that corporate and white-collar crimes were less morally reprehensible or harmful than 'street crimes', or on public acquiescence in non-enforcement. The legislature enacted new laws in recognition of the serious harms that corporate and white-collar crimes posed to society, but also because it was keen to be seen to act and anxious to distance itself from the failings of the past. The rest of this monograph examines how these changed sentiments and beliefs have affected the development of the legal architecture addressing corporate wrongdoing, and the commitment to enforcing it in practice.

6

The new architecture of enforcement

Introduction

The contemporary architecture of enforcement is significantly different from the traditional architecture that preceded it. From the 1990s, the conventional crime monopoly on corporate deviancy became fragmented. Specialist, interdisciplinary agencies with enhanced powers policed and prosecuted wrongdoing. Furthermore, the exclusive dominance of conventional criminal law faded. Regulators increasingly relied on regulatory criminal law, administrative fines and civil orders to sanction companies and their officers. Regulatory criminal law was often imposed on the basis of strict liability and reverse onus provisions required the accused to prove his innocence, or face punishment. Civil sanctions operated independently of the criminal law, in non-adversarial proceedings and were justified on the basis that they were more concerned with preventing future harm than punishing or blaming offenders. Similarly, the traditional adversarial prosecution process could also be avoided through the imposition of huge administrative fines. These orders were often characterised as civil sanctions, although their status was not entirely certain because they seemed to share characteristics of both civil and criminal punishments. This chapter gathers these developments together and shows that regulatory, civil and administrative sanctions were introduced for instrumental reasons, to overcome the difficulties of proving guilt in corporate and white-collar crime prosecutions.

The changes to enforcement in the corporate and financial sectors were gradual and staggered. Discrete developments had their own momentums and moved at different paces. Many of the old threads which characterised traditional corporate enforcement were sewn into the contemporary approach. The traditional commitment to constitutionalism, liberal legalism and human rights persisted and there was a judicial rearguard resistance to some of the more draconian elements of the new architecture. Nevertheless, though the traditional approach to corporate wrongdoing was always characterised by some dualism between conventional and regulatory approaches, it is shown that the contemporary approach was increasingly dominated by regulatory impulses, utilitarianism and instrumentalism. This chapter analyses the instrumental logic underpinning the contemporary architecture. It commences with an examination of the new regulatory agencies and the powers they possessed. This leads the reader into an examination of the regulatory crime strategies and civil sanctions which were employed by these agencies. It is shown that these developments suggest a reorientation of corporate enforcement away from the use of conventional criminal law, which emphasised individualised punishment for blameworthy misconduct, to a regulatory architecture, which was more concerned with efficiency, pragmatism, prevention and risk management. The chapter concludes with an examination of how corporate wrongdoing was politicised in the wake of the recent high profile wrongdoing in the banking sector. It is posited that the recent developments in corporate enforcement, which were introduced as pragmatic and efficient ways of achieving corporate accountability, were colonised by politicians who want to be seen to be 'tough on crime'.

The 'agencification' and enhancement of enforcement

Conventional crime fighters monopolised most of the responsibility for investigating and prosecuting corporate and white-collar crimes in twentieth century Ireland, even though they often lacked the necessary skills, resources and powers to do so effectively. More recently, however, enforcement became more fragmented, parcelled out among many different enforcement bodies specialising in a particular field of corporate enforcement. These included the establishment of the Competition Authority in 1991, the Environmental Protection Agency in 1992, the Office of the Director of Corporate Enforcement (ODCE) in 2001, the Irish Auditing and Accounting Supervisory Authority (IAASA) in 2003, the Irish Financial Services Regulatory Authority in 2003, the Health and Safety Authority in 2005 (formerly the National Authority for Occupational Safety and Health established in 1989), the National Consumer Agency in 2007 (formerly the Office of the Director of Consumer Affairs since 1978), the National Employment Rights Authority in 2008 and, most recently, the Central Bank of Ireland in 2010 (amalgamating the Central Bank and Financial Regulator). A number of regulatory bodies were also given some responsibility for tackling corruption though the Garda Bureau of Fraud Investigation continued to play a central role also (Higgins, 2012). Though the USA was once the leader in regulatory agency creation, a recent study by Scott (2008) revealed that Ireland is 'the world champion for creation of agencies, surpassing even the United States'.

Moreover, unlike previously, many of these enforcers have the specialist knowledge, training and skills to deal with corporate wrongdoing. In some cases, the enforcement of corporate obligations is their core priority. For example, the ODCE is the first agency since the foundation of the State dedicated to enforcing the Companies Acts and it is staffed by teams of civil servants, lawyers, accountants and Gardaí. Many regulatory agencies communicate and interact with each other in order to detect the commission of corporate and white-collar crimes. The Stock Exchange, the CRO, the IAASA, the Competition Authority, An Garda Síochána, the Revenue Commissioners and the courts may disclose information or report suspected offences to the ODCE and these bodies increasingly work together on matters of mutual interest (ODCE, 2014: 20–2). However, they can also be fiercely independent and can only be held accountable in limited ways. For example, in accordance with the Company Law Enforcement Act 2001, the Director of Corporate Enforcement (DCE) could be appointed for a five-year term (s. 8) and was only accountable to the extent that the DCE was required to submit an annual report and account to Oireachtas committees if requested to do so (s. 71). Even then the DCE maintained some independence because it was not required to furnish any information that would prejudice its ability to discharge its functions or information which it discovered in the execution of his functions and which had not come to the attention of the public (s. 17).

Furthermore, these regulatory agencies had extensive powers. Since the Primary Act, the CRO had the power to apply for court orders to compel companies to comply with the Companies Acts (s. 371) and to direct an unincorporated company to cease carrying on business where it was falsely asserting that it was a limited liability company (s. 381). In accordance with the Companies Act 1990, it had the power to apply for disqualification orders where companies had been persistently in default of their filing requirements (s. 160(6)). It was empowered by section 16 of the Companies (Amendment) Act 1982 to prosecute a number of filing offences and this ambit was also subsequently increased (Cahill, 2008: 545–9). Its powers were boosted further when section 66 of the Company Law Enforcement Act 2001 empowered it to impose on-the-spot fines instead of pursuing prosecutions. Also under this Act, the ODCE colonised the power previously possessed by the Minister to summarily prosecute all offences under the Companies Acts (s. 14(4)). This gave it the power to investigate and prosecute crimes. It also had the power to impose on-the-spot-fines in preference to pursuing prosecutions (s. 109(1)). The DPP generally only prosecuted indictable crimes in the Companies Acts that were referred to it by the ODCE. The Minister was still responsible for drafting company law, and to a limited extent to devise policy for the ODCE and the CRO (Cahill, 2008: 561). However, authority possessed by the Minister to petition the High Court to appoint an inspector to a company, and to make decisions relating to the qualification and recognition of auditors, were transferred to the ODCE and the IAASA respectively. All of this suggested that regulatory agencies shared or had colonised significant powers that were once possessed by the Gardaí, DPP and the Minister.

The ODCE is empowered to direct companies to produce any documents it requires, sometimes without court involvement if, for example, it believes that the company is being run to defraud creditors. It can also require third parties, company officers and employees to explain these documents (s. 29). However, the statements and explanations can only be used in civil proceedings and in trials for the specific offences of refusing to make a statement or making a false statement. Failure to supply the documents, or to alter or destroy them is a criminal offence, as is the failure to explain them. The ODCE can also apply to the District Court for a search warrant if the documents are not produced (s. 30). It does not need to suspect that a criminal offence was committed but any evidence collected can be used in both criminal cases and civil proceedings (Cahill, 2008: 622–3). This search order is valid for up to one month, which is considered at the upper end of the scale (Walsh, 2002: 414). It can also be executed multiple times where usually such warrants are considered exhausted when executed once.

The unusually long duration of the warrant and the fact that it can be exercised repeatedly prompted Cahill (2008: 628–9) to question whether the legislation is disproportionate to the ends it sought to achieve. In addition, Gardaí are seconded to the ODCE to support its endeavours and maintain their full ordinary powers of arrest and detention. The maximum term of imprisonment was raised to five years in 2001 in respect of offences which imposed a shorter period of imprisonment (s. 104(c)). As only offences punishable by up to five years imprisonment were defined as arrestable offences under section 4 of the Criminal Justice Act 1984, this allows Gardaí to arrest and question suspects for these offences without a warrant, when previously they could only be questioned with their consent (Courtney, 2012: 1764).

The ODCE can also apply to the court to have an inspector appointed to investigate the affairs of the company in accordance with section 8 of the Companies Act 1990, as amended by section 21 of the Company Law Enforcement Act 2001. Such orders can be granted where, for example, the DCE suspects there is misconduct prejudicing the company shareholders. However, 'There is no reference to evidence of the existence of such a situation being required, or even to the existence of reasonable grounds; it is merely necessary that circumstances suggest such a situation exists' (Cahill, 2008: 654). Given that this threshold is so low, it is remarkable that the powers of the inspector are so strong. The inspector can compel a wide variety of companies, and not just the company under investigation, including all its officers and agents (such as bankers, auditors, legal and accounting professionals, book-keepers, and tax advisers) to produce a wide variety of books and other documents. They can also be compelled to appear before the inspector and can be required to answer questions under oath under section 10(4) of the Companies Act 1990. Failure to comply, whether by refusal or otherwise, with any of these provisions can result in the court making 'any order or direction it thinks fit' in accordance with section 23 of the 2001 Act. Until such point as the inspector makes adverse findings against persons or determines conflicts of evidence, then inspection is inquisitorial and not quasi-judicial, so individuals are not entitled to the usual protections available in adversarial proceedings, like the privilege against self-incrimination, because this would 'unduly hamper the effective regulation in the public interest of complex financial and commercial activities' (*Re National Irish Bank Ltd (No. 1)* [1999] 3 I.R.145: para. 67). However, answers to these questions cannot be used in any criminal trials other than for perjury (s. 28). Reflecting on these developments, corporate enforcers have significant powers to investigate crimes when previously the Gardaí complained that they were hamstrung by outdated and ineffective laws.

In accordance with section 45 of the Companies (Auditing and Accounting) Act 2003, directors of companies that had a balance sheet in excess of €7 million or an annual turnover of €15 million were also required to file statements specifying their procedures to secure compliance with company law and which acknowledged their personal responsibility in this regard. Courtney described these requirements as the most 'uniquely stringent' corporate monitoring requirement anywhere in the developed world (Downes, 2007). They were not subsequently commenced because it was thought that they would be too onerous for many businesses (Devlin, 2003; Brennan, 2003). However, their enactment still reflected the strength of public and political appetite for enhanced standards of corporate governance. In any event, other methods of monitoring have proven more acceptable.

While liquidators had been under a duty to report suspected indictable offences to the DPP since the Primary Act (s. 299), the ability to detect corporate and white-collar crime is greatly enhanced by new rules requiring legal and accounting professionals to report their suspicions that criminal offences had taken place. Under section 6 of the Criminal Justice Act 1994 (s. 32) Regulations 2003 on the Prevention of the use of the Financial System for the Purpose of Money Laundering, solicitors shall report their clients' suspicious transactions to the Revenue Commissioners and the Gardaí if it is suspected that they involve money laundering. Similarly, under section 1079 of the Taxes Consolidation Act 1997, the company auditor shall report suspected breaches of the Tax Acts to the Revenue Commissioners if the company does not remedy these breaches. Under section 74 of the Company Law Enforcement Act 2001, auditors shall report to the DCE if they suspect that a company, its officers or agents have committed an indictable offence under the Companies Acts and give reasons for this opinion. Section 37 of the

Companies (Amendment) Act 2003 provides that they also shall give further information such as books and documents to the director to assist with his investigation if he requires them.

Similarly, disciplinary committees of recognised accounting bodies are also under an obligation in section 58 of the Company Law Enforcement Act 2001 Act to report to the ODCE and provide any information it requires if they believe that one of their members has committed an indictable offence. Liquidators of insolvent companies are also required to report to the DCE on the behaviour of the company officers under section 56 of that Act. Auditors and other 'relevant persons' are under an obligation to report to the Gardaí the suspected commission of offences under section 59 of the Criminal Justice (Theft and Fraud Offences) Act 2001. These reporting obligations have proved very useful to the ODCE in helping it detect corporate wrongdoing. Auditors and accounting bodies made 40 per cent of all complaints to the DCE in 2006 and 30 per cent of all complaints in 2007 (ODCE, 2008: Appendix 2.1). These complaints were often more useful than complaints from the public, which often did not translate into breaches of 'public company law' (16). The use of legal and accounting professionals reflected a significant orientation of who is expected to police corporate and white-collar crime. Auditors, for example, were traditionally required to realign information asymmetries by providing investors with independent verification of the companies' financial information. This meant that management could not misrepresent the position of the company that they were seeking capital for, that investors could make informed accurate decisions about whether their investment was viable, and continued audits ensured that the management was not misappropriating funds from the company thereafter (Coffee, 2006). Recent initiatives, however, suggest that accounting and other professionals have transitioned from private watchdogs, reporting to shareholders and directors, to public 'information reporters' (Kilcommins *et al.*, 2004: 166), private police who either prevent wrongdoing or report it after the fact for public protection.

The material analysed thus far reflects a greater emphasis on redesigning and retooling the institutions of enforcement to make them more effective. Despite putting this architecture in place, however, these enforcers still do not seem to be adequately financed and this has affected their ability to hire enough skilled staff to do the work that is expected of them. In 2007, the DCE asked for an additional twenty staff but only received four (*Irish Times*, 1 March 2007: 8). In its Annual Report from 2011, the Office acknowledged that the substantial resources required to conduct the Anglo investigation had placed it under considerable strain (2012: 3). In its most recent report, the DCE stated (2014: 7) that the office needed to be 'further professionalised' beyond its approved complement of two accountants and 'will require the appointment of an additional five, suitably qualified and experienced, accountants over and above its current approved complement if it is to be capable of operating credibly and on a sustained basis at the level to which it aspires'. Furthermore, as of 2010, the Garda Bureau of Fraud Investigation was staffed by sixty-five officers, a considerable increase on previous decades, but not enough to deal with the level of work they had. They complained that 'they [were] "completely snowed under" with credit card and other equally complex computer and internet frauds. The amount of fraud under investigation is so great that cases involving less than €200,000 have been temporarily sidelined' (*Sunday Independent*, 13 September 2009: 26).

Financial services regulation was also severely under-resourced. Though the number of staff working in the Banking Supervision Department of the Central Bank and Financial Services Authority of Ireland rose from 38.5 in 2000 to 56.5 in 2008, this was not a match for the increased workload that it was expected to address. The total value of assets at the regulated institutions more than trebled from €355 billion in 2000 to €1.4 trillion in 2008 (Honohan, 2010: 61–2). Consequently, front-line staff at the Financial Regulator was thin and on-site inspections were infrequent (Honohan, 2010: 66; Regling and Watson, 2010: 38). The under-resourcing of financial regulators also impacted on the ability to hire and retain staff with the necessary skills to do the job, especially because the private financial sector could afford to pay them more (Honohan, 2010: 63; Regling and Watson, 2010: 38). Unsurprisingly, it was concluded that 'the considerable asymmetry in expertise and seniority between the staff of the [Financial Regulator] and the regulated institutions … is likely to have hampered effective supervision' (Honohan, 2010: 75).

In summary, it was shown that policing and prosecution monopolies held by the Gardaí and the DPP became fragmented as numerous specialist regulatory agencies were created to police and prosecute corporate and white-collar crimes. Unlike the Garda Fraud Squad during most of the twentieth century, these agencies are interdisciplinary in nature, employ a range of legal and accounting professionals, exploit 'information reporters', have considerable powers to investigate corporate wrongdoing and investigate and prosecute crimes. This fragmentation and enhancement of regulatory enforcement does not mean that the State is divested of its power, or 'hollowed out' in some way (Braithwaite, 2008: 28). Instead, the State has amassed more power, has more enforcers to do its bidding and has more instruments of control. It suggests that the State is being 'rolled out' rather than 'rolled back' (Hudson, 2003: 56). There is, however, a greater separation between government and enforcement. The transfer of ministerial enforcement powers to regulatory agencies, for example, suggests that the government is now more concerned with devising general policy but is no longer directly involved in enforcement. This suggests that the State 'governs at a distance' (Rose, 1999: 9), preferring to steer rather than row when fighting corporate and white-collar crime (Osborne and Gaebler, 1992:

25). In reality, of course, regulatory agencies have significant capacity to pursue their own objectives, while also implementing government or departmental policies, so perhaps multiple centres of power exist (Foucault, 1991a: 102), which both steer and row (Braithwaite, 1999: 80). Gathered together, these features of the new enforcement architecture are significant departures from the old regime in which the ordinary police complained that they were hamstrung by limited resources and archaic laws. Specialist interdisciplinary agencies have been given significant powers to make it easier to hold white-collar criminals to account. Nevertheless, increased expertise and investigative powers are insufficient in themselves to address corporate and white-collar crimes. Regulators must also be able to sanction corporate criminals. The next section examines the increased prominence of regulatory criminal law.

Regulatory criminalisation

The Company Law Enforcement Act 2001 criminalised more forms of corporate wrongdoing. The number of separate criminal offences increased to approximately 400, a significant increase from the 280 criminal offences in the Companies Acts 1963–1990 (CLRG, 2001: para. 8.1.1). Penalties also increased. Section 385 of the Primary Act defined a summary offence as one punishable by a maximum of six months' imprisonment and a £100 fine. There was also a £50 minimum fine for offenders who were convicted of repeatedly committing offences contrary to the Primary Act (s. 386). Section 240(1)(a) of the Companies Act 1990 increased the penalties on summary conviction to a maximum fine not exceeding £1,000 and a maximum term of imprisonment not exceeding 12 months. Section 240(1)(b) increased the penalty on conviction on indictment to a fine not exceeding £10,000 and imprisonment for a term not exceeding three years.

However, these provisions did not affect particular offences that specified other penalties. Section 104 of the Company Law Enforcement Act 2001 then increased the maximum period of imprisonment for all indictable offences to at least five years. The penalties for specific offences also increased significantly. For example, conviction on indictment for fraudulent trading was punishable by two years' imprisonment and a £500 fine in the Primary Act but was punishable by seven years' imprisonment and a £50,000 fine in accordance with section 137 of the Companies Act 1990. Furthermore, maximum sentences of ten years were available for market abuse, contrary to section 32 of the Investment Funds, Companies and Miscellaneous Provisions Act 2005. Section 242 of the Companies Act 1990 specified that furnishing false information in order to appear in compliance with company law was punishable by seven years' imprisonment. More recently, the Fines Act 2010 specified that the maximum fine for summary offences will not be defined by a specific amount but rather classified in terms of gravity and linked to inflation. It also increased the fines for indictable offences.

Crucially, however, many of the offences in the Companies Acts do not use conventional crime methods. In the past, section 383 of the Primary Act defined an 'officer in default' of his obligations under company law as one who 'knowingly and wilfully' allowed or permitted the default. The prosecution had the burden of proving that the company officer was subjectively culpable and this was considered a significant barrier to prosecution. As observed by Courtney (2002: 661), 'the instance of prosecuting officers in default has been very rare, largely due to the high evidential hurdle set by the original Companies Act 1963, s 383'. However, reverse onus provisions have now 'become a more regular feature of regulatory statutes' (Horan, 2011: 322). Section 100 of the 2001 Act repealed and replaced this provision removing the need to prove that company officers have acted intentionally in over ninety offences that applied to both companies and to every officer in default (Courtney, 2002: 660). So, while the State once had to prove that the accused had acted knowingly and wilfully, this amendment meant that the accused not only had to prove that he did not act intentionally, but also that he did not act recklessly or negligently (Cahill, 2008: 784).

This blanket reversal of the burden of proof requires officers to prove their own innocence by showing that they did everything they could reasonably have done to prevent the wrongdoing from occurring. Moreover, as noted by Cahill (784), section 383(3) specifies that 'whenever a company fails to comply with a requirement of the Companies Acts, every director has automatically committed a breach of duty. This heightens considerably the likelihood of enforcement of the provisions of the Companies Acts against individual directors.' Strict liability is also employed in offences not employing the 'officer in default' provision. For example, in *Director of Corporate Enforcement* v. *Gannon and Gilroy Gannon* ([2002] 4 I.R.439), O'Caoimh J. in the High Court held that one act of auditing by one auditor of the company, when the auditor is unqualified to do so, is sufficient to render all partners of the firm criminally liable regardless of whether they knew such auditing was taking place. Gathering these threads together, the blanket reversal of the burden of proof and the increased tendency to employ strict liability mechanisms suggests that regulatory crime stratagems are increasingly employed for reasons of accountability and efficiency. The traditional requirement that prosecutors had the burden of proving that wrongdoer were subjectively culpable is avoided, enabling convictions to be achieved with greater ease.

Further efforts to streamline criminal procedures and facilitate successful prosecutions are also evident in amendments to the rules on when prosecutions can be taken, where they can be taken and the manner in which evidence can be presented to the jury at trial. Section 240 of the Companies Act 1990 provides that summary prosecutions of company offences shall be taken within three years of the commission of the offence but section 41 of the Companies (Amendment) (No. 2) Act 1999 provides that this period can be extended if the accused has not been in the jurisdiction or where the prosecutor determines that the evidence needed to ground the prosecution has arisen outside of this period. A statement signed by the prosecutor that the evidence came into his or her knowledge or possession on a certain date is prima facie evidence of this fact. Courtney observed that this exception is 'far-reaching' and 'may have a significant impact on the numbers of prosecutions' (Courtney, 2002: 663).

Furthermore, section 105 of the Companies Law Enforcement Act 2001 amends section 240 of the 1990 Act and provides that prosecutions can be taken in any court area where the offence is committed, or where the accused is charged, arrested, resided or where the company is registered. Previously, the District Court Rules required prosecutions to be taken in either the area where the accused resided or where the crime was committed. In corporate cases, it was not clear whether this referred to the area where the company's office was registered or where the directors lived, so the practice developed of initiating cases in both areas, resulting in the unnecessary duplication of work and the depletion of already scarce resources for regulators. Finally, section 110 of the 2001 Act allows evidence to be provided to juries 'in any form that judges deem appropriate'. Juries can also be supplied with affidavits by accountants to explain complex financial transactions (Cahill, 2008: 797). All of this suggests that efforts have been made to streamline the criminal justice system to make it easier to hold company officers accountable.

Some due process rights were also curtailed in response to concerns about 'ordinary' organised crime and drug-related crimes. When the level of recorded crime peaked in 1983, the Criminal Justice Act 1984 was introduced to increase the powers of Gardaí and increase penalties on conviction. However, O'Donnell and O'Sullivan (2001: 2) explained that this brief concern with 'law and order' was short-lived until the 1990s when politicians engaged in a more sustained 'zero-tolerance' 'war on crime' which was 'inflated by increasingly aggressive reporting of crime issues by the media'. The tipping point was reached in 1996 when Garda Gerry McCabe and investigative journalist, Veronica Guerin, were murdered within two weeks of each other. The public remained concerned when the high-profile murder trial of Liam Keane in 2003 collapsed because witnesses refused to testify against him. The Taoiseach, Bertie Ahern, called for tougher 'anti-terrorist type laws' because the Gardaí 'cannot take on a crowd of gangsters with their peann luaidhes [pencils]' (*Irish Times*, 6 November 2003, 6–7).

These initiatives also aided the prosecution of white-collar crimes because they applied to all criminal cases. Suspects can be detained for up to twenty-four hours in accordance with section 9 of the Criminal Justice Act 2006, an increase from twelve hours since 1984, and prior to 1984 could only be arrested to secure their presence in court (Vaughan and Kilcommins, 2008: 122). Until recently, people accused of crimes had the constitutional right to reasonable access to a lawyer but this was interpreted in a restrictive way so that the accused had access to a lawyer for one only hour in every four to six hours that they were in custody, and lawyers were not entitled to be present when the accused was being questioned (124). However, the Supreme Court has recently rolled back against these practices in *DPP* v. *Gormley* ([2014] IESC 17) finding them to breach the constitutional entitlement to a trial in due course of law. Erosions were made into the right to silence. In accordance with sections 18 and 19 of the Criminal Justice Act 1984, adverse inferences could be drawn from the accused's failure to account for marks on his person, or objects in his possession, or his whereabouts at a particular place. Section 19A of the Criminal Justice Act 1984, as amended by section 30 of the Criminal Justice Act 2007, provided that adverse inferences could also be drawn from the defendant's failure to mention particular facts when being questioned by the Gardaí which he or she later relied on in his or her defence at trial. Furthermore, the State also embraced preventative detention to a greater degree than ever before. Traditionally, bail could only be denied on the basis that the accused would abscond or interfere with evidence and witnesses. However, since a referendum in 1996, it could be denied on the basis that the accused could commit future serious offences (Vaughan and Kilcommins, 2008: 126). All of this suggested that many due process rights were increasingly being curtailed. Though the curtailments specified in this paragraph were designed to make ordinary crime easier to prosecute, they applied in all criminal cases and have also made it easier to hold corporate and white-collar criminals to account.

It has been shown that the State criminalised corporate wrongdoing extensively. The Companies Acts specified over 400 criminal offences and many of these crimes were underpinned by regulatory mechanisms. There was a much greater employment of strict liability and reverse onus provisions so that prosecutors were less frequently required to prove beyond a reasonable doubt that the company officer acted intentionally to break the law. This suggested that the silken and golden threads were pulled out of the fabric of criminal law in regulatory contexts to make enforcement easier. In addition, new rules were introduced on when and where prosecutions could be taken and what evidence could be presented at trial. These rules were also introduced to surmount the difficulties caused by delays in assembling evidence, complications of locating the offence and the complexity of explaining the issues to a jury without adequate tools of interpretation.

Furthermore, the due process rights of the accused had been restricted or avoided where possible. Detention periods were increased, access to legal representation was limited (though very recent judicial rearguard resistance to this practice has ameliorated the position of the accused), and the right to silence was curtailed. Cumulatively, these restrictions required accused persons to spend more time in Garda custody where they were obliged to explain themselves with limited legal advice. It is difficult to avoid the conclusion that this situation was designed to maximise the probability that an accused would incriminate himself and make it easier for the State to achieve a conviction. Though some of these developments were introduced to address conventional crime concerns, they also applied in corporate cases. Taken together, these developments reflected an instrumental ethos in the laws governing corporate criminality. Governance was rearranged into 'a right manner of disposing things so as to lead … to an end which is "convenient" for each of the things that are to be governed' (Foucault, 1991: 95). The next section shows that the same emphasis on instrumentalism has informed developments in the civil jurisdiction of law.

The 'civil'isation of corporate enforcement

In addition to the increased criminalisation of corporate wrongdoing, there has also been a parallel tendency to 'civilise' law by channelling wrongdoing into the civil jurisdiction of law (Vaughan and Kilcommins, 2008: 134). In the past, arguably the most significant civil order in the Primary Act was a kind of disqualification order which could only be triggered by the criminal conviction of the accused (O'Connell, 2009). The Companies Act 1990 now specifies a much wider range of civil sanctions and orders. Insider dealing is a civil wrong (s. 109). Reckless trading is a civil wrong (s. 138). Company officers can be disqualified entirely from managing companies even if they have not been convicted of a criminal offence (s. 160(2)). Company officers can be restricted from participating in the management of a company which is not sufficiently capitalised (s. 150/1990). While some older civil orders have existed since the Primary Act, like the power to strike off a company from the register of companies (s. 311) and injunctions to compel compliance (s. 371), they only became significant tools for achieving corporate accountability following recent changes in law and enforcement. Moreover, gathering these threads together, it can be shown that some of these sanctions can be triggered automatically for events that are not necessary considered blameworthy, imposed for a mandatory period, with limited judicial input and in proceedings that are considered non-adversarial. It is also shown that 'administrative' sanctions were created which allow corporate enforcers to impose enormous fines, without judicial input unless resisted or appealed. Much like the changes in the criminal justice system, these 'streamlined' civil and administrative sanctions are designed to secure accountability with greater ease.

The restriction order was created by section 150 of the Companies Act 1990 to address the 'phoenix syndrome'. This arises when business people use limited liability companies to hide from their debts, only to rise from the ashes of insolvency to do the same again with a new company in the same business. The order is designed to prevent dishonest and irresponsible persons from acting as a director or secretary and from being concerned with the management or formation of the company, unless that company is capitalised by a certain amount. However, few orders were actually sought or granted until section 56 of the Company Law Enforcement Act 2001 specifically charged liquidators with the responsibility to take proceedings, even if liquidators believed that such proceedings were not justified, or be criminally liable themselves, unless relieved of this responsibility by the ODCE. The liquidator was not obliged to produce any evidence of wrongdoing. All he had to do was show that the company was in insolvent liquidation and that the respondent was a director of the company during the preceding twelve months. As such, the application was trigged by the insolvent liquidation of the company, an event which could arise without any fault on the part of the respondent. By contrast, it must be proven that the director acted honestly and responsibly and the negative proposition that there was no just or equitable reason why he ought to have been restricted must also be refuted. The respondent shall be restricted unless the court is convinced he or she acted honestly and responsibly. The order must be imposed for a mandatory period of five years. The court has no discretion to impose a lesser period of restriction at this point and the respondent can only appeal the length of the restriction period within the first year. The protective rather than punitive rationale appears to permit these instrumental mechanisms to avoid the adversarial process, evade due process safeguards for the accused, boost executive discretion and limit judicial input.

The same emphasis on streamlining procedures to achieve accountability is also evident in the procedures underpinning deemed and discretionary disqualification orders created by the Companies Act 1990, albeit to varying degrees. Directors are deemed to be disqualified when they are convicted on indictment of an offence relating to a company or involving fraud or dishonesty (s. 160(1)). They are prohibited from any involvement with companies for a fixed period of five years though prosecutors can apply for a longer period of disqualification. Unlike deemed disqualification, discretionary disqualification is entirely unshackled from the criminal justice system and is available as a stand-alone civil sanction (s. 160(2)). Numerous forms of misconduct justify a discretionary disqualification order, including defrauding the members or creditors of a company or perpetually defaulting on corporate filing obligations. Unlike in cases of restriction, however, the onus is on the applicant to prove the respondent should be disqualified (*Re CB Readymix Ltd, Cahill* v. *Grimes* [2002] 1 I.R. 372). These orders also pursue a preventative and non-punitive rationale because they 'protect the public against the future conduct of companies by persons whose past records as directors of insolvent companies have shown them to be a danger to others' (Brown Wilkinson VC, *Re Ro-Line* [1988] Ch 477: 485–6). The Irish courts have endorsed this approach but also clarified that a consideration of the past actions of the director is important because it is the best indication of whether he or she would commit future wrongdoing (*Director of Corporate Enforcement* v. *McCann* [2010] IESC 59). Much like the criminal law, which is increasingly being used as a means-ended instrument, these civil orders are justified on the basis that they achieve a particular public good.

The other prominent civil sanctions are also justified by reference to non-punitive consequentialist goals. The Primary Act provided that if companies or company officers have not complied with the Companies Acts within fourteen days of receiving a notice from a shareholder, creditor or the Registrar of Companies to do so, then that person can apply to the High Court to oblige the company or company officer to 'make good' this default within a particular period of time or be held in contempt of court (s. 371). Therefore, the injunction to compel compliance is explicitly compliance-orientated, existing only to remedy problems that can be 'made good'. To the extent that the contempt of court can be a punishment, it is only employed where the wrongdoer cumulatively refused to obey company law, the initial order to comply and the subsequent order from the superior courts to comply. It is doubtful that those who commit 'real' crimes would be asked to obey the law so often before they are punished.

Similarly, companies are also asked to obey the law before being struck off the register of companies (s. 311). Notwithstanding the view of one commentator that the strike-off remedy is 'just deserts' (McCormack, 1991: 11), the sanction is better regarded as a compliance-orientated strategy rather than one of punitive orientation because companies can be reinstated to the register when they observe their legal obligations (O'Higgins, 2001). The evolution of this order since 1963 also indicates the tighter restrictions and decreased tolerance for corporate wrongdoing. Initially, companies could only be struck off for not carrying on business but they could subsequently be struck off for failing to file annual returns and for failing to file certain returns with the Revenue Commissioners. Furthermore, not only can companies be struck off for more kinds of wrongdoing but they can also be removed for shorter periods of wrongdoing. The Companies (Amendment) Act 1982 provided that companies could only be struck off if they failed to file annual accounts for three consecutive years. This was reduced to two years in 1990 (s. 245), and to one year by the Companies (Amendment) (No. 2) Act 1999 (s. 46), facilitating an 'enhanced strike-off process' (DETE, 2000: 11). The strike-off mechanism, which in many ways is the corporate equivalent of the death penalty, has been called 'the most powerful weapon in the war of attrition against non-compliance with filing and other requirements' (Courtney, 2012: 1677). All of this suggested that the legislature has introduced a range of instrumental civil sanctions which are designed to force compliance with the law or prevent corporate wrongdoing, rather than punish corporate wrongdoers. Prevention is achieved by denying further participation in corporate life, either by stopping those persons who have shown that they cannot be trusted in corporate affairs from holding positions of authority with companies or by removing the privilege of corporate personality.

The emphasis on instrumentalism also gave rise to the creation of administrative sanctions or so-called 'on-the-spot fines'. These sanctions channelled cases out of the criminal justice system, creating what some commentators have called 'low visibility justice' (Vaughan and Kilcommins, 2008: 125). Companies and company officers are informed that it is suspected that they have breached company law and they are required to pay a fine or face prosecution. If the fine is paid, no prosecution is taken, notwithstanding the fact that a criminal offence has been committed. Sections 66(1) and 109 of the Company Law Enforcement Act 2001 empower the CRO and the ODCE to invoke these sanctions for any filing offence or as an alternative to summary prosecutions respectively.

Similar steps have also been taken to bypass the criminal justice system in the financial sector for more serious corporate wrongdoing like insider dealing, market manipulation and wrongs relating to prospectuses in company law, addressed by the Investment Funds, Companies and Miscellaneous Provisions Act 2005. The Financial Regulator, now structured within the Central Bank, is empowered by the Central Bank and Financial Services Authority of Ireland Act 2004 to hold an 'examination' to establish if reasonable grounds exist to believe that a contravention of law has occurred. The Regulator can decide not to impose any sanctions if the wrongdoer cooperates fully and remediates its wrongdoing. If no agreement is reached, and grounds exist to warrant further investigation of wrongdoing, the Regulator can establish an 'inquiry' to determine if the contravention did occur and to decide on the sanctions that should be imposed. Despite the fact that these inquiries are not bound by the criminal law rules of evidence, the regulator can impose fines of up to €5 million on companies and unincorporated bodies and individuals may be fined €500,000 (s. 10). These fines increased to €10 million and €1 million respectively under the Central Bank (Supervision and Enforcement Act) 2013. The Financial Regulator acknowledged in its *Outline of Administrative Sanctions Procedure* (2005, para. 2.2.5) that this streamlined administrative system was more punitive than the criminal justice system, 'In light of the limited penalties available pursuant to summary criminal prosecutions [so] … [o]nly in exceptional circumstances will the Financial Regulator pursue a prescribed contravention via the criminal courts.'

Administrative orders are welcomed as highly efficient sanctions that hold corporate wrongdoers to high standards of accountability without the need to institute costly legal proceedings (Courtney, 2002: 666). However, they also pose particular constitutional difficulties in Ireland. Article 34.1 requires that 'Justice shall be administered in courts established by law by judges appointed in the manner provided by this Constitution, and, save in such special and limited cases as may be prescribed by law, shall be administered in public.' Article 37.1 provides that 'Nothing in this Constitution shall operate to invalidate the exercise of limited functions and powers of a judicial nature, in matters other than criminal matters, by any person or body of persons duly authorised by law to exercise such functions and powers, notwithstanding that such person or such body of persons is not a judge or a court appointed or established as such under this Constitution.' Taken cumulatively, these provisions have been interpreted by a former DPP, James Hamilton, to require that 'anything which may be categorised as a power or function in relation to a criminal matter must be exercised by a judge or court, no matter how limited the power or function may be' (Hamilton, 2010: 24). The indicia of crime were already well canvassed in the first chapter of this monograph so it is sufficient to note that the punitive nature of administrative sanctions suggests that they share some characteristics with criminal sanctions. Administrative sanctions have survived so far on the assumption that they are civil fines but their status is still uncertain. Nevertheless, Hamilton (28) has suggested that there is a 'substantial risk' that these sanctions could be found to be unconstitutional in contexts outside of enforcing revenue law. McDowell (2010: 138, 141) suggests that the system of licensing, whereby financial and corporate operators agree to regulatory laws, legitimises administrative sanctions, though they could be unconstitutional if used in other contexts.

All of this suggests that the State is legislating to ensure that corporate laws are easier to enforce for regulators in order to compensate for decades of failing to properly govern the corporate sector. This, however, is not the whole answer. The courts operate as a check on the development of more control-orientated laws. In *Re USIT World Plc.* ([2005] I.E.H.C. 285), Peart J. refused to restrict two company directors who had not participated in the restriction proceedings. He stated that there is no presumption in favour of punishment. Despite this, however, section 150 of the Companies Act 1990 provides that 'the court shall [grant the order] unless it is satisfied … that the person concerned has acted honestly and responsibly'. Given that there are no special provisions for directors who do not resist proceedings, it is difficult to see how there is no presumption in favour of granting the order against the respondent. He also reasoned that the court can make its own determination on matters of honesty and responsibility without assistance from the directors. It is true that the legislation did not specify that the respondents must prove their own honesty and responsibility so the court can potentially be satisfied of the respondents' honesty and responsibility from a variety of sources. However, it is unclear where else this evidence would usually come from, apart from the respondent directors themselves. After all, the liquidator is not required to participate in the proceedings except to show that the company is insolvent and that the respondent was a director of that company in the twelve months prior to its entering insolvency. The court seemed to take a benevolent view of the legislation which arguably strained its meaning to do justice in the individual case before it.

The very mechanisms which Peart J. sought to avoid and deny were subsequently criticised by the Supreme Court. In *Re Tralee Beef and Lamb* ([2008] IESC 1), Hardiman J. criticised the 'draconian' statutory mechanisms that commence a chain of events likely to lead to punishment, whereby liquidators are obliged to take proceedings unless exempted and then the judiciary is obliged to grant the order unless persuaded otherwise. This statutory mechanism, Hardiman J. complained, is being used to indiscriminately target and stigmatise honest professionals and 'the effect of the restriction order will be much greater than if he is a "cowboy" director, the class at whom the statutory provision was originally directed'. On this basis, he questioned the constitutionality of the restriction order and granted the appeal (McGrath, 2007: 8). It is unclear what impact this will have, if any, on corporate enforcement because subsequent orders for restriction have been upheld by the Supreme Court (*Mitek Holdings Ltd & The Companies Acts* [2010] IESC 31). The judiciary also seems to have adopted a less challenging tone in such cases though no direct challenge has yet been taken to contest the constitutionality of the restriction order.

The courts have also sought to preserve and expand their discretion in cases concerning disqualification orders. In *Wood Products (Longford) Limited* v. *Companies Act* ([2008] 4 I.R. 598), the directors had failed to make annual returns for a period of thirteen consecutive years and had failed to comply with a subsequent court order to do so. Fennelly J. observed, 'The parliamentary intention to improve managerial standards ... is clear ... The statutory climate is stricter than it has ever been.' While the court concluded that the officers had persistently defaulted on their obligations and had met the statutory requirements for disqualification, it refused to exercise its discretion to disqualify them. Though the court was motivated by a variety of practical reasons for its decision, like the interests of employees in the continuance of the company, this case and the others also evinced a judicial rearguard resistance at the highest levels to more control-orientated mechanisms, particularly when they encroached on judicial oversight of potentially punitive processes. Of course, this is just a limited check on government power. Nevertheless, it is important to acknowledge that constitutionalism, human rights and judicial oversight continue to act as checks on the developing architecture.

In considering the evidence so far on the civilisation of corporate law enforcement, it is evident that the State has sought to introduce and enhance its civil enforcement strategies as part of the emphasis on promoting compliance with company law, and to avoid the more difficult aspects of criminal law enforcement. In the past, the civil sanction of disqualification could only be triggered by the criminal conviction of the accused, and even then only on the application of a criminal prosecutor. However, the contemporary system of corporate enforcement expanded and significantly diversified into the civil jurisdiction of the law. Though some differences are readily apparent between the different forms of civil sanctions, together they indicate a profound departure from the conventional crime approach in the twentieth century. They are not designed to punish past misbehaviour. They are orientated either to protect against future wrongdoing or to compel wrongdoers to comply with their existing obligations. The restriction and disqualification orders protect investors, creditors and other stakeholders from the repeated wrongdoing of corporate officers. Both the injunction to compel compliance and the strike-off mechanism remind companies and their officers of their obligations to obey the law or be held in contempt of court and lose corporate personality.

Administrative sanctions are also created to channel wrongdoing from the criminal to the civil jurisdiction of law. Though these sanctions are also a manifestation of the desire to avoid adversarial proceedings, it is more difficult to avoid the idea that they deserve less judicial supervision, especially given the highly punitive fines that can be imposed. Civil orders and administrative sanctions emerge in a context in which law is fashioned into a means-ended instrument. In much the same way as a ship must be guided to port through rocks and storms, so too must the wrongdoer be brought to justice through the obstacle course of the legal system (Foucault, 1991a: 95). The creation and enhancement of the orders, their automatic nature, the preventative and protective rationale, their non-adversarial nature, increased executive power and lack of judicial discretion in their execution, all signify a move towards increasing corporate accountability and strengthening corporate compliance and enforcement. Unlike criminal prosecutions, these orders are more instrumental than expressive, less severe but more certain in their application.

Instrumental and expressive governance

Traditionally, corporate obligations were substantially underpinned using criminal sanctions, employing conventional crime methods, and were enforced by ordinary police and prosecutors. Criminal punishment was legitimate because the accused could take advantage of due process safeguards to prevent against wrongful conviction (Berlin, 2005: 232; Habermas, 1996: para. 9.1.3). The operation of criminal procedure was more concerned with 'how to hold down the administration of punitive justice and protect the individual from oppression under the guise thereof, rather than how to make the criminal law an effective agency for securing social interests' (Pound, 1913: 308). However, it was thought to be too difficult to hold corporate wrongdoers to account using conventional criminal law mechanisms. The old way of addressing corporate wrongdoing was not suited to addressing the contemporary challenges faced by an advanced industrial society. Increased regulatory intervention ran alongside 'larger socio-economic developments, not least industrialisation and the shift from a rural to a predominantly urban population' (Zedner, 2004: 3). The regulatory architecture became 'juridified', a phenomenon which 'refers quite generally to the tendency toward an increase in formal (or positive, written) law that can be observed in society', whereby the expansion of law is matched by its density, specialisation and detail (Habermas, 1987: 357; 1996, para. 9.3.1).

Since the 1990s, corporate and white-collar crimes have been policed by numerous specialist agencies, with enhanced powers, employing a wider array of sanctions to surmount the difficulties posed by onerous conventional criminal law procedures. This new style of governance corresponds to Foucault's (1991) theory on governmentality, which suggested that regulation is also increasingly exercised through numerous centres of power to solve problems and achieve particular ends. This model of instrumental governance emerged 'to organize the administration of justice so that there may be an efficient machine to dispose of the great volume of litigation in the modern city, to enforce the great mass of police regulation required by the conditions of urban life, and make the criminal law effective to secure social interests' (Pound, 1913: 310). Law had been used to hold down State power but now it was used in a more explicit way to service the political system for the pursuit of particular policy ends, operating 'as a "technically rational apparatus which [was] continually transformable in the light of expediential considerations and devoid of all sacredness of content' (Weber, 1968: 895).

Though it was increasingly recognised that corporate wrongdoing is morally reprehensible, the State was primarily concerned with making the law enforceable. This instrumental logic was clear when Deputy McDowell (Dáil Deb 17 November 1988, vol. 384, col. 1000–1002) called for presumptions of guilt to help the prosecution, changes to rules on the admissibility of company records, curtailments on the rules on hearsay, curtailments on the right to silence, and questioned the wisdom of having trials by lay jury without accounting expertise. For the most part, McDowell was not concerned with issues of morality. He was approaching the issue pragmatically to achieve convictions. Without limiting due process rights and changing procedures to facilitate the prosecution of white-collar criminals, he claimed it would be 'impossible unless the defendant makes widespread confessions of guilt, effectively puts his head in the noose and kicks the lever as he goes down, to secure convictions' (Dáil Deb 17 November 1988, vol. 384, col. 1000–1002). The issue of corporate wrongdoing was being addressed practically in terms of how to achieve desirable ends.

However, the enforcement context radically changed again when serious corporate wrongdoing in the financial services sector came to light in 2008, some of which has already resulted in prosecutions and convictions and some of which continues to be subject to ongoing criminal investigations (ODCE, 2011, 2012, 2013, 2014). It was alleged that assets were being temporarily moved between banks prior to the end of the financial year to mask financial difficulties, that directors had taken out enormous secret loans to buy bank shares and that bank shares were being sold privately to keep the prices artificially high. These tactics seem to have been designed to make Anglo Irish Bank appear to be in better financial health than was really the case. Banks were also lending money irresponsibly to property developers without requiring adequate security or diversifying into other areas of lending (Honohan, 2010). This fuelled a property bubble which destabilised the entire banking system and damaged the financial security of the State. The national economy declined and the rate of unemployment soared from 4.9 per cent in 2007 to 18.1 per cent by 2012 (CSO, 2013: 31). Polemicists suggested that Ireland had joined the 'new third world' (Lewis, 2011).

Meanwhile, senior bankers were walking away from their failed institutions with significant bonuses, or severance packages, or were simply abandoning their debts (*Irish Independent*, 9 February 2009: 14; Lyons and Curran, 2013: Ross, 2009). These events were the tipping point that crystallised sentiments which had been growing for some time. The public understood that 'crimes in the suites' could damage the security of the State in ways that were at least as harmful as 'street crime'. Hundreds of people took to the streets to protest outside Anglo Irish Bank headquarters and the national Parliament (*Irish Times*, 19 May 2010: 7). White-collar crime became politicised. The Minister for Justice in 2009, Dermot Ahern, emphasised that the law would 'bring to justice those who may have played hard and fast with the financial security of this country [and] that, whether you have a balaclava, a sawn-off shotgun or a white collar and designer suit, the same rules apply' (*Irish Times*, 25 February 2009: 1). Another Minister, Noel Dempsey, opined that the bankers were guilty of 'economic treason' (*Irish Times*, 24 February 2009: 1). Not to be outdone, opposition spokesman, Leo Varadkar stated that they did more damage to the State than the IRA and should be treated like subversives (*Irish Times*, 29 October 2010: 10).

These revelations prompted criminal investigations into wrongdoing in the banking sector, particularly into wrongdoing at Anglo Irish Bank. However, these investigations also revealed the continuing difficulties of prosecuting white-collar crimes and this had the effect of concentrating the political mind on increasing accountability in company law. In particular, it was reported that the volume and detail of the documents seized from Anglo Irish Bank created significant difficulties for investigators, that some of it was inadmissible because it was protected by professional legal privilege and that former employees of the bank refused to provide the passwords to encrypted files (*Irish Independent*, 11 April 2009: 12; *Irish Times*, 11 November 2010: 6). Despite instrumental measures to boost corporate accountability, there were still significant legal issues that the legislature had to address if corporate misconduct was to be addressed effectively. Consequently, the legislature again introduced tougher new laws to enhance regulatory supervision of corporate and financial activity and to punish wrongdoing with greater ease.

The Companies (Amendment) Act 2009 gave the ODCE the right to inspect and copy the books which detail directors' interests in contracts or proposed contracts with the company, and criminalised the failure to deny this (s. 2). Despite concerns that the existing powers of search and seizure possessed by the DCE were disproportionate to the ends they sought to achieve (Cahill, 2008: 628–9), these powers were enhanced. The law was amended to allow the District Court to extend the one-month period of validity for the exercise of the search warrant (s. 5). The power of seizure was also extended such that material which is only possibly of relevance may be seized for examination elsewhere, if it is not possible to make this determination on site. Both seizable and non-seizable information can also be taken where it is impractical to separate them, say where both sets of information are stored on the same computer. The seizing officer has up to three months and one week to return the non-material information which is seized. Furthermore, legally privileged information must be produced and can be seized on a sealed basis pending a determination by the High Court on whether the information qualifies as privileged (s. 6). The purpose of this amendment is to make it easier to challenge legally privileged material. Furthermore, section 7 of the Companies (Amendment) Act 2009 amended section 40 of the Companies Act 1990, making the illegal use of company assets by directors a strict liability offence, when previously company officers had to commit it 'knowingly and wilfully'. The Companies (Miscellaneous Provisions) Act 2009 was subsequently introduced to tighten up accounting rules. It empowered the Minister to make regulations governing transitional accounting standards for parent companies.

In relation to money laundering, the Central Bank was empowered by section 63 of the Criminal Justice (Money Laundering and Terrorist Financing) Act 2010 to 'take measures that are reasonably necessary for the purpose of securing compliance'. It indicated (2010: 16) that it would use administrative sanctions to achieve this statutory objective. Furthermore, the Central Bank Act 2010 empowered the Central Bank to investigate the appointment of key influential figures to see if they are fit and proper to hold their positions. This requirement applies to all persons in financial institutions that had a 'controlled function'. People have 'controlled functions' when they hold influential positions, when they monitor compliance with the law, when they advise consumers and when they deal with the property of the financial institution (s. 20). People are not fit and proper when they do not have the necessary experience, qualifications or skills; if they have participated in serious financial misconduct; provided information to the Central Bank which they knew or ought to have known was false or misleading, whether directly or indirectly; or if they were convicted of a serious offence, such as fraud (s. 25). In these circumstances, the Central Bank can suspend the officer from his position in a financial institution for up to three months if confirmed by the Head of Financial Regulation (s. 29), and for a further three months if confirmed by the High Court (s. 31). The chief executive, secretary, directors and other highly influential personnel must have their appointments pre-approved by the Central Bank (ss. 22 and 23). It can also serve an 'evidentiary notice' to summon a person to appear before the Head of Financial Regulation, to answer questions and provide information documents (s. 32). The failure to do so is a criminal offence (ss. 33, 36 and 37). The Central Bank is also more accountable to the Oireachtas and is obliged to provide it with an annual Performance Statement (sch. 1).

Furthermore, detailed statutory codes now regulate the financial services industry, setting out 'statutory requirements aimed at improving the performance of boards and directors and at ensuring appropriate independence and challenge at board level' and new rules which set 'more demanding corporate governance standards here than those in place in other jurisdictions' (Elderfield, 2010). The Central Bank also limits the number of directorships that any one person can hold. Major domestic banks and insurers are required to retain a majority of independent non-executive directors on their boards to independently investigate and challenge the accuracy of financial information, controls and risk management systems in the company. Regulated banks and insurers can be required to submit compliance statements to show that they are obeying the Code. All of these developments show that 'the light touches that Ireland was so proud in the past are no longer in vogue' (*Irish Times*, 11 June 2010: A3).

The investigative and enforcement powers possessed by the Central Bank were further consolidated and enhanced by the Central Bank (Supervision and Enforcement) Act 2013. Part 2 and Part 3 specified that the Central Bank can require independent reports written by experts on relevant matters and set out broad new information gathering powers to require materials in such forms and at any times that the Central Bank specifies. Authorised officers are empowered to enter premises, search and seize records, and summon persons to provide information and explain decisions and records. Additionally, it empowers the Central Bank to apply to the High Court for a determination as to whether material is subject to legal privilege and, if not, to seize it. Part 4 specifies that auditors can also be directed to verify whether institutions are complying with financial services legislation and particular protections are detailed for whistle-blowers in Part 5 of the legislation. Part 8 empowers the Central Bank, with prior consultation with the Minister, to set regulations for financial service providers. Part 11 of the legislation increases the maximum penalties under the administrative sanctions regime to €10 million or 10 per cent of annual turnover in the case of regulated institutions and €1 million in the case of individuals.

The Criminal Justice Act 2011 also strengthens the investigative powers of regulators and reduces delays in the investigation and prosecution of white-collar crimes. It empowers Gardaí to break up detention periods into segments so that suspects can be re-questioned after release if interim investigations require it. The period of detention can be suspended twice and the total period of the suspension cannot exceed four months (s. 7). The Act confirms that adverse inferences can be drawn from the refusal to explain suspicious circumstances involving the accused, provided that he has been informed of this beforehand and has had the opportunity to consult a solicitor (s. 9). The Gardaí have the power, on application to the District Court, to require people with relevant information to provide this information and answer questions about it (s. 15(1)), an initiative designed to secure the cooperation of reluctant witnesses. Furthermore, the Act provides that if significant volumes of documentation are involved, the District Court can require the information providers to organise and categorise it for the Gardaí (s. 15(2)). This is designed to prevent suspects providing regulators with more information than they can address, hiding relevant information among irrelevant information and delaying investigations. Furthermore, the Gardaí can also apply to the court to determine if material is subject to legal privilege and if not, to seize it (s. 16(2)). If the volume of documents is substantial, the court can appoint an independent expert to examine it and prepare a report for the court on whether the documents are privileged (s. 16(5)). The judgment of the District Court can be appealed to the Circuit Court but no further (s. 16(8)). Moreover, the Act makes it a criminal offence, punishable by up to five years' imprisonment, for people to fail to report information to the Gardaí pertaining to corporate or financial crime (s. 19).

A number of other initiatives and laws have also been proposed. The DPP, James Hamilton, suggested removing the right to trial by jury in complex corporate cases explicitly for reasons of efficiency. With Ireland moving towards a more robust system of corporate and financial regulation, he said that corporate prosecutions will be taken more often and that the State cannot justify the time, effort and expense of providing this constitutional right in complex lengthy trials that they might lose. Accordingly, he recommended that a panel of judges or specialist experts should determine the guilt of those accused of white-collar crimes (*Irish Times*, 19 May 2010: 5). While such an approach is not without difficulties, this proposal has received some support and could be preferable to both judge-only trials and those involving lay juries (Howlin, 2012). Another noteworthy feature of the new legal landscape is the Companies Act 2014. When enacted, this will consolidate, simplify and modernise the existing legislation and place a number of common law principles on a statutory footing. Most significantly, it will recognise that private companies are the dominant corporate form in Ireland and will rewrite company law from this perspective. This is significant because it means that Irish laws are finally being written to address the specific Irish context and are no longer merely an imitation of the British approach (*Irish Times*, 6 June 2011: 14).

These new laws and proposals for reform show that an active legislature is adopting a stricter attitude to corporate and financial regulation. Drawing some of these provisions together, the State is boosting the investigative powers of the police and is seeking to avoid and limit due process rights to the greatest extent possible. While the legislature cannot nakedly abandon constitutional rights entirely, it does seem to be testing their boundaries to the greatest extent possible. These new provisions are designed to make it easier to challenge legally privileged information, to confirm that the right to silence can be limited for white-collar crime suspects, to manipulate detention periods, to increase the prevalence of strict liability, to expand out the use of information reporters and to enhance search and seizure powers that were already thought to be excessive. To a degree, these developments are merely an extension of the existing trajectory.

However, the mentality underpinning these developments is different. First, these initiatives are clearly specific to addressing corporate and white-collar crimes. For example, allowing investigators to seize information when it is inseparable from other material or when its relevance is unclear, clearly applies to the seizure of corporate files in a way which it does not to, say, the seizure of drugs. It is a significant departure from when conventional criminal law addressed corporate wrongdoing without reflection or amendment. Similarly, the suspension of detention periods is specifically suited to the corporate context. If, for example, the corporate suspect states during questioning that certain material is in a large volume of complex files, it could take the Gardaí longer than the remaining period of detention to verify this and follow up with the suspect. The suspension of detention periods facilitates this. This tinkering with the right to liberty to specifically address corporate wrongdoing issues is also a significant change from when due process erosions applied only coincidentally to corporate investigations and prosecutions.

Moreover, unlike previously, when initiatives were introduced for mostly instrumental reasons, to address problems with proving guilt in white-collar crime cases, these initiatives reflect the recognition that corporate and white-collar crimes threaten the economic security of the State. Previously, similar mechanisms were introduced to protect businesses from each other and were therefore designed to protect Ireland's reputation as a desirable place in which to do business, but more recently there has been an emphasis on protecting society from systemic risks posed by corporate wrongdoing. Consequently, there is a further shift away from individual protection and human rights to protecting the interests of society, away from only addressing 'personal references and towards system relations' (Habermas, 1996: 432). Finally, these developments also have ostentatiously political purposes. The 'heating up' of political debates means that politicians have to follow through on their 'tough on crime' approach with something more tangible than rhetoric. Cracking down on due process rights and limiting conventional criminal procedure is the convenient way of blaming regulatory failure on something outside of politics. Therefore, these developments, in addition to responding to issues which have been long neglected, also reflect the political desire to 'tool up' executive power and 'act out' for public approval in an attempt to 'govern through crime' (Simon, 2007). Instrumental justice has been colonised by the political establishment for expressive purposes.

Conclusion

The legal and institutional architecture addressing corporate wrongdoing has changed significantly and corporate wrongdoing is governed in new ways. Previously, corporate and white-collar crime was mostly monopolised by conventional policing agencies and generally prosecuted by the DPP. However, the ordinary police were under-resourced, under-skilled and lacked the necessary powers to enforce the law. To the extent that regulatory agencies existed, they often played an administrative role in addressing corporate wrongdoing. More recently, however, specialist interdisciplinary agencies tackle corporate wrongdoing and have significant powers to detect, investigate and prosecute corporate and white-collar crime. Corporate enforcers also recruited accountants, lawyers and other professionals to act as their eyes and ears. Though once fulfilling private roles, reporting to managers and shareholders, they are obliged to report their suspicions that their clients are breaking the law. Though the Minister and the DPP continued to play some important functions in enforcement, their role declined because other agencies, such as the ODCE, share the right to exercise their powers, and in certain circumstances, have colonised their powers entirely. Furthermore, these regulatory agencies are highly independent and operate with limited oversight. All of this suggests that governance is now being exercised through new centres of power and that a whole network of discrete but interconnected regulatory agencies and private law enforcers has been created.

Regulators also employ a much wider array of sanctions than were traditionally available. Previously, corporate wrongdoing was addressed almost exclusively through criminal sanctions and the State often had the burden of proving beyond a reasonable doubt that the accused had knowingly and wilfully committed the crime. More recently, however, corporate wrongdoing has been addressed by regulatory criminal law, civil orders and administrative sanctions. In addition, corporate wrongdoing is more extensively criminalised than ever, with higher penalties, using regulatory stratagems. Reverse-onus provisions and strict liability mechanisms are employed so that the burden is on the accused to prove that he acted within the law. Furthermore, though the restrictions on access to legal advice have been rolled back (and even then only recently), suspects can be detained for longer, the right to silence is curtailed, hearsay evidence can be admitted in certain circumstances, and bail can be more readily denied. These strategies were designed to make the accused more likely to incriminate himself because he was obliged to spend more time in Garda custody in circumstances where he could have to explain himself with limited legal advice.

Other procedures relating to when and where prosecutions can occur, and in what form evidence can be made available to juries, are also streamlined to facilitate corporate prosecutions. Indeed, such is the emphasis on results and efficiency, that in certain cases enforcers are empowered to impose administrative or 'on the spot' fines that entirely avoid the traditional prosecution process, the adversarial setting of the courtroom and the careful weighing of evidence by the judiciary. Similarly, greater accountability is achieved through the use of civil orders that boost executive discretion and limit judicial oversight, pursuing preventative and protective rationales in supposedly non-adversarial settings that do not require a high level of due process protections. Taken together, these developments suggest that corporate wrongdoing is being governed in new ways. Mechanisms and procedures are rearranged and reformulated to streamline accountability.

The creation of specialist regulatory agencies with significant powers of investigation and prosecution, and the creation of a variety of sanctions designed to achieve corporate accountability, reflect the strong emphasis on instrumentalism underpinning the contemporary corporate enforcement architecture. Though the public perception and understanding of corporate wrongdoing was changing prior to the financial crisis, many of these developments were not principally introduced to address the immorality of corporate and white-collar crime or to protect the security of the State. The goal was to convince corporate interests that their investments were safe so the State could continue to attract foreign direct investment and grow the economy. Sentiments, opinions and beliefs about corporate wrongdoing have since changed significantly. The scale and impact of corporate wrongdoing in the financial services sector crystallised the existing sentiments demanding increased corporate accountability. It was understood that corporate wrongdoing is morally reprehensible, causes significant harm and is a threat to the security of the State. For the first time in the history of the State, corporate and white-collar crime became politicised. Politicians competed to be more outraged by corporate wrongdoing. They wanted to be tough on white-collar criminals.

More legislation was passed to boost the powers of the enforcement agencies, to increase corporate supervision and to hold corporate wrongdoers to account with even greater ease. This represented a continuation of the recent legal trajectory, albeit underpinned by a new rationale. What once was exclusively instrumental is also expressive. The State is attempting to 'govern though crime' by 'tooling up' executive power, 'ratcheting up' punishment and 'acting out' to be tough on corporate and white-collar crimes. This approach constitutes a significant departure from the hands-off regulatory style which characterised most of the last century. The result of these developments, however, is a highly contradictory legal architecture which recognises the morally reprehensible nature of corporate wrongdoing but which uses regulatory criminal law, administrative sanctions and civil orders to address it. This approach is contradictory because these strategies are more concerned with prevention and risk management, not blame and punishment, and usually address wrongs which are *mala prohibita* rather than *mala in se*. On the other hand, they may prove to be shrewd methods of boosting corporate accountability. If this is to be the case, the law must be enforced or very little will have really changed in Ireland. Chapter 7 explores whether this architecture represents what one author has called 'all law and no enforcement or the dawn of a new era' (Lynch Fannon, 2002).

7

'Responsive' enforcement

Introduction

Ireland traditionally had a culture of corporate non-compliance with the law and corporate regulations were rarely enforced. Though corporate wrongdoing was addressed by the State's most powerful weapon of moral censure, the criminal law, and by the same agencies which addressed serious crimes, the Gardaí and the DPP, prosecutions were rare and there is no record of anyone receiving a custodial sentence for breaching the Companies Acts prior to the 1990s. The traditional system did not cope effectively with the detection, investigation, prosecution and punishment of corporate crime in practice. The contemporary approach employs a new legal architecture and new institutions of enforcement to address corporate wrongdoing. Specialist interdisciplinary agencies tackle corporate misconduct and employ a variety of enforcement mechanisms to do so. These sanctions include regulatory criminal law, civil orders and administrative sanctions. This chapter shows that regulatory agencies adopt a highly sophisticated, graduated approach to wrongdoing, first attempting to educate and persuade officers of corporate and financial institutions to obey the law. If wrongdoers fail to obey the law, or remediate their wrongdoing, then enforcers are supposed to respond by using a sanctioning approach, of incremental severity, progressing from civil sanctions to severe criminal punishment.

The purpose of this chapter is to explore how this tiered approach is employed in practice. It is shown that corporate enforcers successfully employed educative and civil strategies to increase compliance with the law but that there was some reluctance to prosecute wrongdoers, particularly on indictment. In the financial services sector, regulatory responses rarely escalated from compliance to sanctioning approaches, even for persistent non-compliance. Since 2008, however, there has been a greater willingness to employ more severe sanctioning approaches against corporate and financial wrongdoers and the judiciary seems to be initiating a process to reconfigure sentencing rules so that white-collar criminals are more likely to be imprisoned. Though these developments do not indicate that the entire landscape of punishment and sentencing is being redrawn, they may indicate the beginning of a new culture, one which is more willing to recognise the harm posed by corporate wrongdoing and punish it accordingly.

Compliance and sanctioning models of corporate regulation

Regulatory agencies like the ODCE have adopted a highly sophisticated, graduated approach to wrongdoing (Appleby, 2010). This model corresponds approximately to the responsive regulatory model advanced by Ayres and Braithwaite (1992) (see Figure 7.1). According to this model, regulators first attempt to educate and persuade people to obey the law and warn them of the consequences for non-compliance. If wrongdoers fail to do so or remediate their wrongdoing, then enforcers respond by using a sanctioning approach which is tiered in terms of severity. Penalties escalate from civil and administrative sanctions to criminal prosecutions. The ultimate sanction facing a large organisation, like a bank, is the suspension or revocation of its licence. However, this sanction is 'such a drastic one … that it is politically impossible and morally unacceptable to use it with any but the most extraordinary offences' (36). Therefore, it is unlikely to be a credible threat and, if relied upon to enforce obligations, might actually lead to under-regulation (Ogus, 2004: 53). Criminal prosecutions, particularly on indictment, are probably the sanction of last resort in most contexts, particularly for company officers who are more concerned about themselves than their institution or company.

A number of ideas underpin the regulatory pyramid. Firstly, Ayres and Braithwaite (1992: 19) submit that both compliance and sanctioning approaches are necessary for effective enforcement because corporate actors are motivated by a variety of objectives. Sometimes they want to obey the law because it is the right thing to do or because they identify as law-abiding persons. Other times, they are willing to break the law if it maximises their profits. The sanctioning model is necessary because it speaks to the 'bad man' who wants to break the law (Holmes, 1897). It deters rational corporate actors who want to avoid sanctions and incapacitates irrational actors (through imprisonment) who refuse to obey the law. The compliance-orientated model, by contrast, guides the behaviour of the 'good man' who wants to obey the law. If he is always punished by the sanctioning model, it might undermine his good will to comply with the law (Ayres and Braithwaite, 1992: 19). It could make him hostile to legal regulation and make him want to challenge it in court. This is undesirable for under-resourced regulators who wish to avoid costly legal proceedings. For these reasons, both compliance and sanctioning models of enforcement are important and compliance-orientated approaches are

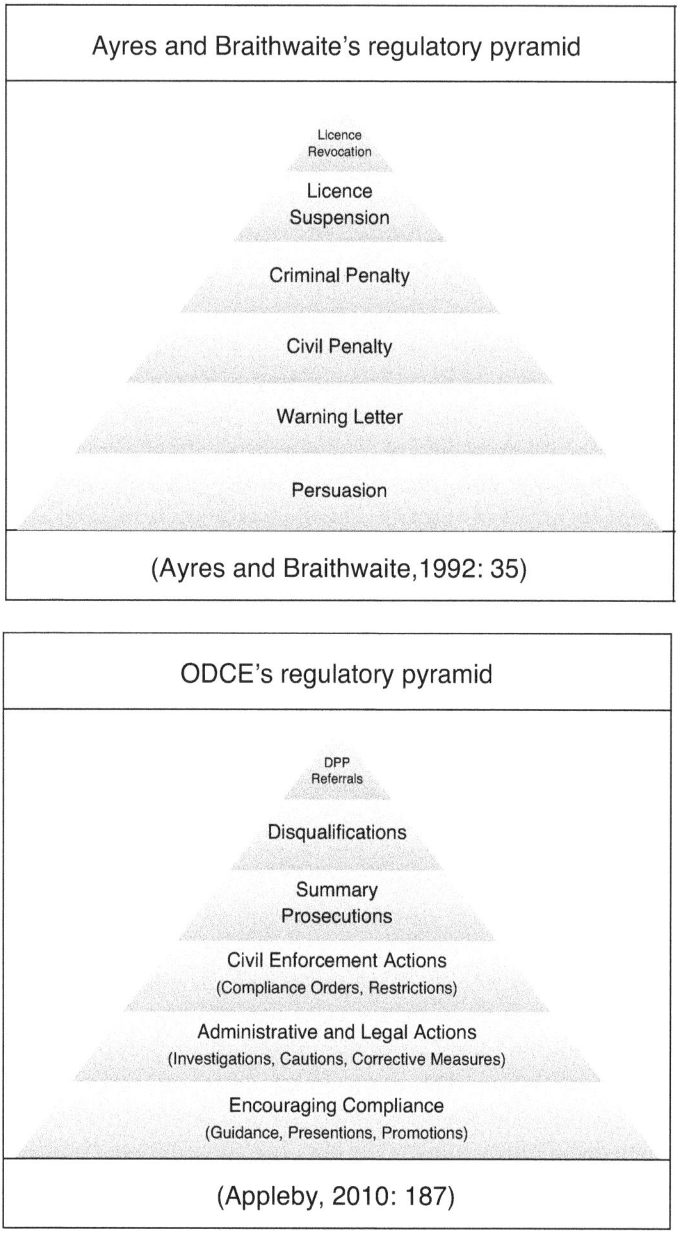

Figure 7.1 The responsive regulatory model

attempted first (24–7). Braithwaite (1990–91) posits that this approach works best when regulators are 'benign big guns' who 'speak softly but carry big sticks' (and a variety of lesser sticks). Regulators need to possess very severe sanctions which they are often, but not always, disinclined to use. They must also possess a variety of 'smaller sticks' which are politically possible to use because they address wrongdoing proportionately. The idea is that most regulatory activity is concentrated in promoting compliance and the more severe the sanction, the less likely it is to be employed. Crucially, however, enforcers must be willing to invoke these sanctions when necessary and 'fire the big gun'. This is especially important in cases they know they will win, thereby appearing invincible. It is thought that the willingness to criminally prosecute gives regulatory agencies credibility and makes the use of lesser sanctions and compliance-orientated strategies possible.

Hawkins, for example, notes that the compliance-orientated approach only really works when the sanctioning approach sits in the background as a threat. He states (2002: 13) that: 'it is the device that makes all other law enforcement possible by granting credibility to more private and informal practices and thereby, in the great majority of cases, foreclosing the possibility of costly prosecution and trial'. The idea is ultimately to make corporate actors realise that compliance is in their interests because they avoid the regulator's 'stick'. As stated by Ayres and Braithwaite (1992: 50), the goal is to make corporate actors internalise governance norms because '[e]ffective regulation is about finesse in manipulating the salience of sanctions and the attribution of responsibility so that regulatory goals are maximally internalized, and so that deterrence and incapacitation works when internalization fails.' In this highly sophisticated framework, governance is 'a question not of imposing laws on men, but of disposing things: that is to say, of employing tactics rather than laws, and even of using laws themselves as tactics – to arrange things in such a way that, through a certain number of means, such and such ends may be achieved' (Foucault, 1991a: 95). This chapter examines how this approach has been applied in addressing corporate and financial wrongdoing in practice. In particular, to what extent are regulators willing to escalate to sanctioning approaches, given that the criminal law was previously so under-utilised in the corporate environment?

The compliance-orientated approach

The criminal sanction was the primary tool of enforcement in the twentieth century. A sanctioning model of justice was employed, premised on a 'command and control' logic. More recently, however, regulators have employed a more sophisticated approach and enforcement has many layers and many instruments. The ODCE, for example, is statutorily charged by section 12(1)

(b) of the Company Law Enforcement Act 2001 to encourage compliance with the Companies Acts and does so by providing guidance on how best to comply with company law and by improving company law and practice. Since its establishment, the ODCE has had an admirable history of actively publishing guides informing officers of their legal powers and responsibilities and explaining legislative amendments. Representatives of the ODCE have also made themselves available for media interviews and public comments and delivered hundreds of presentations to a wide variety of interested parties over its lifetime.

The ODCE also developed a practical presentation for company officers entitled 'Corporate Health Check'. This identified specific key areas of compliance for corporate actors and it proved popular with company directors (ODCE, 2006: 6). A flyer of the same name was produced in 2008 which posed a series of key questions that all company officers should ask themselves in reflecting on their compliance with company law (2009: 7). In its most recent report for the year of 2013, the ODCE noted that it had produced six new guidance and information publications and had delivered sixty information presentations to various stakeholder groups (2014: 18–9). Similar educative, compliance-orientated strategies have been implemented by other regulatory agencies. The CRO has published a variety of guides on incorporation (2012), filing returns (2009) and related matters. It has also stepped up its advertising drive at peak filing times, using a promotion called 'You've Got a Date' to remind people that their annual filing date was approaching (2006: 25). Similarly, the Central Bank also recently published regulatory guidance on its new risk-based supervisory approach called Probability Risk and Impact System (PRISM) (2011).

These initiatives show that the current regulatory approach is radically different from the sanctioning approach previously employed by the Gardaí and the DPP. Corporate compliance with law is boosted first and foremost through educating company officers on their obligations. Recognising this shift in focus and orientation, 60 per cent of directors surveyed in 2007 stated that the primary role of the ODCE was encouraging compliance (ODCE, 2008: 9–10). Moreover, it seems that the compliance-orientated approach is working because 87 per cent of directors surveyed in 2007 believed that compliance had increased over the previous five years, an 11 per cent increase on 2005. Moreover, 100 per cent of the accountants and liquidators surveyed believed that compliance had increased over this period (2008: 9–10). The ODCE itself acknowledges, 'The Office's compliance work is a primary driver in its attempts to support a growing culture of compliance in the State' (2009: 10). This approach represented change that would have been unthinkable only a decade beforehand when apathetic legal and political institutions largely ignored the regulation of the corporate sphere, when company law existed only on paper and when people were unaware of their obligations, when complicated legal provisions were not explained to corporate actors and when the system pursued a sanctioning model of corporate enforcement. This departure is a positive development that evidences a joined-up approach to corporate compliance. It also indicates that the State is willing to play a more preventative role in corporate enforcement, one that goes beyond simply punishing offenders after the fact.

A compliance-orientated approach was also adopted in the regulation of the financial sector, in particular, a principles-based approach, underpinned by some specific technical rules. This 'encourage[d] adherence to the spirit of sound regulatory standards, without being overly bureaucratic' (Financial Regulator, 2006: 12). The principles required financial service providers to act in a transparent and accountable manner with prudence and integrity in the best interests of consumers, to have sufficient financial resources, sound corporate governance structures, risk management policies and oversight systems and internal controls. Additionally, they were required to obey the rules set down by the financial regulator and provide accurate information to him when requested to do so (Financial Regulator, 2007: 33). In essence, financial service providers were allowed to make their own decisions about how to manage risk provided they had effective systems and models for monitoring that risk. The 'preferred approach to enforcement was to seek voluntary compliance with legislation, codes and rules ... To this extent, the underlying philosophy was orientated towards trusting a properly governed firm' (Honohan, 2010: 44–5). The rules-based approach, by contrast, was criticised by the CEO of the Financial Regulator as being 'a very legalistic approach' which was costly, inflexible, and slow to react to changed circumstances (O'Reilly, 2005: 4–5).

The preference for a compliance-orientated approach meant that the relationship between the Financial Regulator and credit institutions was largely collaborative. The Financial Regulator identified problems and concerns in credit institutions through audits, inspection reports or external reviews. The regulator and the regulated institution exchanged letters, arranged meetings and discussed the problems with a view to resolving them. A solution would be negotiated and drawn up into an 'action plan'. The regulated institution would later assure the regulator that the plan had been implemented and these assurances would be accepted because the regulator trusted that 'those running the banks and building societies were honourable persons striving to do their best to comply with the principles ... [and] it was assumed that those in charge of institutions would, after careful consideration, do their best to comply' (Honohan, 2010: 55–6). In general, 'threats of action by the [Financial Regulator] in the absence of compliance were not typically part of the process ... It was considered much better to resolve regulatory issues through voluntary compliance and discussion' (55).

The compliance-orientated strategies discussed so far centre on educating companies and their officers about their legal obligations and on the use of dialogue to encourage compliance. However, a number of other non-punitive compliance-orientated strategies, like ministerial directions and warning letters, are also employed by regulatory agencies. These mechanisms seem to be replacing criminal law mechanisms, at least in certain circumstances, as the preferred approach to achieving corporate compliance. For example, in accordance with section 131(3) of the Primary Act, three ministerial directions were issued to companies to hold AGMs in 1999 and only those companies that failed to comply with the direction were prosecuted (CRO, 2000: 44). Similarly, in 2000, in accordance with section 302 of the Primary Act, the CRO sent thirty warning letters to liquidators to compel them to file reports on their work. If the liquidator did not comply, an application could be made to the High Court for an order directing the liquidator to comply. The CRO indicated that the compliance model would be given preference over a sanctioning model in future years. It proposed 'to continue with this enforcement campaign during 2001, and to make use of the section 302 procedure where necessary. No District Court prosecutions are, therefore, planned' (CRO, 2001: 60). Despite the fact that these mechanisms specified in sections 301 and 302 existed in the Primary Act, previous Companies Reports did not specify their use, suggesting that they were employed for the first time in 1999 and 2000.

The ODCE also prefers compliance-orientated approaches to criminal prosecutions, provided that the company or company officer in question has voluntarily rectified its or his non-compliance. For example, where a shareholder had not received financial statements from the company, or notice of an AGM, where there was a refusal to provide access to the register of the company's members, the failure to file financial statements with the Registrar, and the failure to notify the Registrar of the identities of the company directors who were actually directing the company, were also not prosecuted when the matters were voluntarily rectified (ODCE, 2003: 13). Similarly, liquidators were not prosecuted for failing to submit a report on their work despite the fact that this was also a criminal offence under section 56 of the Company Law Enforcement Act 2001. Again, the ODCE indicated a preference for engaging in dialogue to secure compliance and, in the alternative, a preference for seeking orders under section 371 of the Primary Act to enforce duties specified in the Companies Acts (2004: 23). The CRO has also found these orders useful to compel the filing of outstanding annual returns (2014: 14). In particular, the ODCE has had significant success in pursuing rectification and compliance instead of more punitive strategies. For example, €100 million in illegal directors' loans was paid back to companies in 2003 and 2004 (2005: 3). This approach continued to bear fruit. In 2012 and 2013, the ODCE secured the repayment of €117 million in loans through voluntary rectification (2013: 43; 2014: 39).

In summary, it was shown that the primary enforcers in the corporate and financial sectors adopted a compliance-orientated approach. The ODCE produced numerous publications, delivered papers at speaking engagements and ran various other services to educate companies and their officers about their legal obligations and to warn them of the consequences of non-compliance. A compliance-orientated approach was also adopted in regulating the financial services sector. In this instance, regulation was explicitly cooperative in nature. Regulated institutions were trusted to comply with general principles that promoted fairness and transparency. If problems arose, conciliatory strategies were adopted to devise plans that would curb non-compliance. When faced with non-compliance, regulatory agencies wrote warning letters to advise corporate actors that they were in breach of their legal obligations but refrained from sanctioning them if they rectified their wrongdoing. All of these tactics were designed to assist corporate and financial actors to obey the law and to build continuing positive relationships with companies and financial institutions, such that they would not resist regulation and would internalise legal norms. Of course, as noted at the outset of this chapter, compliance strategies speak to the 'good man' who wishes to obey the law, not to the 'bad man' who wishes to disregard it. Regulators must occasionally employ sanctioning strategies when faced with serious or persistent wrongdoing. This deters rational wrongdoers who wish to avoid punishment and makes compliance-orientated strategies more effective. It also incapacitates those who cannot be rationally deterred from wrongdoing. The next section explores the extent to which corporate and financial enforcers have been willing to civilly sanction wrongdoers.

Civil sanctions

In certain cases, encouragement and warnings are not sufficient to ensure corporate compliance with law. In these circumstances, regulators tend to seek civil orders or apply a variety of civil sanctions to offenders for non-compliance, even where the wrongdoing is defined in the Companies Acts as a crime. For example, though the failure to file annual returns to the CRO is a criminal offence, the CRO announced in September 1998 that it was initiating a large-scale operation to strike companies off the register of companies, rather than prosecute them or their officers. It initially targeted companies that had not filed annual returns in two years and initiated strike-off procedures against 500 of these companies every day. Over 25,000 notices were issued between September 1998 and the end of the year (DETE, 1999: 47). The strike-off policy continued in 1999 when a further 28,731 companies were struck off the register. The Companies Amendment (No. 2) Act 1999 then gave the Registrar the power to strike companies off the register after failing to file a return in one year. This facilitated an enhanced strike-off process in 2000 when 41,217 companies were struck off for failure to file returns. Of these, 32,937 companies were involuntarily struck off. This approach seems to have been relatively

Table 7.1 Number of companies involuntarily struck off by CRO (2003–13)

Year	Strike-offs
2003	14,836
2004	1,401
2005	9,415
2006	5,255
2007	4,085
2008	5,804
2009	5,729
2010	6,272
2011	7,938
2012	7,333
2013	7,077

Sources: CRO, Annual Reports (2004–14)

successful. Though only 60 per cent of companies filed their returns from 1999 on time, 90 per cent had filed them by the end of the year 2000 (2001: 60).

Though the CRO did prosecute some companies it expressed a marked preference for non-criminal enforcement mechanisms and the Registrar of Companies 'announced that he will concentrate his efforts in the future on persuading all companies to file their returns on time' (2001: 60). Emphasising risk management strategies, it was suggested that the CRO would also attempt to target those who might potentially be repeat wrongdoers, 'paying particular attention to those companies which had been restored to the register having been struck off for failure to file returns in the past and to the degree of lateness in filing previous returns' (2001: 60). By 2001, the CRO stopped striking companies off the register almost entirely, finding that 'it had substantially achieved its desired effect in clearing defunct companies from the register and in ensuring compliance from those remaining' (2002: 18). However, it cautioned that 'the strike off process remains a valid response to non-compliance and will be used again if needed' (2002: 18). As shown in Table 7.1, though 14,836 companies were involuntarily struck off for failing to file annual returns in 2003 (2004: 14; 2006: 1), this fell to 4,085 in 2007 (2008: 13) before gradually rising again to 7,077 in 2013 (CRO, 2014: 5).

These figures indicate that striking companies off the register remains a valid response to non-compliance with the Companies Acts. This approach, when combined with other educative, compliance-orientated strategies, seems to have worked because the level of compliance with filing annual returns has consistently improved. Though just 13 per cent of companies had filed on time for 1997, this had risen to 63 per cent for 2002 and 77 per cent for 2007. For

Table 7.2 Late filing penalties (2001–13)

Year	Fines in millions of euros
2001	1.8
2002	12.5
2003	27.8
2004	18.2
2005	21.4
2006	20.7
2007	17.9
2008	17.67
2009	12.8
2010	11.31
2011	11.759
2012	11.346
2013	10.61

Sources: CRO, Annual Reports (2004–14)

the year 2012, the CRO reported a 'historically high outcome of 90.8 per cent of companies being up-to-date in terms of filing of annual returns had been achieved' (2013: 1).

Despite the fact that compliance generally seems to have improved, the CRO has imposed significant administrative fines or 'late filing penalties'. As shown in Table 7.2, these fines peaked in 2003, totalling €27.8 million (2004: 12), before declining to €10.61 million in 2013 as a result of greater compliance and the advent of electronic filing (2014: 3). However, they remain much higher than those ever imposed as a result of summary prosecutions in the past. For example, the Companies Reports reveal that the total sum of fines imposed in 1980 for the offence of failing to file annual returns amounted to just £2,482 (1981: 11). By contrast, in 2005, the CRO collected €21.4 million in administrative late filing penalties (2006: 25). This shows the power of administrative fines to secure accountability and the frequency with which they are used to achieve corporate compliance in recent times.

Notwithstanding the significant use of strike-offs and administrative fines, the most significant civil sanctions frequently employed to date have arguably been restriction and disqualification. Restriction was introduced by the Companies Act 1990 but was rarely applied against irresponsible and dishonest directors in its early years because no one was statutorily charged with the responsibility to apply for these orders (Courtney, 2012: 1791). However, in accordance with section 56 of the Company Law Enforcement Act 2001, liquidators are obliged to take restrictions proceedings against directors of insolvent companies unless they are relieved of this responsibility by the ODCE. The number of persons on the register of restricted persons has increased significantly since then. By the end of 2002, there were just fifty-four people on this register (ODCE, 2007: 31). However, this rose to 791 by the end of 2007 (2009: 26). The number of restricted persons fell slightly to 613 by 2012 as previously restricted persons were removed from the register when they completed their five-year restriction period (CRO, 2013: 34). Given the substantial reliance on this order, it is perhaps unsurprising that the ODCE views the restriction order as 'the primary legal sanction for irresponsible behaviour in insolvent companies' (ODCE, 2005: 31).

Disqualification is also a 'useful complementary option to those of restriction and criminal prosecution' and one the ODCE increasingly relies on 'in order to sanction suspected misconduct and alert the market to past misbehaviour' (ODCE, 2005: 31). Just ten company directors were named on the register of disqualified persons in 2004 (2006: 34) but by the end of 2012 this number had risen to 3,908 (CRO, 2013: 34). While this was certainly attributable in part to the greater number of disqualification proceedings being taken by the ODCE and liquidators, a significant increase in this figure is also attributable to more joined-up thinking and greater cooperation between the Courts Service and the Registrar of Companies. In 2005, the ODCE secured agreement between these two agencies that those automatically disqualified following conviction for indictable offences in relation to a company, or involving fraud or dishonesty, would also be added to the Register of Disqualified Persons (ODCE, 2006: 34).

The vast majority of persons are automatically disqualified without any input from the courts. By the end of 2010, 3,200 of the 3,444 disqualified persons were automatically disqualified (approximately 93 per cent of the total number) and only 244 persons were disqualified as a result of an order from the High Court (2011: 29). To the extent that the High Court imposes such orders, it is not shy about imposing them for lengthy periods. In 2007 one company director was disqualified for twelve years, the longest period imposed in an action taken by the ODCE (2008: 30, 32). In another case where a company director refused to cooperate with the liquidator and paid himself €200,000 when the company was insolvent, the court decided to disqualify him for seven years, even though the ODCE had only applied for a restriction order for five years (2006: 33). More recently, in in the case of *DCE* v. *Bailey* ([2013] IEHC 561) concerning the systematic falsification of books of account and significant frauds against the Revenue Commissioners, Finlay Geoghegan J. indicated that the appropriate period of disqualification for the two respondent directors was fourteen years. However, upon consideration of the mitigation factors, relating to the lapse in time since the commission of the wrongs and the subsequent compliance of the directors with their legal obligations, she reduced the periods of disqualification to seven years. The significant periods of disqualification evidenced the willingness of the judiciary to sanction directors harshly and apply high standards of corporate governance.

The evidence considered so far shows that that the number of restricted and disqualified persons has increased significantly in recent years. This is partially due to the tenacity of regulators seeking to enforce the law. However, it is also a consequence of the fully automatic construction of deemed disqualification orders and the instrumental nature of restriction orders. Both of these phenomena explain the extraordinarily high levels of success in obtaining civil sanctions. In 2005, the High Court granted restriction orders and disqualification orders against 74 per cent of the 192 directors who were proceeded against for these sanctions (2006: 33). In 2006, 77 per cent of all directors pursued were restricted or disqualified (2007: 30). In 2008 and 2009, the High Court restricted or disqualified 91 per cent and 92 per cent of all people that had been brought before it (2010: 24). In 2010, 96 per cent of all directors brought before the courts were restricted or disqualified (2011: 27). Civil sanctions like restriction and disqualification are often championed on the basis that they are the best shot at achieving corporate accountability (Lynch Fannon, 2010; Macrory, 2006). The percentage of orders affirmed by the courts appears to confirm this.

However, civil sanctions are not always the panacea they appear to be, especially when they are used to target very high profile directors of large corporations or financial institutions. In Chapter 5, it was shown that National Irish Bank (NIB) and National Irish Bank Financial Services (NIBFS) encouraged and facilitated their clients to commit serious tax offences. Inspectors appointed by the High Court investigated the affair and reported in 2004 that the senior management were aware of the use of bogus non-resident accounts for the purposes of tax evasion. In 2005, acting on the basis of this report, the ODCE sought to have nine directors and senior managers of NIB and NIBFS disqualified for their roles in the wrongdoing. In one case, the director consented to his disqualification (*DCE* v. *D'Arcy* [2006] 2 I.R. 163). Most cases, however, appear to have been hotly contested. The courts have refused on a number of occasions to grant orders against the former NIB directors or to quash them on appeal (*DCE* v. *Boner* [2008] IEHC 151; *DCE* v. *Curran* [2007] IEHC 181; *DCE* v. *Byrne* [2009] IESC 57). At the start of 2012, only two cases had been fully concluded (ODCE, 2013, 46). Later that year, the Supreme Court allowed an appeal against a decision by the High Court to disqualify a director for nine years, instead substituting it for restriction order (*DCE* v. *Seymour* [2011] IESC 45). The ODCE subsequently withdrew a pending case in the High Court and also withdrew two Supreme Court appeals against decisions of the High Court that no disqualification should be imposed (ODCE, 2013: 46; 2014: 43). In addition, some of these cases continue to limp on as three more Supreme Court appeals are awaited (ODCE, 2014: 43). The failure to bring to justice many of those involved in the NIB scandal suggests that the ODCE has had mixed success in achieving civil orders against high profile company executives who are willing to vigorously contest these proceedings.

In another case that may cast some certainty on the utility of civil sanctions for the ODCE, *Fyffes Plc* v. *DCC Plc & ors* ([2007] IESC 36), the Supreme Court held that Fyffes had proven its case for insider dealing against Mr Flavin on the civil balance of probabilities. The ODCE applied to be joined as a notice party to the proceedings and reminded the court that it had the power to disqualify Flavin of its own motion, effectively 'piggy-backing' a civil case between private parties to turn it into a regulatory action. Presumably, the ODCE chose this avenue because it was cheaper than having to prove the wrongdoing again in separate civil proceedings to disqualify Flavin. The case had already run for eighty-seven days in the High Court and the plaintiff's legal fees alone were later settled for approximately €3.4 million. This was more than the €3.355 million it cost to run the ODCE in 2006 (ODCE, 2007: 36). However, when the Supreme Court decided that the ODCE would have to prove its own case for disqualification against him, the cost and uncertainty of action did not seem to justify the proceedings, particularly when a subsequently commissioned inspector's report concluded that Flavin had acted lawfully, despite his 'error of judgment' (Shipsey, 2010: 967). Notwithstanding the conventional view that civil strategies can be preferable to criminal law for pragmatic reasons, this case demonstrated that civil regulatory actions can still be expensive, lengthy and onerous for applicants, especially when wrongdoing can seem ambiguous and when corporate defendants are more likely to have the resources to resist the case.

Financial wrongdoers have also not always been held to account by the Financial Regulator, though in these instances the lack of accountability has stemmed more from an unwillingness to escalate from compliance and dialogue to sanctioning approaches. In particular, the Financial Regulator has failed to regularly impose administrative sanctions or reach 'settlement agreements' of any severity. By the end of 2007, it reached just seven settlement agreements and the largest fine imposed was €5,000 (2008: 10). Even if the Financial Regulator was willing to use administrative sanctions to discipline wrongdoers, it had a limited ability to do so. Remarkably, the key principles underpinning the regulator's compliance-based principles approach, requiring transparency, integrity and oversight, were not codified and therefore breaches of these principles were not subject to administrative sanction procedures (Honohan, 2010: 46). Furthermore, it seems that regulators were reluctant to take cases to court because they were afraid they would lose. Instead of testing the law and identifying areas which had to be improved by the legislature, the approach of the regulator was characterised by timidity; it would 'walk softly and carry no stick' (55). Regulators were too deferential to the regulated, 'moving very far in the direction not just of "principles-based" but of "light-touch" supervision' (Regling and Watson, 2010: 18). When serious issues were identified with regulated entities, the regulator collaborated with institutions to draft action plans remedying these problems. However, even though these action plans were often not implemented, or sometimes only partially, regulators did not enforce the original plan but simply accommodated institutions by devising new action plans. Furthermore, no action was taken when the regulated institutions also failed to implement the revised action plans (Honohan, 2010: 72–3).

In addition, serious breaches of liquidity rules and sectoral concentrations were not treated with urgency when 'correspondence was batted backwards and forwards in what appears to be a quite leisurely manner. It often took several months for a letter to be issued and at least as long for a response to arrive' (73). The regulation of the financial sector was characterised by 'inconclusive engagement ... and a lack of decisive follow-through' (75). The regulator was so deferential to bankers that it even appeared to approve irresponsible behaviour, albeit without realising the full implications of doing so. For example, the issue of 'balance sheet management', whereby banks transfer capital to each other to enhance the appearance of each other's financial health, and which has now become the subject of criminal investigations, seems to have been approved by the regulator. In 2008, when the Finance Director of Anglo Irish Bank, Willie McAteer, met the then Financial Regulator, Pat Neary, to tell him that the bank would be 'managing the balance sheet at the year end', Neary replied: 'Fair play to you, Willie' (O'Toole, 2009: 210).

It has been shown that corporate and financial regulators first educated company officers about their legal responsibilities and encouraged them to comply with the law. Prosecutions were not pursued even when criminal offences were committed, provided that offenders voluntarily rectified their non-compliance. When educative strategies failed, and wrongs were not being voluntarily rectified, corporate enforcers, such as the ODCE and the CRO, relied on civil sanctions instead of prosecuting offenders. The CRO, for example, successfully struck off a large number of companies or fined them for failing to file their annual returns. These fines were significantly larger than those imposed in the past as a result of criminal prosecutions. Similarly, the ODCE was, in general, remarkably successful in securing restriction and disqualification orders, though it did have difficulties when these proceedings were hotly contested by well-resourced respondents. All of this confirms that corporate enforcers have had tremendous success in relying on civil sanctions as an alternative to prosecution. However, the successes of these regulators must be distinguished from the enforcement activities undertaken by the Financial Regulator. The regulation of the financial services sector was characterised by deference to regulated institutions and their officers. The regulator did not ensure that remedial action was taken when wrongdoing was detected. Given that there was no commitment to following through on the compliance-orientated approach, perhaps it is unsurprising that there was also no serious or sustained recourse to administrative sanctions in their early years.

It was emphasised at the outset that compliance-orientated approaches work best when backed by sanctioning strategies. These strategies include 'little sticks' like civil sanctions so that regulators can respond proportionately to lesser forms of wrongdoing. However, regulators also need to be able to draw upon 'big sticks' with harsh penalties. It is this willingness to invoke harsh sanctions in practice that convince corporate actors to voluntarily comply with the law. In the Irish corporate enforcement context, criminal sanctions, particularly prosecutions for indictable offences, are probably the largest viable sticks that regulators can employ. The next section analyses the willingness to criminally prosecute company officers. This is of particular interest given the traditional unwillingness to criminally sanction corporate wrongdoers in the past and may indicate the true extent to which there is a new approach to corporate enforcement.

Criminal prosecutions

For much of the twentieth century, corporate wrongdoing was addressed almost exclusively by the criminal law. However, it subsequently became merely one element of a diverse range of enforcement options for regulators. Nevertheless, it is also the most crucial sanction. Criminal law, particularly when prosecuted on indictment, is generally considered the sanction of last resort to address only the most persistent wrongdoers or the most serious wrongdoing. The existence of this sanction is important but it is the willingness of regulators to use it that makes the graduated corporate enforcement architecture effective in practice. The greater the willingness to use the 'big gun', when necessary, and to use it successfully, the more likely it is thought to push regulatory activity down to the cooperative base of the regulatory pyramid (Ayres and Braithwaite, 1992: 40). This is because regulators appear to be invincible and ruthless when faced with non-compliance. The idea is that rational corporate actors wish to avoid severe punishment and are persuaded that compliance with the law is in their best interests. The purpose of this section is to investigate the extent to which regulators have been willing to pull the trigger on criminal sanctions in practice and the extent to which they have been successful in doing so. Furthermore, the severity of penalties applied against convicted wrongdoers is also analysed. Owing to the unwillingness of the Financial Regulator to employ civil sanctions with any regularity, it is unsurprising that it did not criminally prosecute wrongdoers. For this reason, this section focuses on prosecutions taken by the ODCE, the CRO, the Gardaí and the DPP.

In its First Report, the CLRG (2001: 143, 147) stated, 'no prosecutions on indictment had been taken during the life of the 1963 Act' and that in the context of subsequent Acts, 'there does not appear to be any recorded instance of prosecution on indictment'. However, an unreported prosecution for an indictable offence in the Companies Acts was successfully taken in 1996. The case, *DPP* v. *Mark A Synnott*, was not officially reported in the Company Reports and is not discussed in the leading company law and criminal law textbooks, with the exception of that written by Courtney (2012: 942), perhaps reflecting the lack of importance ascribed to the case. Nevertheless, the case was significant for a number of reasons. The defendant's company collapsed with debts of over £2 million, having traded while insolvent for approximately ten years (*Irish Times*, 8 May 1996: 1, 5, 14; 11 May 1996: 2, 5). He pleaded guilty to three charges (one charge of fraudulent trading and two of fraudulent conversion) out of a total of thirty-nine on the indictment. He was imprisoned for four years and three months and disqualified from acting as a company director, auditor or manager for ten years. The case represented a departure in many ways from the hegemony of the traditional period. It was the first successful prosecution of fraudulent trading and the first prosecution on indictment. It was also the first prison sentence imposed for an offence in the Companies Acts. The criminality of the defendant's actions was not swept away by the Probation Act. In fact, it was emphasised. The case was prosecuted in a criminal court with teeth, not in the District Court. The involvement of the Garda Fraud Squad as investigators of real crime was emphasised and a large photo of a besuited, bespectacled man in handcuffs led away by members of An Gardaí Síochána featured in Ireland's leading broadsheet newspaper (*Irish Times* 8 May 1996: 14). Was this prosecution the first step of a long journey towards criminal accountability for white-collar wrongdoers or was it merely an aberration? Would more prosecutions on indictment follow and if so, would offenders be regularly imprisoned? These issues are teased out in the following paragraphs.

In the late 1990s, the CRO revealed a new willingness to prosecute a variety of offences not previously pursued. In addition to prosecuting for failure to file returns, offences prosecuted by the CRO in 1998, 1999 and 2000 included the failure to maintain proper books and accounts, failure to hold general meetings, trading as a limited company despite having been struck off the Register or abuse of limited liability, failure to comply with the Register of Members, failure of liquidators to file returns, acting as an auditor while not qualified, failure to provide a copy of the register of Directors' interests, failure to notify the Registrar of the cessation of status as a single member company, trading under a misleading name (misuse of PLC), and failure to comply with a direction to change a company name. The CRO (2001: 52) announced that: 'the year 2000 saw the highest number of convictions obtained for non-filing offences ever. The continuing trend towards greater enforcement of the Acts is evident in the number of prosecutions taken in the wider range of offences which were prosecuted'.

Similarly, the ODCE has, since its establishment in 2001, also prosecuted a variety of offences never previously prosecuted. In 2003, the ODCE announced 'the first case of its kind' in which it secured five convictions for transmitting false information to the Registrar of Companies (2004: 17). The ODCE also commenced its first case against a company director for fraudulent trading, among other offences, in 2003. The accused pleaded guilty to this charge, among others, and was sentenced to two concurrent sentences of six months, suspended for twelve months (19). In 2004, the ODCE secured its first conviction against a person for acting as a director while restricted, without complying with the necessary statutory conditions (2005: 17). In 2005, the ODCE initiated the first prosecution for using a falsified document affecting or relating to the property of a company (2006: 22). In 2006, two new offences were prosecuted for the first time (2007: 21). The ODCE prosecuted one person for acting as a director while disqualified and one person for falsely representing financial statements as being audited to the company's bank. In 2008, the ODCE successfully prosecuted, for the first time, a company director for knowingly using company assets in breach of the legal restrictions on the giving of loans to directors (2009: 17). All of this shows that a wider variety of criminal offences were being prosecuted by regulatory agencies and particularly, the ODCE, as it managed to gain more experience of how to prosecute new offences for the first time.

The increased willingness to apply the criminal law was also evident in the punishments imposed for corporate wrongdoing. The ODCE reported that the average fine imposed following conviction was 35 per cent higher in 2003 than 2002 (2004: 16). In 2004, the ODCE noted that this trend was continuing. It noted that in one case, the District Court imposed fines and costs totalling €6,500 on an individual. It also remarked that for the first time, the District Court was much more willing to consider imposing custodial sentences. It imposed two suspended sentences of six months for fraudulent trading and a three-month suspended sentence for acting as an auditor while unqualified (2005: 18). The trend towards higher fines increased in 2005 when the total amount of fines increased by 70 per cent, compared to the previous year, despite the fact that fewer cases in 2005 resulted in convictions (2006: 22). In 2008, the courts imposed a custodial sentence on a man convicted of acting as a director of a company while disqualified from doing so. It was the first time that the sentence had not been suspended by the courts in a prosecution undertaken by the ODCE but it was later suspended on appeal (2009: 18; 2010: 53). In 2011, in a prosecution taken by the DPP referred to it by the ODCE, a custodial sentence became effective in respect of a company law offence. This was the first time this had happened since the ODCE was founded. The

Circuit Court imposed a three-year period of imprisonment for filing false information with the CRO, suspending the last year of the sentence (2012: 4, 34).

Reflecting on these developments, it can be seen that a new emphasis on criminal law enforcement and punishment was clearly evident. Enforcers demonstrated a greater desire to prosecute and punish corporate criminals to a greater extent than before. A wider range of crimes was being prosecuted, and with greater frequency. However, the tendency towards the criminal punishment of offenders was not applied in as frequent, consistent and meaningful a manner as might initially have been thought. Though the material considered here suggests that the Gardaí, DPP and CRO were seeking to criminally punish corporate offenders at the end of the twentieth century, their activities in this regard declined thereafter. For example, while 748 companies and 184 directors were convicted as a result of CRO prosecutions in 2001 (CRO, 2002: 41), this had dropped to ninety-seven and zero respectively by 2008 (CRO, 2009: 16). Similarly, the number of offences for breaches of the Companies Acts recorded by the Gardaí dropped from thirty-eight in 2003 to two in 2009 (CSO, 2008: 42). These declines approximately coincided with the development of the ODCE and it may have been the case that the ODCE effectively colonised some of the functions of the Gardaí and the CRO as it sought to establish itself as the primary corporate law enforcer in the State.

Furthermore, though the ODCE had prosecuted a variety of offences since its establishment, this point should not be overstated. Over 400 offences now exist in the Companies Acts and when viewed in this context, very few of them were prosecuted. Furthermore, the occasional prosecution of new misbehaviour was largely symbolic. In 2002, the ODCE acknowledged that 70 per cent of the cases that it sought to pursue involved only three types of offence: the failure to keep books of account, failure to produce various company registers and failure to hold AGMs or EGMs (2003: 17). In 2005, the ODCE received 1,992 reports from auditors which disclosed that fifteen different types of offences had been committed but 98 per cent of the reports were concerned with only five offences, and more than 80 per cent were concerned with the failure to file returns with the Registrar of Companies (2006, 12). The obligation to report the failure to file returns ceased in 2005. By 2013, 78 per cent of all indictable offences reported to the ODCE by auditors concerned illegal loans to company directors and a further 12 per cent of these offences concerned the failure to maintain proper books of account (2014: 30). While the ODCE also received a substantial number of complaints from the public, these could be of a general and sometimes irrelevant nature (2008: 16). It seems that the principal source of useful information regarding breaches of company law comes from auditors' reports. However, audits are

Table 7.3 Criminal and civil enforcement of the Companies Acts (2002–13)

	Number of summary convictions secured by ODCE	Number of persons on the register of restricted persons at end of year	Number of persons on the register of disqualified persons at end of year
2002	14	54	4
2003	43	295	5
2004	66	487	10
2005	49	600	1,010
2006	48	685	1,781
2007	28	791	2,111
2008	32	624	2,679
2009	6	538	3,134
2010	8	589	3,483
2011	19	546	3,651
2012	16	613	3,908
2013	17	767	3,951

Sources: ODCE CRO, Annual Reports (2003–14)

often of a financial rather than a legal nature and therefore are likely only to reveal certain types of wrongdoing. As such, perhaps it is unsurprising that the offences prosecuted by the ODCE were limited to a very concentrated field of misbehaviour.

Moreover, the number of convictions achieved by the ODCE has significantly declined in recent years. Though the ODCE secured sixty-six convictions in 2004 (2005: 17), this gradually declined and the ODCE secured just eight convictions in 2010. Seven of these eight convictions were against one individual so just two people were convicted that year (2011: 27). Matters have improved slightly more recently. In 2013, the ODCE secured seventeen convictions in just five cases, ten of which were against one individual (2014: 44). The commencement of this decline corresponded with the stated decision by the ODCE in 2005 that is would 'rebalance' its enforcement strategy and employ civil sanctions more often (2006: 24). This was evinced by the high levels of civil sanctions which had been granted from approximately that time, discussed above, and outlined in Table 7.3.

The effect of these prosecutions was limited because most prosecutions initiated by the ODCE were for summary offences in the District Court where penalties were limited. Imprisonment was the exception to the rule and offenders were rarely visited with the same stigma as if they had been prosecuted in a higher court. Though the McDowell Group recommended that the Probation Act 1907 should not apply to persons summarily convicted of company offences, this recommendation was not given force of law. District

Court judges have regularly invoked the Probation Act in favour of corporate defendants. For example, the Probation Act was applied in favour of defendants on thirty-five charges in 2005, not much less than the forty-nine convictions secured by the ODCE (2006: 3). Similarly, in 2006, the Probation Act was applied on thirty-six charges, compared to forty-eight convictions achieved by the ODCE (2007: 18). This suggests that corporate offenders, even when convicted, often did not receive a criminal record.

Gathering these developments together, there was a greater willingness to prosecute company officers for corporate wrongdoing in summary proceedings at the turn of the twenty-first century. The ODCE and CRO prosecuted a variety of summary offences which had never been prosecuted before. Convictions resulted in some significant fines and suspended sentences were occasionally handed down. However, no offenders were imprisoned in the first decade of the operation of the ODCE and the increased tendency to prosecute and punish wrongdoers declined after 2005 when civil sanctions were more regularly employed. In general, the range of offences in the Companies Acts which continued to be prosecuted was very limited and most cases were processed in the District Court where punishments are often small fines. Prosecutions on indictment were rare and custodial sentences were exceptional. The first effective custodial sentence during the lifetime of the ODCE was not handed down until 2011. For these reasons, the Synnott case in the late 1990s seems more of a false dawn than the beginning of a new era. Corporate enforcers often failed to pull the trigger on its harshest criminal sanctions. This may undermine the credibility of the regulatory architecture and make compliance-orientated approaches more difficult in time. If regulators never punish, then companies will have less reason to respond to the compliance-orientated approaches.

A new willingness to punish?

In the opening chapter of this monograph, it was argued that the criminal law attached to behaviour only when there was a social response to it that labelled that activity as criminal. Similarly, rules were only enforced when infractions were brought to the attention of the public in such a way that they could not be ignored. Though a number of corporate scandals emerged since the 1990s, no single trigger overhauled enforcement practices such that companies and their officers were regularly prosecuted and imprisoned for their wrongdoing. Regulators and companies found mutual benefit in non-enforcement when compliance-orientated sanctions worked instead. When sanctions were required, civil mechanisms were employed. Compliance-orientated mechanisms and civil orders allowed companies to avoid the punitive side of regulation and regulators avoided costly criminal prosecutions.

However, a new emphasis on enforcement was triggered by the financial crisis of 2008. The resultant social and political outrage required regulators to demonstrate a greater willingness to employ the more punitive aspects of the regulatory architecture in practice. The DPP has successfully prosecuted, on indictment, two former directors at Anglo Irish Bank for breaches of the Companies Acts. Similarly, the Financial Regulator, now the Central Bank, has also shown a new willingness to impose severe administrative sanctions on financial service providers when they break the law. Moreover, there are some early indications that the judiciary are reformulating sentencing rules such that white-collar criminals are more likely to receive custodial sentences for serious wrongdoing. This section explores these emerging indications of a more adversarial and punitive approach to corporate and financial regulation.

Regulators raided the offices of Anglo Irish Bank in February 2009 (ODCE, 2010: 15). Since that time, they have been investigating a number of alleged crimes perpetrated by senior management there (ODCE, 2011: 16). In particular, regulators were investigating the provision of loans to members of the Quinn family and ten prominent business people (informally dubbed the 'Maple Ten') by Anglo so that they could buy shares in the bank from prominent Irish businessman, Sean Quinn. The shares were sold privately and not on the stock exchange. If this volume of shares had been sold publicly at that time, it would have undermined confidence in the bank and damaged the share price. It could be alleged that the shares were sold privately to keep their price artificially high. The ODCE was investigating whether these loans breached the laws preventing companies from purchasing their own shares. The Garda Bureau of Fraud Investigation was investigating the market abuse aspects of the transactions. In addition, the chairman of Anglo, Seán Fitzpatrick, was alleged to have hidden €87 million in personal loans from the bank by transferring them off the bank's books to Irish Nationwide before the end of the financial year. Furthermore, Irish Life and Permanent Bank provided Anglo with €7.45 billion in deposits. Anglo was alleged to have made representations that these deposits were customer and commercial deposits rather than inter-bank transfers. If this was the case, Anglo could have misrepresented its financial health at the end of the financial year to the Financial Regulator. Following separate investigations conducted by the ODCE, the Financial Regulator and the Garda Bureau of Fraud Investigation, three former senior officers with Anglo Irish Bank were arrested, sometimes on multiple occasions, and in dawn raid on their homes.

Though various other strands of the ODCE's investigations are ongoing (ODCE, 2014: 46), these three executives, Sean Fitzpatrick (the former Chairman of the bank), Willie McAteer and Pat Whelan were prosecuted in early 2014 for providing loans to the Quinn family and the Maple Ten. It was alleged that these loans were in breach of section 60 of the Companies Act 1963, a prohibition on the provision of financial assistance by a company to purchase its own shares, an offence then punishable by five years' imprisonment and a fine of €3,174. Counsel for the three defendants mounted a vigorous defence against the charges over an eleven-week trial. They contended that the executives had been advised by a leading commercial law firm that the deal was permissible, that the Financial Regular had approved the deal and that a leading investment bank had executed the deal. As such they had not knowingly committed an offence, were *mens rea* or culpability required. They asserted this would also show that they had taken reasonable steps to comply with the law, thereby allowing them a due diligence defence, were the offence to be one employing strict liability.

However, Judge Nolan asked the jury to disregard the evidence it had heard on legal advice and stated that it was no defence for the men to say they had not known that they were committing a crime. In effect, this seemed to transform the offence into one of absolute liability, punishable by up to five years' imprisonment, even though the Supreme Court in *CC* v. *Ireland* ([2006] I.E.S.C. 33) held that it was unconstitutional to employ absolute liability for offences where the accused could be subject to a substantial custodial sentence. In addition, the defence argued that the loans were issued in the ordinary course of business, a permitted exception for financial assistance under section 60 of the Primary Act. Much evidence also centred on this issue. Unlike the loans to members of the Quinn family, which had to be repaid in full, the Maple Ten were only personally liable to repay 25 per cent of the loans they received, raising the question as to whether these loans were subject to normal commercial terms in the ordinary course of business.

In any event, it seems that no evidence was provided that Mr Fitzpatrick, who was not responsible for the day-to-day running of the company, knew of the details of these arrangements and he was acquitted on all charges. Mr McAteer and Mr Whelan were also subsequently acquitted on six counts of illegally loaning money to the Quinns but found guilty on ten counts of illegally lending to the Maple Ten (*Irish Times*, 18 April 2014). Nevertheless, though convicted, Mr McAteer and Mr Whelan did not receive custodial sentences. There was uproar among the public and 'social media went slightly berserk' (*Irish Independent*, 20 April 2012: 24). It was said that the system addressing corporate and white-collar crimes was broken (*Sunday Independent*, 4 May 2014: 24), and that Ireland was plagued by 'a botched and broken regulatory culture' (*Sunday Business Post*, 4 May 2014). It was opined, 'As a matter of urgency, we need to enable our gardaí and provide investigators with the wide resources and tools required for them to make absolutely clear that Ireland is an intolerable country in which to commit a corporate crime … we must then legislate for new corporate crimes, so that victims of future reckless lending can, at a very minimum, live in a country where justice will be served' (*Irish Daily Mail*, 19 April 2014: 25).

Nevertheless, the case does not reflect a 'broken system'; it is a significant symbolic statement of the more aggressive contemporary approach to corporate enforcement in practice. The State persevered over a six-year investigation, despite limited resources and considerable difficulties securing evidence, to prosecute for the first time, breaches of the Companies Acts on illegal lending. As noted by the ODCE itself, it could be described as 'the largest "white collar" criminal trial ever to have been mounted in the history of the State, and it is, therefore, of considerable significance' (ODCE, 2014: 7). Moreover, the State had proven its case beyond a reasonable doubt and secured convictions against some of the most senior figures in Irish banking, finally 'pulling the trigger on the big gun'. Perhaps of most significance, the ODCE (Press release, 27 May 2014) seems to be indicating that its resistance to such prosecutions is subsiding because it is implementing new enforcement principles 'to result in a gradual shift away from summary prosecutions in the District Court in favour of prosecutions on indictment'.

The Financial Regulator and the Central Bank of Ireland have also shown an increased willingness to sanction wrongdoers and have employed administrative sanctions more frequently since 2008. It reached twenty-eight settlement agreements between 2008 and 2010 pursuant to its administrative sanctions procedures under the Central Bank Acts and the securities market legislation (Central Bank: 2010: 27; 2011: 50–1; Financial Regulator, 2009: 85). In 2011 and 2012, it reached a further twenty-six settlement agreements of this nature; and in 2013, a further sixteen (2014: 40). Fines also increased significantly. In 2008, the Financial Regulator fined Quinn Insurance Ireland €3.25 million and Sean Quinn was personally fined €200,000 for failing to notify the Financial Regulator prior to providing loans to related companies (McDonald, 2010). In 2009, Merrill Lynch International Bank Limited was fined €2.75 million for two incidents in which it failed to adequately supervise one of its traders who had inaccurately valued his positions (2010: 27). In 2010, AIB was fined €2 million for failing to exercise adequate control mechanisms to prevent or rectify overcharging (Central Bank, 2011: 50). It imposed fines totalling €5.05 million in 2011 (2012: 54), €8.5 million in 2012 (2013: 54) and €6.35 million in 2013 (2014: 40).

It appears that the Central Bank is now demonstrating a more assertive attitude. In a document entitled *Our New Approach*, it promises to adopt a 'challenging, and where necessary, intrusive stance' (2010: 2). The Central Bank's Enforcement Strategy 2011–12 also assures (2010: 3), 'a more vigorous application of enforcement effort backed by sufficient resources to represent a credible threat of action. Where serious breaches of regulatory requirements occur, regulated entities and their management can expect that those serious matters will be investigated fully and vigorously followed through to conclusion.' However, it still expresses a preference for administrative sanctions to discipline financial wrongdoing, stating that wrongdoing will only be channelled through the criminal courts in 'exceptional circumstances' though it is 'currently scrutinising this policy to ensure that criminal prosecutions are pursued in all appropriate cases taking into account the seriousness, intent and wilfulness of the contravention involved' (20).

The argument so far is that corporate and financial regulators seem more willing than previously to sanction serious cases of wrongdoing in the aftermath of the financial crisis of 2008. There may be an increased tendency to more regularly incarcerate corporate offenders for serious corporate wrongdoing too. This approach was evident in the case of *DPP* v. *Duffy* ([2009] IEHC 208). Though the courts would normally impose a custodial sentence only if a fine would prove ineffective, McKechnie J. suggested that the courts should generally consider imposing a mixed sanction, comprising both a fine and a period of imprisonment, for white-collar criminals because 'prison, in particular for those with unblemished pasts, for those who are respected within the community, and for those who are unlikely to re-offend can be a very powerful deterrent … and can carry a uniquely strong moral message' (para. 42). He also emphasised that he saw 'no room for any lengthy lead in period before use is commonly made of this supporting form of sanction' (para. 43). Moreover, instead of tailoring punishment to the particular facts of the offence and the offender in the usual way, an approach that tended to privilege white-collar offenders without previous convictions, he seemed to suggest that the courts should now focus more on the harm caused by crimes to determine the duration of custodial sentences. Offenders also could not claim that the wrongdoing was out of character where it was premeditated and sustained. Therefore, mitigating factors, such as the absence of previous convictions and apparent good character, were de-emphasised because white-collar offenders, by their very nature, would always take advantage of them and would be systemically under-punished by the law. The case is controversial. In one debate on the case, the majority of attendees (mostly lawyers) did not support the imprisoning of white-collar criminals (First Law, 2009: 57). Nevertheless, without overstating the significance of the Duffy decision, it indicates an initial step towards a new way of thinking, one which recognises that corporate and white-collar crimes are harmful, immoral and must be punished severely. As noted by Kilcommins and Vaughan (2010: 92), this case 'may be indicative of the fledgling emergence of a new approach to tackling white-collar crime'.

In a similar vein, in *DPP* v. *Paul Murray* ([2012] IECCA 60), Finnegan J. (para. 19) drew upon corporate wrongdoing and the financial crisis to recommend custodial sentences for both 'crimes in the streets' and 'crimes in the suites' because, at a time of economic crisis, 'widespread tax evasion by the wealthy and well-to-do can gravely threaten social solidarity and, as a consequence, the very stability of a state itself'. Consequently, he suggested 'for the future guidance of sentencing courts that significant and systematic frauds directed upon the public revenue – whether illegal tax evasion on the one hand or social security fraud on the other – should generally meet with an immediate and appreciable custodial sentence' (para. 22). More recently, in *DPP* v. *Paul Begley* ([2013] IECCA 32), a case where the defendant labelled garlic as apples to evade an unusually high level of customs duty, McKechnie J. again emphasised that offenders without previous convictions would not get significant credit for these mitigating factors where they were common among those who committed similar crimes. This was the case even where they were rehabilitated and unlikely to offend again (para. 71). He clarified, however, that mitigating factors could not be ignored. While the court may wish to impose punitive sentences on white-collar criminals to generally deter them from committing such crimes in the first place, sentencing an offender with regard only to rationales of punishment and deterrence alone, without proper consideration of other relevant factors, was an error of principle. The court noted that the offender had cooperated with the investigation, was repaying the Revenue Commissioners, pleaded guilty at the earliest reasonable time, and therefore reduced his period of imprisonment from six to two years. The fledging approach advanced in Duffy was being confirmed but also clarified.

The recent decision of Judge Martin Nolan not to imprison the Anglo bankers William McAteer and Pat Whelan is not inconsistent with the tougher sentencing principles that have emerged since 2008. It certainly does not necessarily represent a judicial resistance to imposing custodial sentences in serious white-collar crime cases; Judge Martin Nolan was the sentencing judge in the aforementioned Begley case, in which he had sentenced the businessman to six years' imprisonment. Indeed, it seems likely that having had his severe sentence reduced by Judge McKechnie in that case, he was undoubtedly conscious that he should be influenced by the mitigating factors at play in the matter before him when it came to the Anglo bankers. Unsurprisingly, in light of this, lawyers for the two former Anglo directors emphasised that their clients did not have previous criminal convictions, acted in good faith without malign motives, had cooperated with the authorities and had not personally benefited from the transaction. However, the sentence did not turn on these mitigating factors. Judge Nolan stated that imprisonment would be unjust because the offenders were not motivated by 'greed, avarice or the pursuit of profit' but were acting in accordance with legal advice and the Financial Regulator had given the 'green light'. These factors distinguish this case from other white-collar crime sentencing hearings that have resulted in imprisonment. Far from representing a failure of the rule of law, the case represents the triumph of proportionality over public opinion. The court resisted the urge to sate the popular demand for retribution.

The developments discussed above demonstrate that corporate and financial regulators are more willing than ever to invoke the harsher elements of the corporate enforcement architecture to assuage popular concerns. The instrumental architecture was maintained but a more expressive pressure was also being applied. The ODCE and the Garda Bureau of Fraud Investigation dedicated substantial resources to investigating the wrongdoing associated with the financial crisis in 2008 and were determined to assemble enough evidence to allow the DPP to prosecute particular wrongdoers, securing convictions against two former directors of Anglo Irish Bank. The Central Bank also demonstrated an increased willingness to employ its administrative sanctions which were among the harshest available to it. Furthermore, the Central Bank also seemed to be reconsidering its enforcement policy such that criminal prosecutions will be more regularly taken for corporate wrongdoing; and there have been some initial moves to reformulate the sentencing rules which apply to white-collar criminals. In determining the suitability and period of the custodial sentence, the courts appeared to place a greater emphasis on the particular harm caused by the offence and less emphasis on the background of the offender. This formulation is less likely to privilege white-collar wrongdoers who are frequently considered pillars of the community and are unlikely to have previous convictions. All of this suggests that they are more likely to be prosecuted and jailed than ever before.

Conclusion

Regulators have adopted a sophisticated pyramidal approach to corporate and financial enforcement. Regulators first educate their officers about their legal obligations through accessible publications, engagement with the media and public presentations. They also encourage companies and their officers to obey the law and to remedy non-compliance where this is possible. It seems that wrongdoers are generally only sanctioned if non-compliance persists or where that wrongdoing is considered especially serious. In circumstances where a sanctioning approach is required, regulators envisage that civil orders, such as restriction, disqualification or administrative fines, mostly suffice. According to this model, law, and particularly criminal law, is the sanction of last resort, though it is also the sanction that makes the system effective. Criminal sanctions allow the regulator to be a 'benign big gun', prompting corporate and financial officers to respond to compliance strategies and lesser sticks to avoid the 'big stick' of criminal prosecution and punishment. However, the extent to which this architecture is fully utilised has varied until recently. In particular, this chapter has shown that there was a reluctance to escalate from compliance-orientated strategies to prosecutions and especially prosecutions on indictment. In the financial sector, the compliance-orientated approach has proven to be too deferential to credit institutions and the principles-based techniques it advanced have been ineffective. In essence, the failure to escalate from dialogue to sanctioning undermined its value and creditability. When administrative sanctions were employed, the fines imposed were very small. Prior to 2008, the largest fine imposed was €5,000, even though the regulator was empowered to impose fines of up to €5 million at that time. No criminal prosecutions were ever initiated by the Financial Regulator against financial institutions or their officers.

The Honohan and Regling Reports of 2010 mirror the McDowell Report of 1998 and the Cox Report of 1958, all of which detail widespread non-compliance with the law, the deferential approach of regulators to respectable corporate elites and the chronic reluctance to prosecute corporate wrongdoers who broke the law. Though there was clearly a willingness to employ civil sanctions against companies and their officers by the ODCE and the CRO, there continued to be a reluctance to employ the harshest penalties at the upper levels of the enforcement pyramid. For example, some very serious cases, such as those involving officers at NIB and Fyffes, continued to be addressed by civil sanctions, and not always successfully. Very few of the 400 offences in the Companies Acts have ever been prosecuted. Those offences that were prosecuted were pursued in the District Court where punishments were limited. For example, no one has been imprisoned following a DCE prosecution in its first decade and only five cases were referred to the DPP for prosecution on indictment. Even then, these cases generally resulted in acquittals or suspended sentences.

However, the banking crisis in 2008 changed the landscape of enforcement. Legal changes and social sentiments requiring higher standards in business have recently coincided. This development prompted changes in enforcement practices. The Financial Regulator has shown a tendency to take a stricter approach to supervision by disciplining misconduct through administrative sanctions with significant fines, and it is reconsidering its aversion to criminal prosecutions. The ODCE, the Garda Bureau of Fraud Investigation and the Central Bank were all involved in investigating the wrongdoing associated with the financial crisis and these efforts have resulted in convictions for two former executives at Anglo Irish Bank. Moreover, the judiciary has recently indicated that it is reformulating sentencing rules such that white-collar criminals are more likely to be imprisoned for serious wrongdoing. Though offenders continue to enjoy the constitutional right to proportionate sentencing, taking into consideration both the particular facts of the offence and the particular circumstances of the offender, the weight given to each seems to be changing. It is suggested that the courts now give particular consideration to the harm caused by the offence and less to the particular background of the offender. This development, if it is more regularly adopted, means that white-collar criminals are less likely to receive suspended sentences because they do not have previous convictions. Though these developments are still in their infancy, they indicate the emergence of a greater willingness to apply harsher criminal sanctions when necessary.

Nevertheless, it may be too early to tell whether this willingness will be sustained or if most enforcement will continue to be channelled through the civil jurisdiction of law. The reliance on civil mechanisms is understandable. Civil orders often have the advantage of being cost-effective and efficient ways of enforcing corporate obligations. Regulators avoid lengthy and costly criminal trials, as well as the difficulties involved in onerous criminal law procedures, such as proving intent to commit the wrong beyond a reasonable doubt. These sanctions are particularly useful for regulators and politicians who want to get results and be seen to be tough on corporate misconduct, especially in a climate where the electorate is clamouring for corporate accountability. Nevertheless, notwithstanding the capacity of such measures to achieve instrumental objectives in an efficient manner, it is difficult to escape the conclusion that the compliance-orientated approach, especially when not supported by the regular prosecution of serious cases which merit it, creates a two-tier legal system privileging elites in the corporate and financial sector. White-collar criminals continue to be treated far more deferentially than conventional criminals because they are usually only prosecuted after non-legal enforcement techniques and civil sanctions have failed, if at all. Political rhetoric on corporate accountability rings hollow when the public has lost its most powerful weapon of censure. Criminal prosecutions make it easier for the public to identify corporate and white-collar crimes as wrongs against society, to allow them to blame wrongdoers for their actions, and thereby reinforce the common sense of right and wrong. If public shaming of corporate and white-collar criminals does not occur then 'crime in the suites' continues to be of a different character to 'crime in the streets'.

Summary of Part II

Part II of this monograph took a socio-legal approach in order to examine the contemporary practice of corporate enforcement. It gathered together changed ways of thinking, new legal instruments and regulatory responses addressing corporate wrongdoing. This brief summary forges these elements together to capture the momentum of the contemporary period. This facilitates the juxtaposition of traditional and contemporary paradigms in the conclusion to this monograph, which offers an assessment of developments that would not otherwise be apparent. Excavating the character of this period has necessitated a broad examination of political, economic and cultural life in Ireland, concentrating on significant events rather than exhaustive detail. Inevitably, that approach will face the criticism that some deviation has not been considered or that more detail is needed. Nevertheless, it is hoped that the analysis undertaken in Part II, moving between the general and the particular, has put shape and order on events that might otherwise be considered erratic and disjointed.

This Part demonstrated that a new model of corporate and financial regulation started to emerge, as Ireland transitioned from an inward-looking rural State, with low levels of corporate activity, to a more professionally orientated open centre for international commerce and finance. However, as more people moved off the land and into white-collar jobs, more opportunities for white-collar crime arose. This induced a greater awareness of issues of corporate deviancy. Ireland acted to protect its reputation as an attractive place in which to do business, to reassure market players operating within the law that they would be safe from the deviant behaviour of others operating outside it. The conventional crime monopoly became fragmented because specialist interdisciplinary agencies, with enhanced powers, were established to police and prosecute corporate wrongs, colonising functions formerly held by government departments and conventional crime fighters. The State also diversified its regulatory arsenal. Over 120 offences have been added to the Companies Acts since 2001, with over 400 criminal offences now in the Companies Acts 1963–2013. These offences frequently employ regulatory strategies like strict liability and 'reverse onus' provisions, avoiding the more onerous issue of proving subjective culpability in order to streamline accountability. This suggests that the silken and golden threads are increasingly being pulled out of the fabric of the criminal law. Furthermore, corporate and financial wrongdoing is now increasingly dealt with through administrative sanctions and civil orders. These sanctions are employed to avoid the high level of proof and evidence that are sometimes required in criminal trials. Unlike criminal prosecutions, these orders are more protective than punitive in orientation, and more certain, though apparently less severe, in their application.

Enforcement has also become much more sophisticated, moving away from the 'command and control' model to a 'responsive' or compliance-orientated model of enforcement. Enforcers first educate company officers about their responsibilities and encourage them to comply with their obligations. Generally, it is only if this approach is unsuccessful, that regulatory responses escalate up the enforcement pyramid, to warning letters, civil sanctions and ultimately to criminal liability on indictment. By design, most corporate and financial wrongdoing is addressed in the civil jurisdiction of the law rather than in the criminal courts. Non-legal and civil sanctions were being used in preference to criminal sanctions because they are more efficient and effective methods of corporate enforcement than lengthy expensive trials where more onerous criminal standards of proof are required. Nevertheless, notwithstanding the capacity of such measures to achieve instrumental objectives in an efficient manner, corporate wrongdoers were being treated more deferentially than ordinary wrongdoers because they were generally only prosecuted, if at all, after non-legal techniques and civil sanctions had failed.

However, the enforcement context appears to be changing again. When extensive wrongdoing in the financial services sector was revealed in 2008, corporate wrongdoing became politicised. When the State assumed the debts of Anglo Irish Bank, people burned effigies outside its headquarters and protested outside the national Parliament. Members of the public were frustrated that banks were being bailed out for corporate irresponsibility when cuts were being made to public expenditure. Politicians responded that white-collar criminals were guilty of economic treason and should be treated like terrorists. More new laws were introduced to make it even easier to challenge legally privileged information, to confirm that the right to silence can be limited, to increase detention periods, to increase the prevalence of strict liability, to expand out the use of information reporters and to enhance search and seizure powers. To a degree, these developments were merely an extension of the existing trajectory. However, the mentality underpinning these developments is different. Previously, regulatory initiatives were introduced for mostly instrumental reasons, to address problems with proving guilt in corporate crime cases.

However, while these initiatives also continue to address neglected issues, they also have ostentatiously political purposes. They reflect the political desire to 'tool up' executive power and 'act out' for public approval. Instrumental justice now has an expressive hue.

There are also some early indications of a more aggressive sanctioning approach in practice. Senior managers of Anglo Irish Bank have been successfully prosecuted on indictment and other investigations into alleged crimes at Irish banks continue. Moreover, the judiciary has also emphasised, in a subtle reformulation of existing sentencing principles, that white-collar criminals should more frequently receive custodial sentences in appropriately serious cases. In particular, while noting that mitigating factors cannot be ignored, the Superior Courts have emphasised that white-collar criminals should not benefit from particular mitigating factors in sentencing where such matters are common to that class of offender. To do otherwise, would mean that white-collar criminals, by their nature and the nature of their crime, will always take advantage of them and corporate wrongdoing will be systemically under-punished by the law. This approach, if adopted and advanced in the future, may mean that white-collar criminals are more likely to go to jail than ever before. Therefore, in concluding Part II of this monograph, it would appear that legislative reform, social and political sentiments requiring increased corporate accountability, and judicially initiated reform, have recently aligned.

Conclusion

This monograph has shown that a new way of governing corporate wrongdoing emerged to address Ireland's changed social, political and economic context. For most of the twentieth century Ireland was a rural economy. The State experienced low levels of corporate activity as a result of protectionist policies advanced in the decades following independence from Britain. Protectionism was initially advanced as an assertion of sovereignty to prevent the British from seizing control of the Irish economy. However, these policies were abandoned in order to boost the prosperity of the State. Ireland also seized the opportunities presented by increased globalisation and access to the European common market. It aggressively marketed Ireland as an attractive place in which to do business, drawing particular attention to its facilitative corporate regulations, low corporate tax regime and highly educated workforce. Though company law was of little political interest and corporate wrongdoing was generally treated with apathy, increased corporate activity was viewed positively.

By the 1990s, Ireland had been transformed from a closed rural State to a highly open commercial society. It was home to some of the largest corporations and financial institutions in the world and there were more white-collar workers than farmers. Traditional methods of laying blame in the rural Irish State were no longer capable of addressing the contemporary challenges of an advanced industrial society which was more willing to recognise the risks posed by increased corporate activity. The State became aware of the need to ensure that the business environment was sufficiently well regulated to ensure it could continue to attract significant amounts of foreign investment. It had to reassure legitimate businesses that they were protected from the deviant behaviour of their competitors. Consequently, the approach to addressing corporate wrongdoing changed significantly.

Corporate and white-collar crimes were addressed by ordinary criminal law mechanisms for most of the twentieth century. The burden of proof was on the prosecution to prove beyond a reasonable doubt that company officers had knowingly and wilfully broken the law. The presumption of innocence and the requirement that offenders had to be found subjectively culpable of wrongdoing were so essential to criminal liability that they were considered the golden and silken threads running through the fabric of criminal justice. The accused also took advantage of an array of other constitutional rights, including the right to privacy, the right to liberty, the right to silence, the right to access a lawyer and to pre-trial disclosure. Since the 1990s, however, corporate wrongdoing has increasingly been addressed by regulatory crime mechanisms which avoid onerous due process safeguards. Regulatory crime mechanisms reversed the onus of proof in many corporate cases such that company officers must show that they should not be convicted and prosecutors do not need to prove that the accused acted with intent. Furthermore, the right to silence was restricted and the laws on hearsay and bail have changed in favour of prosecutors. The rules on when and where prosecutions may be taken and the manner in which evidence can be presented to the jury at trial have also been reformulated to facilitate the prosecution of crime. These developments seem designed to keep the accused in Garda custody with limited legal advice, in circumstances where they may be required to explain themselves, in the hope that they will incriminate themselves. Others required the accused to prove their innocence before the courts.

It was also shown that corporate enforcement in the twentieth century was underpinned almost exclusively by criminal sanctions and that the Companies Acts contained hundreds of distinct criminal offences. Penalties on conviction were relatively mild, with penalties so low for some indictable company offences that offenders often could not be arrested without a warrant. Where civil sanctions existed, they sometimes had to be triggered by the criminal conviction of the accused. Breaching a civil order was also a criminal offence, reflecting the dominance of criminal punishment in the traditional approach to corporate wrongdoing. More recently, however, enforcers were given a wider variety of sanctions with which to tackle corporate wrongdoing. While corporate misconduct continued to be extensively criminalised, and was subject to increasingly severe penalties, corporate deviancy could also be addressed by a variety of civil and administrative sanctions. Both companies and their officers could be civilly fined for sums of money that are higher than those imposed by the criminal courts. Company officers could be restricted or disqualified and companies could be directed to comply with the law or be struck off the register of companies. Some of these sanctions were triggered automatically for events which were not necessarily considered blameworthy, imposed for mandatory periods, with limited judicial input and in circumstances that were considered non-adversarial. These procedures were justified on the basis that the State was protecting the public from the repeated wrongdoing of those who have shown that they could not be trusted, but without punishing or stigmatising the wrongdoer.

Not only was corporate and white-collar crime predominantly addressed by conventional criminal law in the twentieth century, it was also mostly enforced by the ordinary police. The Gardaí investigated corporate and white-collar crimes and the DPP prosecuted them. However, conventional policing agencies were unsuited to addressing corporate wrongdoing. The Gardaí were not staffed with accountants and lawyers who were trained to detect corporate wrongdoing. They also refrained from consulting professionals outside the force because it was thought unprofessional to seek advice from civilians. Furthermore, auditors and other professionals were not required to report that they suspected a corporate offence had been committed, a major impediment given that companies themselves were unlikely to admit the commission of fraud within their organisations. In addition, the Gardaí were constrained by antiquated laws. They often could not arrest persons they suspected had committed indictable white-collar crimes and had to interview suspects by appointment in the presence of their solicitors. The laws on fraud were so old that they predated the foundation of the State and were therefore often unsuited to addressing contemporary illegalities. Moreover, the Garda Fraud Squad was perpetually under-resourced and understaffed.

To the extent that regulatory agencies existed, they mostly played an ancillary or administrative role and were also so under-resourced as to be ineffective. Since the 1990s, however, numerous specialist agencies were established to police corporate elites. Though resourcing continued to be an issue in some respects, these agencies were better staffed and resourced than ever. Moreover, these agencies were interdisciplinary in nature, staffed by accountants, lawyers, civil servants and police. They also had extensive powers of inspection, search, seizure, and could summarily prosecute crime in their respective areas. This was a significant departure from the traditional approach when the police complained that they were hamstrung by limited and outdated laws. Furthermore, the ability to detect crime was enhanced by new laws requiring lawyers, accountants, auditors and others to report their suspicions that crimes had been committed by their clients. Professionals who traditionally acted privately for shareholders and directors became 'information reporters', recruited into a private police force which acted for public protection.

The way in which the regulatory model was enforced was a significant departure from that of the traditional approach. Previously, the conventional crime model was almost exclusively sanction-orientated, premised on a 'command and control' logic, but rarely enforced. Of the hundreds of offences in the Companies Acts, only the failure to file annual returns was prosecuted with any regularity. Convictions were rare, fines were low, and offenders often availed themselves of the Probation Act. The traditional approach to enforcement was sanctioning in theory and non-existent in practice. Since then, enforcement has diversified, employing both compliance-orientated and sanctioning approaches. Enforcers first educated companies and their officers about their legal obligations and encouraged compliance with the law. If the law was broken, enforcers required offenders to remedy their non-compliance. In general, companies and their officers were only sanctioned when they refused to obey the law or refused to remediate their wrongdoing. In these circumstances, regulators were supposed to respond by escalating enforcement action to civil sanctions and ultimately criminal prosecutions. The idea was that regulators were most effective when they were 'benign big guns' who 'speak softly and carry a big stick'. This means that regulators appealed to the law-abiding nature of corporate actors but without hesitating to severely punish those who refuse to comply, if needed. Nevertheless, there remained a considerable reluctance to punish wrongdoers severely in practice. The financial regulator did not escalate from a principles-based compliance approach to a sanctioning approach, refusing to impose administrative sanctions or prosecute wrongdoers. To the extent that the sanctioning model was employed for corporate wrongdoing outside the financial sector, most enforcement took place in the civil jurisdiction of law. When criminal prosecutions were taken against company officers, the cases were heard in the lower courts. Consequently, fines were small, custodial sentences were rare and offenders often left court without a criminal record. Prosecutions on indictment were particularly rare. In general, there was no commitment to using the harsher elements of the new architecture in practice.

However, the enforcement context has changed again since the banking crisis in 2008. Owing to the absence of effective regulatory oversight, corporate and financial wrongdoing in the banking sector severely damaged the economy and required the banks to be rescued. People lost their jobs, their homes were devalued, they became more indebted, their taxes increased and their economic security was jeopardised. If corporate wrongdoing was not pursued in the past because there was no public demand for 'respectable' company officers to be criminally prosecuted like ordinary criminals, then this had changed. It was understood that corporate wrongdoing could damage the security of the State in ways that are at least as harmful as 'street crime'. People wanted accountability and corporate and financial crime became politicised. Politicians stated that white-collar criminals were guilty of economic treason and should be treated like terrorists. The State pledged to be tough on white-collar crime and introduced tougher new laws involving the increased use of strict liability, stronger investigative powers, more stringent accounting rules, increased powers of supervision, greater regulatory accountability, the manipulation of detention periods, independent verification of legal privilege, confirmation of inroads into the right to silence and the expanded use of information reporters. All of these developments evinced the desire to 'tool up' executive power and 'act out' for public approval in an attempt to 'govern through crime'. The expressive approach, where justice must be seen to be done and corporate wrongdoers must be seen to be punished, now competes with instrumental policies.

Since the banking crisis, the Financial Regulator (and now the Central Bank) has more regularly imposed administrative sanctions against financial services providers and individuals for non-compliance with the law and its policy of avoiding criminal prosecutions is being revisited. Former directors at Anglo Irish Bank have been convicted on indictment for breaking company law and other strands of this investigation are continuing. There are also some early indications from the judiciary that sentencing rules were being reformulated so that white-collar criminals were more likely to receive custodial offences for serious white-collar crimes. Judges now seem more willing to focus on the potential harm caused by the offence rather than the personal background of the offender, a development that is less likely to privilege corporate wrongdoers. These measures suggest that there is an increased willingness to invoke a harsher sanctioning approach to corporate and financial wrongdoing, though it may be too early to tell if this approach will be sustained.

Ireland has developed from an inward-looking, rural State into a global economy with significant levels of corporate activity and the architecture addressing corporate wrongdoing changed accordingly. Traditionally, Ireland uncritically imitated the British approach to regulating corporate conduct. Corporate wrongdoing was criminalised using conventional criminal justice methods and the ordinary police were charged with the responsibility of enforcing the law. The failure to design a specialised framework reflected the traditional apathy in corporate matters and the lack of expertise in company law which characterised the agrarian Irish State. There was no cultural recognition that corporate wrongdoing could cause serious harm so company law was rarely enforced. This traditional model could not adequately address the contemporary challenges posed by an entrepreneurial society in the twenty-first century. Consequently, a new architecture of justice was created. The conventional crime monopoly on corporate deviancy became fragmented because a variety of specialist, interdisciplinary agencies with enhanced powers were created to address corporate wrongdoing. The exclusive dominance of conventional crime methods also faded because corporate wrongdoing was specifically addressed by a pyramidal enforcement architecture, taking compliance-orientated and sanctioning approaches, using both civil and criminal enforcement mechanisms, for instrumental and expressive reasons. However, the traditional approach to defining crime exclusively in terms of conventional crime indicia has not been adapted or updated for the contemporary approach to regulatory enforcement. In particular, it does not reflect the new social and political willingness to recognise that corporate wrongdoing can be morally reprehensible and at least as harmful as 'conventional crime'.

This monograph has gathered together the contemporary structures, practices and mentalities relating to the policing and punishment of corporate wrongdoing and has shown that the State seems to have transitioned from one paradoxical model of corporate enforcement to another. The traditional system of corporate enforcement invoked the State's most powerful weapon of censure, the criminal law, but was remarkably lenient in practice because the law was rarely enforced. The contemporary model is more concerned with accountability and less with blame, is explicitly conciliatory but incorporates remarkably punitive, instrumental and expressive elements. Nevertheless, the new method of governing corporate wrongs is a striking departure from the traditional approach of the twentieth century. A new architecture exists.

References

Adler, F. (1983) *Nations Not Obsessed by Crime* (Littleton: Rothman).

Allen, G. (1999) *The Garda Siochana* (Dublin: Policing Independent Ireland (Dublin: Gill & Macmillan).

Appleby, P. (2005) 'Corporate regulation in Ireland', in O'Brien, J. (ed.), *Governing the Corporation: Regulation and Corporate Governance in an Age of Scandal and Global Markets* (West Sussex: John Wiley & Sons).

Appleby, P. (2010) 'Compliance and enforcement – the ODCE perspective', in Kilcommins, S. and Kilkelly, U. (eds), *Regulatory Crime in Ireland* (Dublin: First Law).

Ashworth, A. (1999, 2006, 2009) *Principles of Criminal Law*, 3rd, 5th and 6th edns (Oxford: Oxford University Press).

Ashworth, A. (2000) 'Is the criminal law a lost cause', *Law Quarterly Review* 116.

Ashworth, A. and Player, E. (1998) 'Sentencing, equal treatment, and the impact of sanctions', in Ashworth, A. and Wasik, M. (eds), *Fundamentals of Sentencing Theory* (Oxford: Clarendon Press).

Ayres, I. and Braithwaite, J. (1992) *Responsive Regulation: Transcending the Deregulation Debate* (Oxford: Oxford University Press).

Bacik, I. and O'Connell, M. (eds) (1998), *Crime and Poverty in Ireland* (Dublin: Round Hall Sweet and Maxwell).

Bacik, I., Kelly, A., O'Connell, M. and Sinclair, H. (1998) 'Crime and poverty in Dublin: an analysis of the association between community deprivation, District Court appearance and sentence severity', in Bacik, I. and O'Connell, M. (eds), *Crime and Poverty in Ireland* (Dublin: Round Hall Sweet and Maxwell).

Baldwin, R., Cave, M. and Lodge, M. (2010) 'Introduction: regulation – the field and the developing agenda', in Baldin, R., Cave, M. and Lodge, M. (eds), *The Oxford Handbook of Regulation* (Oxford: Oxford University Press).

Bannon, A. (2006) *'Company Law Offences' Corporate Crime Elective in Professional Practice Course Part 2* (Dublin: Law Society of Ireland).

Barnes, E. M. (2002) 'Reflections on twenty five years as Ireland's first Director of Public Prosecutions', in O'Mahony, P. (ed.), *Criminal Justice in Ireland* (Dublin: Institute of Public Administration).

Beck, U. (1992) *Risk Society: Towards a New Modernity* (London: Sage).

Becker, H. S. (1991) *Outsiders: Studies in the Sociology of Deviance* (New York: Free Press).

Berlin, I. (2005) 'Two concepts of liberty', in Warburton, N. (ed.), *Philosophy Basic Readings* (New York: Routledge).

Black, J. (2001) 'Decentring regulation: understanding the role of regulation and self-regulation in a "post-regulatory" world', *Current Legal Problems* 54.

Black, J. (2005) 'The emergence of risk based regulation and the new public management in the UK', *Public Law* 512.

Black, J. and Baldwin, R. (2010) 'Really responsive risk-based regulation', *Law and Policy* 32.

Blake, M. and Ashworth, A. (1996) 'The presumption of innocence in English criminal law', *Criminal Law Review* 306.

Blue, J. R. (1999–2000) 'Celtic Tiger roars defiantly: corporation tax in Ireland and competition within the European Union', *Duke Journal of Comparative & International Law* 10.

Box, S. (1983) *Power, Crime, and Mystification* (London: Tavistock).

Braithwaite, J. (1982) 'Challenging just deserts: punishing white-collar criminals', *Journal of Criminal Law and Criminology* 73.

Braithwaite, J. (1984) *Corporate Crime in the Pharmaceutical Industry* (London: Routledge & Kegan Paul).

Braithwaite, J. (1990–91) 'Convergence in models of regulatory strategy', *Current Issues in Criminal Justice* 2.

Braithwaite, J. (1999) 'Accountability and governance under the new regulatory state', *Australian Journal of Public Administration* 58.

Braithwaite, J. (2000) 'The new regulatory state and the transformation of criminology', *British Journal of Criminology* 40.

Braithwaite, J. (2003) 'What's wrong with the sociology of punishment', *Theoretical Criminology* 7.

Braithwaite, J. (2005) *Neoliberalism or Regulatory Capitalism* (Canberra: Regulatory Institutions Network).

Braithwaite, J. (2008) *Regulatory Capitalism: How it Works, Ideas for Making it Work Better* (Cheltenham: Edward Elgar).

Braithwaite, J. and Drahos, P. (2000) *Global Business Regulation* (Cambridge: Cambridge University Press).

Bratton, W. (2004) 'Rules, principles and the accounting crisis in the United States', *European Business Organisation Law Journal* 5.

Brennan, N. (2003) 'Accounting in crisis: a story of auditing, accounting, corporate governance and market failures', *Irish Banking Review* 2.

Brennan, N. (2010) 'A review of corporate governance research: an Irish perspective', in Hogan, J., Donnelly, P. F. and O'Rourke, B. K. (eds), *Irish Business and Society* (Dublin: Gill & Macmillan).

Byrne, E. (2012) *Political Corruption in Ireland 1922–2010: A Crooked Harp* (Manchester: Manchester University Press).

Cahill, N. (2008) *Company Law Compliance and Enforcement* (Haywards Heath: Tottel).

Campbell, L., Kilcommins, S. and O'Sullivan, C. (2010) *Criminal Law in Ireland: Cases and Commentary* (Dublin: Clarus Press).

Carson, W. G. (1974) 'Symbolic and instrumental dimensions of early factory legislation', in Hood, R. G. (ed.), *Crime Criminology and Public Policy: Essays in Honour of Sir Leon Radzinowicz* (London: Heinemann).

Carswell, S. (2011) *Anglo Republic: Inside the Bank that Broke Ireland* (Dublin: Penguin).

Cartwright, P. (2001) *Consumer Protection and the Criminal Law: Law, Theory and Policy in the UK* (Cambridge: Cambridge University Press).

Central Bank of Ireland (2010) *Banking supervision: our new approach* (Dublin: Central Bank of Ireland).

Central Bank of Ireland (2010) *Enforcement Strategy 2011–2012* (Dublin: Central Bank of Ireland).

Central Bank of Ireland (Various Years) *Annual Report* (Dublin: Central Bank of Ireland).

Central Statistics Office (2008) *Garda Recorded Crime Statistics 2003–2006* (Dublin: Stationery Office).

Central Statistics Office (2011) *Garda Recorded Crime Statistics 2005–2009* (Dublin: Stationery Office).

Central Statistics Office (2013) *Statistical Yearbook on Ireland 2013* (Dublin: Stationery Office).

Charleton, P., McDermott, P. A. and Bolger, M. (1999) *Criminal Law* (Dublin: Butterworths).

Clarke, M. (1990) *Business Crime: Its Nature and Control* (Oxford: Polity Press).

Coffee, J. C. (2006) *Gatekeepers: The Professions and Corporate Governance* (New York: Oxford University Press).

Collins, N. and O'Shea, M. (2000) *Understanding Corruption in Irish Politics* (Cork: Cork University Press).

Committee of Public Accounts (1999) *Parliamentary Inquiry into DIRT First Report* (Dublin: Stationery Office).

Committee of Public Accounts (2001) *Parliamentary Inquiry into DIRT Final Report* (Dublin: Stationery Office).

Companies Registration Office (CRO) (Various Years) *Annual Report* (Dublin: Stationery Office).

Companies Report (Various Years) (Dublin: Stationery Office).

Company Law Review Group (CLRG) (2001) *First Report* (Dublin: Stationery Office).
Company Law Review Group (CLRG) (2004) *Second Report* (Dublin: Stationery Office).
Company Law Review Group (CLRG) (2005) *Report on Directors' Compliance Statement* (Dublin: Company Law Review Group).
Company Law Review Group (CLRG) (Various Years) *Annual Report* (Dublin: Stationery Office).
Comptroller and Auditor General (1999) *Report on the Investigation into the Administration of Deposit Interest Retention Tax and Related Matters during the period 1 January 1986 to 1 December 1998* (Dublin: Stationery Office).
Connery, N. and Hodnett, D. (2009) *Regulatory Law in Ireland* (Dublin: Bloomsbury Professional).
Cooper, M. (2009) *Who Really Runs Ireland? The Story of the Elite who Led Ireland from Bust to Boom ... and Back Again* (Dublin: Penguin).
Cooper, M. (2011) *How Ireland Really Went Bust* (Dublin: Penguin).
Costello, D. (1965) *Fine Gael Policy: Towards a Just Society* (Dublin: Fine Gael).
Costello, Mr Justice Declan (1980) *Disaster at Whiddy Island, Bantry Co. Cork: Report of Tribunal of Inquiry* (Dublin: Stationery Office).
Courtney, T. B. (2002, 2012) *The Law of Private Companies,* 2nd and 3rd edns (Dublin: Butterworths).
Cox, A. (1958) *Report of the Company Law Reform Committee* (Dublin: Stationery Office).
Creaton, S. and O'Clery, C. (2002) *Panic at the Bank: How John Rusnak lost AIB $691,000,000* (Dublin: Gill & Macmillan).
Croall, H. (1992) *White Collar Crime* (Buckingham: Open University Press).
Cronin, A. (1954) 'This time, this place', *The Bell* 19.
Crowley, T.P. (1973) *A Guide to the Companies Act, 1963* (Dublin: The Institute of Certified Public Accountants).
Cullen, F. T., Hartman, J. L. and Jonson, C. L. (2009) 'Bad guys: why the public supports punishing white-collar offenders', *Crime, Law and Social Change* 51.
Daly, M. (1994) 'The economic ideals of Irish nationalism: frugal comfort or lavish austerity?' *Eire/Ireland* 29.
Daly, M. E. (1984) 'An Irish-Ireland for Irish business? The Control of Manufactures Acts, 1932 and 1934', *Irish Historical Studies* 24.
Delaney, V. T. H. (1959) 'Company law reform in Ireland', *The Modern Law Review* 22.
Department of Justice (1997) *Tackling Crime: A Discussion Paper* (Dublin: Stationery Office).
Department of Justice (2010) *White Paper on Crime: Organised and White Collar Crime* (Dublin: Stationery Office).

Department of Public Enterprise (2000) *Governance and Accountability in the Regulatory Process: Policy Proposals* (Dublin: Stationery Office).
Department of the Taoiseach (1999) *Action Programme for the Millennium* (Dublin: Department of the Taoiseach).
Department of the Taoiseach (2004) *Regulating Better: A Government White Paper setting out six principles of Better Regulation* (Dublin: Department of the Taoiseach).
Department of the Taoiseach (2009) *Revised RIA Guidelines: How to Conduct a Regulatory Impact Analysis* (Dublin: Department of the Taoiseach).
Department of Transport (1987) *The Merchant Shipping Act 1894. MV Herald of Free Enterprise. Report of Court no. 8074. Formal Investigation* (London: Stationery Office).
Devlin, D. (2003) 'Accounting in crisis: the accountant's perspective', *Irish Banking Review* 18.
Dine, J. (1995) *Criminal Law in the Corporate Context* (Aldershot: Dartmouth Publishing).
DKM Consultants (1984) *The Control of Banking in the Republic of Ireland* (Dublin: Mount Salus Press).
Donnelly, R. (2008) 'Accounting, board independence and contagion affects from adverse comment: the case of Elan', *The British Accounting Review* 40.
Douglas, M. (1992) *Risk and Blame: Essays in Cultural Theory* (London: Routledge).
Downes, D. (2007) *In Conversation with Tom Courtney, CLRG* (Dublin: Chartered Accountants).
Durkheim, E. (1964) *The Rules of Sociological Method* (New York: Free Press).
Dworkin, R. (1987) *Taking Rights Seriously* (Cambridge, MA: Harvard University Press).
Dworkin, R. (1998) *Law's Empire* (Oxford: Hart Publishing).
Elderfield, M. (2010) 'The regulation agenda: update on bank recapitalisation and new corporate governance requirements' (Address by Matthew Elderfield, Head of Financial Regulation to the Association of Compliance Officers in Ireland, 22 November).
Fahey, T. (1992) 'Catholicism and industrial society in Ireland', in Goldthorpe, J. and Whelan, C. (eds), *The Development of Industrial Society in Ireland* (Oxford: Oxford University Press).
Farmer, L. (1996) 'The obsession with definition: the nature of crime and critical legal theory', *Social and Legal Studies* 5.
Fennell, C. (2009) *The Law of Evidence in Ireland*, 3rd edn (Haywards Heath: Bloomsbury Professional).
Ferriter, D. (2005) *The Transformation of Ireland 1900–2000* (Dublin: Profile Books Ltd).

Financial Regulator (2005) *Outline of Administrative Sanctions Procedure* (Dublin: Irish Financial Services Regulatory Authority).
Financial Regulator (2006) *Strategic Plan 2006* (Dublin: Financial Regulator).
Financial Regulator (Various Years) *Annual Report* (Dublin: Central Bank).
First Law (2009) 'Jail is the way to go after *DPP* v. *Duffy*' (Dublin: First Law Debate).
Fisse, B. and Braithwaite, J. (1993) *Corporations, Crime and Accountability* (Cambridge: Cambridge University Press).
Flood, Mr Justice Fergus (2002) *Report of the Tribunal of Inquiry into Certain Planning Matters and Payments* (Dublin: Stationery Office).
Foley, C. P. and Barry, A. G. (1992) *Investigation into the Affairs of Siuicre Eireann CPT and Related Companies: Final Report of Foley, C. P. and Barry, A. G.* (Dublin: Stationery Office).
Forde, M. and Kennedy, H. (2008) *Company Law* (Dublin: Thomson Round Hall).
Forfas (2002) *International Trade and Investment Report 2001* (Dublin: Forfas).
Foucault, M. (1991a) 'Governmentality', in Burchell, G. and Gordon, C. (eds), *The Foucault Effect: Studies in Governmentality* (Chicago: University of Chicago Press).
Foucault, M. (1991b) *Discipline and Punish: The Birth of the Prison* (Harmondsworth: Penguin).
Friedman, L. M. (1975) *The Legal System: A Social Science Perspective* (New York: Russel Sage).
Fuller, L. (1964) *The Morality of Law* (New Haven, CT: Yale University Press).
Gallagher, E. (1999) '"Collaring" the white collar criminal', *Commercial Law Practitioner* 6.
Gallagher, M. and Komito, L. (1996) 'Dail deputies and their constituency work', in Coakley, J. and Gallagher, M. (eds), *Politics in the Republic of Ireland* (Limerick: PSAI Press).
Garland, D. (2001) *The Culture of Control: Crime and Social Order in Contemporary Society* (Oxford: Oxford University Press).
Garland, D. (2003) 'The rise of risk', in Ericson, E. V. and Doyle, A. (eds), *Risk and Morality* (Toronto: University of Toronto Press).
Giddens, A. (2009) *Sociology*, 6th edn (Cambridge: Polity Press).
Girvin, B. and Murphy, G. (eds) (2005), *The Lemass Era: Politics and Society in the Ireland of Sean Lemass* (Dublin: University College Dublin Press).
Glacken, J. A. (1993) *Chestvale Properties Ltd and Hoddle Investments Ltd. Investigation Under Section 14(1), Companies Act 1990 Final Report* (Dublin: Stationery Office).
Gobert, J. (1994) 'Corporate criminality: four models of fault', *Legal Studies* 14.
Gower, L. C. B. (1997) *Principles of Modern Company Law* (London: Sweet and Maxwell).

Greer, D. and Nicolson, J. W. (2003) *The Factory Acts in Ireland, 1802–1914* (Dublin: Four Courts Press).
Gunningham, N. and Grabosky, P. (1999) *Smart Regulation: Designing Environmental Policy* (Oxford: Oxford University Press).
Habermas, J. (1987) *The Theory of Communicative Action Vol. 2 Lifeworld and System* (Cambridge: Polity Press).
Habermas, J. (1996) *Between Facts and Norms* (Cambridge, Polity Press).
Hamilton, C. (2007) *The Presumption of Innocence in Irish Criminal Law: 'Whittling the Golden Thread'* (Dublin: Irish Academic Press).
Hamilton, J. (2010) 'Do we need a system of administrative sanctions in Ireland?', in Kilcommins, S. and Kilkelly, U. (eds), *Regulatory Crime in Ireland* (Dublin: First Law).
Hamilton, Mr Justice Liam (1994) *Report of the Tribunal of Inquiry into the Beef Processing Industry* (Dublin: Stationery Office).
Hanly, C. (2006) *An Introduction to Irish Criminal Law*, 2nd edn (Dublin: Gill & Macmillan).
Hannon, D. and Commins, P. (1992) 'The significance of small-scale landholders in Ireland's socio-economic transformation', in Goldthorpe, J. and Whelan, C. (eds), *The Development of Industrial Society in Ireland* (Oxford: Oxford University Press).
Hardiman, N. (2002) 'The political economy of growth', in Crotty, W. and Schmitt, D. (eds), *Ireland on the World Stage* (Harlow: Longman).
Hawkins, K. (2002) *Law as Last Resort: Prosecution Decision-Making in a Regulatory Agency* (New York: Oxford University Press).
Healy, J. (2004) *Irish Laws of Evidence* (Dublin: Thomson Round Hall).
Higgins, I. (2012) *Corruption Law* (Dublin: Round Hall).
Hogan, G. W. and Whyte, G. F. (2003) *Kelly: The Irish Constitution*, 4th edn (Dublin: Lexis-Nexis Butterworths).
Holmes, O. W. (1897) 'The path of the law', *Harvard Law Review* 10.
Honohan, P. (1999) 'Fiscal adjustment and disinflation in Ireland: setting the macro basis of economic recovery and expansion', in Barry, F. (ed.), *Understanding Ireland's Economic Growth* (New York: St Martin's Press).
Honohan, P. (2010) *The Irish Banking Crisis Regulatory and Financial Stability Policy 2003–2008* (Dublin: Central Bank).
Horan, S. (2011) *Corporate Crime* (Dublin: Bloomsbury Professional).
Howlin, N. (2012) 'White-collar crimes and expert juries: precedents, alternatives and implications', *Irish Criminal Law Journal* 2.
Hudson, B. (2003) *Justice in the Risk Society: Challenging and Re-affirming Justice in the Risk Society* (London: Sage).
IDA Ireland (2004) *Ireland: Vital Statistics* (Dublin: Industrial Development Agency).

IDA Ireland (2011) *Ireland: Vital Statistics* (Dublin: Industrial Development Agency).
IMD World Competitiveness Yearbook 2010 (2010) (Lausanne: International Institute for Management Development).
Inglis, T. (1998) *Moral Monopoly: The Rise and Fall of the Catholic Church in Modern Ireland* (Dublin: University College Dublin Press).
Interdepartmental Inquiry 1950 (1951) (Dublin: Stationery Office).
International Trade Statistics 2003 (2003) (Geneva: World Trade Organization).
Investment in Education. Report of A Survey Team Appointed by the Minister for Education in Conjunction with the OECD (1965) (Dublin: Stationery Office).
Investment in Education. Report of a Survey Team Appointed by the Minister for Education in Conjunction with the OECD (1966) (Dublin: Stationery Office).
Jackall, R. (1988) *Moral Mazes: The World of Corporate Managers* (New York: Oxford University Press).
JUSTICE (1980) *Breaking the Rules: The Problem of Crimes and Contraventions* (London: JUSTICE).
Kahan, D. M. and Posner, E. A. (1999) 'Shaming white-collar criminals: a proposal for reform of the federal sentencing guidelines', *Journal of Law and Economics* 42.
Keane, R. (1985) *Company Law in the Republic of Ireland* (London: Butterworths).
Keane, R. (2007) *Company Law*, 4th edn (Haywards Heath, West Sussex: Tottel).
Kearney, A. T. (2004) 'Measuring globalization: economic reversals, forward momentum', *Foreign Policy* 141.
Kelly, S. (2012) *Breakfast with Anglo* (Dublin: Penguin).
Kennedy, L. (1978) 'The Roman Catholic Church and economic growth in nineteenth century Ireland', *Economic and Social Review*, 10.
Keogh, D. (2005) *Twentieth Century Ireland* (Dublin: Gill & Macmillan).
Kilcommins, S. (2011) 'Regulatory crime', in Butler, M. (ed.), *Criminal Litigation*, 3rd edn (Oxford: Oxford University Press).
Kilcommins, S. and Kilkelly, U. (eds) (2010) *Regulatory Crime in Ireland* (Dublin: First Law/Lonsdale Law Publishing).
Kilcommins, S. and Vaughan, B. (2010) '"The rise of the regulatory Irish state" – a response to Colin Scott', in Kilcommins, S. and Kilkelly, U. (eds), *Regulatory Crime in Ireland* (Dublin: First Law/Lonsdale Law Publishing).
Kilcommins, S., O'Donnell, I., O'Sullivan, E. and Vaughan, B. (eds) (2004) *Crime, Punishment and the Search for Order in Ireland* (Dublin: Institute of Public Education).
Kinsella, S. (2013) 'Modeling moments of crisis: The case of Ireland', *Journal of Economic Issues* 47.
Kinsella, S. and O'Sullivan, K. P. V. (2013) 'Financial and regulatory failure: the case of Ireland', *Journal of Banking Regulation* 14.

Lacey, N. (2003) 'Criminalization as regulation: the role of the criminal law', in Parker, C., Scott, C., Lacey, N. and Braithwaite, J. (eds) *Regulating Law* (Oxford: Oxford University Press).

Lacey, N. (2007) 'Legal constructions of crime', in Maguire, M., Morgan, R. and Reiner, R. (eds), *The Oxford Handbook of Criminology*, 4th edn (Oxford: Oxford University Press).

Lacey, N., Wells, C. and Quick, O. (2003) *Reconstructing Criminal Law: Texts and Materials*, 3rd edn (London: LexisNexis).

Law Reform Commission (LRC 110 – 2013) (2013) *Fourth Programme of Law Reform* (Dublin: Stationery Office).

Law Reform Commission (LRC 43 – 1992) (1992) *Report on the Law Relating to Dishonesty* (Dublin: Law Reform Commission).

Law Reform Commission (LRC 77 – 2005) (2005) *Report on Corporate Killing* (Dublin: Stationery Office).

Law Reform Commission (LRC 87 – 2008) (2008) *Homicide: Murder and Involuntary Manslaughter* (Dublin: Law Reform Commission).

Leahy, T. (1996) *Memoirs of a Garda Superintendent* (Clare: Hero Press).

Lee, G. and Bird, C. (1998) *Breaking the Bank: How the NIB Scandal was Exposed* (Dublin: Blackwater Press).

Lee, J. (1989) *Ireland 1912–1985; Politics and Society* (Cambridge: Cambridge University Press).

Levi, M. (2002) 'Economic crime', in McConville, M. and Wilson, G. (eds), *The Handbook of the Criminal Justice Process (Oxford)* (London: Oxford University Press).

Lewis, M. (2011) *Boomerang: Travels in the New Third World* (New York: W. W. Norton and Company).

Lynch Fannon, I. (2002) 'Enforcement and compliance in Irish company law: all law and no enforcement or the dawn of a new era?' *The Insolvency Lawyer* 14.

Lynch Fannon, I. (2010) 'Controlling risk taking: whose job is it anyway?', in Kilcommins, S. and Kilkelly, U. (eds), *Regulatory Crime in Ireland* (Dublin: First Law/Lonsdale Law Publishing).

Lyons, F. S. L. (1973) *Ireland Since the Famine* (London: Fontana).

Lyons, T. and Carey, B. (2011) *The FitzPatrick Tapes: The Rise and Fall of One Man, One Bank and One Country* (Dublin: Penguin).

Lyons, T. and Curran, R. (2013) *Fingers: The Man Who Brought Down Irish Nationwide and Cost Us 5.4bn* (Dublin: Gill & Macmillan).

Mac Sharry, R. and White, P. (2000) *The Making of the Celtic Tiger: The Inside Story of Ireland's Boom Economy* (Cork: Mercier Press).

Macrory, R. (2006) *Regulatory Justice, Making Sanctions Effective* (London: Better Regulation Executive).

Mahon, Mr Justice Alan (2013) *Report of the Tribunal of Inquiry into Certain Planning Matters and Payments* (Dublin: Stationery Office).

Majone, G. D. (1994) 'The rise of the regulatory state in Europe', *Western European Politics* 17.

Majone, G. D. (1997) 'From the positive to the regulatory state: causes and consequences of changes in the mode of governance', *Journal of Public Policy* 17.

Mann, K. (1985) *Defending White Collar Crime: A Portrait of Attorneys at Work* (New Haven, CT: Yale University Press).

Mann, K. (1992) 'Punitive civil sanctions: the middle ground between criminal and civil law', *The Yale Law Journal* 101.

Mann, K., Wheeler, S. and Sarat, A. (1979–80) 'Sentencing the white-collar offender', *American Criminal Law Review* 17.

McAuley F. and McCutcheon, J. P. (2000) *Criminal Liability: A Grammar* (Dublin: Round Hall Sweet and Maxwell).

McBarnett, D. (2006) 'After Enron will whiter than white collar crime still wash?' *British Journal of Criminology* 46.

McCormack, G. (1991) *The New Companies Legislation* (Dublin: Round Hall).

McCracken, Mr Justice Brian (1997) *Report of the Tribunal of Inquiry (Dunnes Payments)* (Dublin: Stationery Office).

McCullagh, C. (1995) 'Getting the criminals we want: the social production of the criminal population', in Clancy, P., Drudy, S., Lynch, K. and O'Dowd, L. (eds), *Irish Society: Sociological Perspectives* (Dublin: Sociological Association of Ireland).

McCullagh, C. (1996) *Crime in Ireland: A Sociological Introduction* (Cork: Cork University Press).

McCullagh, C. (2002) 'The social analysis of the Irish prison', in O'Mahony, P. (ed.), *Criminal Justice in Ireland* (Dublin: Institute of Public Administration).

McDonald, D. (2010) *Bust: How the Courts Have Exposed the Rotten Heart of the Irish Economy* (Dublin: Penguin).

McDonald, F. and Sheridan, K. (2009) *The Builders: How a Small Group of Property Developers Fuelled the Building Boom and Transformed Ireland* (Dublin: Penguin).

McDowell, M. (1998) *Report of the Working Group in Company Law Compliance and Enforcement* (Dublin: Stationery Office).

McDowell, M. (1999) *Report of the Implementation Advisory Group on the Establishment of a Single Regulatory Authority for the Financial Services Sector* (Dublin: Stationery Office).

McDowell, M. (2010) 'Non-criminal penalties and criminal sanctions in Irish regulatory law', in Kilcommins, S. and Kilkelly, U. (eds), *Regulatory Crime in Ireland* (Dublin: First Law/Lonsdale Law Publishing).

McGrath, D. (2005) *Evidence* (Dublin: Thomson Round Hall).

McGrath, J. (2010) 'The traditional court of crime approach to the definition of a crime', in Kilcommins, S. and Kilkelly, U. (eds), *Regulatory Crime in Ireland* (Dublin: First Law/Lonsdale Law Publishing).

McGrath, J. (2012) 'Sentencing white-collar criminals: making the punishment fit the white-collar crime', *Irish Criminal Law Journal* 22.

McGrath, M. (2007–8) 'Restriction of directors: Tralee beef and lamb', *Irish Business Law Quarterly* 2.

Mcguire, R. (2010) 'White collar crime: the business of crime' in Hogan, J., Donnelly, P. F. and O'Rourke B. K. (eds), *Irish Business and Society* (Dublin: Gill & Macmillan).

McIntyre, T. J. and McMullan, S. (2005) *Criminal Law*, 2nd edn (Dublin: Thomson Round Hall).

McNiffe, L. (1997) *A History of the Garda Síochána* (Dublin: Wolfhound Press).

McWilliams, D. (2005) *The Pope's Children Ireland's New Elite* (London: Gill & Macmillan).

Mitchell, L. E. (2001) *Corporate Irresponsibility: America's Newest Export* (New Haven, CT: Yale University Press).

Mokhiber, R. (1989) *Corporate Crime and Violence: Big Business Power and the Abuse of the Public Trust* (San Francisco: Sierra Club Books).

Moran, M. (2003) *The British Regulatory State: High Modernism and Hyper-Innovation* (Oxford: Oxford University Press).

Moriarty, Mr Justice Michael (2006, 2011) *Report of the Tribunal of Inquiry into Payments to Politicians and Related Matters Parts 1 and 2* (Dublin: Stationery Office).

Morrison, W. (2013) 'What is crime? Contrasting definitions and perspectives', in Hale, C., Hayward, K., Wahidin, A. and Wincup, E. (eds), *Criminology* (Oxford: Oxford University Press).

Moynihan, M. (1975) *Currency and Central Banking in Ireland 1922–1960* (Dublin: Gill & Macmillan).

Moynihan, M. (1980) *Speeches and Statements by Eamon DeValera 1917–73* (Dublin: Gill & Macmillan).

Murphy, D. and Devlin, M. (2009) *Banksters* (Dublin: Hachette Books Ireland).

Murphy, G. (2005) 'From economic nationalism to European Union', in Girvin, B. and Murphy, G. (eds), *The Lemass Era: Politics and Society in the Ireland of Sean Lemass* (Dublin: University College Dublin Press).

National Competitiveness Council (2003) *Annual Competitiveness Report 2003* (Dublin: Forfas).

National Competitiveness Council (2011) *Annual Competitiveness Report 2010: Volume 1: Benchmarking Ireland's Performance* (Dublin: Forfas).

National Social and Economic Council (1984) *The Criminal Justice System: Policy and Performance* (Dublin: National Economic and Social Council).

Nelkin, D. (2007) 'White collar and corporate crime', in Maguire, M., Morgan, R. and Reiner, R. (eds), *The Oxford Handbook of Criminology* (London: Oxford University Press).

Nevin, M. (1967–68) 'A study of the social background of students in Irish Universities', *Journal of the Statistical and Social Inquiry* 21.

Ni Raifeartaigh, U. (2001) 'The convention and Irish criminal law: selected topics', in Kilkelly, U. (ed.), *ECHR and Irish Law*, 2nd edn (Bristol: Jordan Publishing).

Norrie, A. (2001) *Crime, Reason and History*, 2nd edn (London: Butterworths).

O'Brien, A. (1954) *The Vanishing Irish: The Enigma of the Modern World* (London: Allen).

O'Brien, G. (1936) 'Patrick Hogan: minister for agriculture 1922–1932', *Studies: An Irish Quarterly Review* 25.

O'Brien, J. (2007) *Redesigning Financial Regulation: The Politics of Enforcement* (Chichester: John Wiley).

O'Connell, K. (2009) 'Deemed disqualification orders' (10th Annual National Prosecutors' Conference, Dublin Castle Conference Centre).

O'Donnell, I. (1998) 'Crime, punishment and poverty', in Bacik, I. and O'Connell, M. (eds), *Crime and Poverty in Ireland* (Dublin: Round Hall Sweet and Maxwell).

O'Donnell, I. and O'Sullivan, E. (2001) *Crime Control in Ireland: The Politics of Intolerance* (Cork: Cork University Press).

O'Donnell, R. and O'Reardon, C. (2000) 'Social partnership in Ireland's economic transformation', in Fajertag, G. and Pochet, P. (eds), *Social Pacts in Europe* (Brussels: European Trade Union Institute).

O'Grada, C. (1997) *A Rocky Road: The Irish Economy Since the 1920s* (Manchester: Manchester University Press).

O'Grada, C. (2002) 'Is the Celtic tiger a paper tiger?', *Quarterly Economic Commentary*.

O'Grady Walshe, T. (1991) 'Managing a central bank: goals, strategies, and techniques', in Downes, P. and Vaez-Zadeh, R. (eds), *The Evolving Role of Central Banks* (Washington, DC: International Monetary Fund).

O'Hearn, D. (2000) 'Globalisation, "new tigers," and the end of the development state? The case of the Celtic Tiger', *Politics and Society* 28.

O'Higgins, K. (2001) 'How to restore a struck-off company to the register', *Gazette of the Law Society of Ireland* 1.

O'hOgartaigh, C. (2011) '"Everything and nothing spoken": tales from the Celtic Tiger twilight', *Irish Economic and Social History* 38.

O'Mahony, P. (1998) 'Punishing poverty and personal adversity', in Bacik, I. and O'Connell, M. (eds), *Crime and Poverty in Ireland* (Dublin: Round Hall Sweet and Maxwell).

O'Malley, Eoin (1992) 'Problems of industrialisation in Ireland', in Goldthorpe, J. and Whelan, C. (eds), *The Development of Industrial Society in Ireland* (Oxford: Oxford University Press).

O'Malley, T. (2006) *Sentencing Law and Practice*, 2nd edn (Dublin: Thomson Round Hall).

O'Malley, T. (2009) *The Criminal Process* (Dublin: Round Hall).

O'Neill, A. (2007) *The Constitutional Rights of Companies* (Dublin: Thomson Round Hall).

O'Nuallain, L. (1946–47) 'A comparison of the economic position and trend in Eire and Northern Ireland', *Journal of the Social and Statistical Inquiry Society of Ireland* 99.

O'Reilly, L. (2005) 'The future of financial regulation: principles or rules issues for the Irish financial services sector' (Finance Dublin Conference, Dublin Castle).

O'Toole, F. (2010) *Ship of Fools: How Stupidity and Corruption Sank the Celtic Tiger* (London: Faber & Faber).

ODCE (2008) *Whistle-blowing and Irish Company Law – A Review of National and International Research on Whistle-blowing* (Dublin: Office of the Director of Corporate Enforcement).

ODCE (2003–14) *Annual Reports* (Dublin: Stationery Office).

OECD in Figures 2001: Statistics on Member Countries (2001) (Paris: OECD).

OECD in Figures 2003: Statistics on Member Countries (2003) (Paris: OECD).

OECD, *Economic Surveys: Ireland 1996* (1996) (Paris: OECD).

OECD, *Regulatory Reform in Ireland* (2001) (Paris: OECD).

Ogus, A. (2004) 'Enforcing regulation: do we need the criminal law', in Sjögren, H. and Skogh, G. (eds), *New Perspectives on Economic Crime* (Cheltenham: Edward Elgar).

Olsen, J. P. (2002) 'The many faces of Europeanization', *Journal of Common Market Studies* 40.

Osborne, D. and Gaebler, T. (1992) *Reinventing Government: How the Entrepreneurial Spirit is Transforming the Public Sector* (Reading, MA: Addison-Wesley).

Packer, H. L. (1968) *The Limits of the Criminal Sanction* (Stanford, CA: Stanford University Press).

Pierce, A. (2003) 'Elan corporation: A case study in corporate obfuscation', *Corporate Governance International* 6.

Posner, R. A. (1979–80) 'Optimal sentences for white collar criminals', *American Criminal Law Review* 17.

Pound, R. (1913) 'The administration of justice in the modern city', *Harvard Law Review* 26.

Programme for Economic Expansion Laid by the Government before each House of the Oireachtas, November 1958 (1959) (Dublin: Stationery Office).

Punch, M. (2008) 'The organisation did it: individuals, corporations and crime', in Minkes, J. and Minkes, L. (eds), *Corporate and White Collar Crime* (London: Sage).

Quinn, R. (1997) 'Celtic tiger in a global jungle – address by the Minister for Finance' (IBEC Annual Business Conference, Dublin Castle).
Ramsay, I. (2007) *Consumer Law and Policy: Text and Materials on Regulating Consumer Markets*, 2nd edn (Oxford: Hart Publishing).
Reddan, F. (2008) *Ireland's IFSC: A Story of Global Financial Success* (Dublin: Mercier Press).
Regling, K. and Watson, M. (2010) *A Preliminary Report on the Sources of Ireland's Banking Crisis* (Dublin: Stationery Office).
Report of the Inspectors Appointed To Enquire into the Affairs of Ansbacher (Cayman) Ltd (2002) (Dublin: Stationery Office).
Rhode, D. L. and Paton, P. D. (2003) 'Lawyers, ethics, and Enron', *Stanford Journal of Law, Business and Finance* 8.
Rose, N. (1999) *Powers of Freedom: Reframing Political Thought* (Cambridge: Cambridge University Press).
Ross, S. (2009) *The Bankers: How the Banks Brought Ireland to its Knees* (Dublin: Penguin).
Ross, S. (2012) *The Untouchables: The People who Helped Run Ireland into the Ground – and are Still Running the Show* (Dublin: Penguin).
Ross, S. and Webb, N. (2012) *Wasters* (Dublin: Penguin).
Rottman, D. B. and Tormey, P. F. (1986) 'Respectable crime: occupational and professional crime in the Republic of Ireland', *Studies: An Irish Quarterly Review* 75.
Rottman, D. B., Hannan, D. F., Hardiman, N. and Wiley, M. M. (1982) *The Distribution of Income in the Republic of Ireland: A Study in Social Class and Family-Cycle Inequalities* (Dublin: Economic and Social Research Institute).
Sayre, F. B. (1932) 'Mens Rea', *Harvard Law Review* 45.
Sayre, F. B. (1933) 'Public welfare offences', *Columbia Law Review* 33.
Scott, C. (2008) 'Regulating everything' (Inaugural Lecture of the Chair in EU Regulation and Governance, University College Dublin).
Scott, C. (2010) 'Regulatory crime – history, functions, problems, solutions', in Kilcommins, S. and Kilkelly, U. (eds), *Regulatory Crime in Ireland* (Dublin: Lonsdale).
Second Programme for Economic Expansion: laid by the Government Before each House of the Oireachtas, July, 1964 (1964) (Dublin: Stationery Office).
Shipsey, B. (2010) *Inspector's Report into the affairs of DCC* (Dublin: Office of the Director of Corporate Enforcement).
Simon, J. (2007) *Governing Through Crime: How the War on Crime Transformed American Democracy and Created a Culture of Fear* (New York: Oxford University Press).
Smith, N. J. (2005) *Showcasing Globalisation: The Political Economy of the Irish Republic* (Manchester: Manchester University Press).

Snider, L. (2008) 'Corporate economic crimes', in Minkes, J. and Minkes, L. (eds), *Corporate and White Collar Crime* (London: Sage).
Stadler, W. A. Benson, M. L., and Cullen, F. T. (2013) 'Revisiting the special sensitivity hypothesis: the prison experience of white-collar inmates', *Justice Quarterly* 30.
Stanley, C. (1992) 'Serious money: legitimation of deviancy in financial markets', *International Journal of the Sociology of Law* 20.
Stigler, G. J. (1971) 'The theory of economic regulation', *Bell Journal of Economics and Management Science* 2.
Sutherland, E. (1940) 'Is "white collar crime" crime?' *American Sociology Review* 10.
Sutherland, E. (1949) *White Collar Crime* (New York: Dryden Press).
Tansey, P. (1998) *Ireland at Work: Economic Growth and the Labour Market, 1987–1997* (Dublin: Oak Tree Press).
Thaler, R. H. and Sunstein, C. (2008) *Nudge: Improving Decisions About Health, Wealth, and Happiness* (New Haven, CT: Yale University Press).
The Report of the Review Group on Auditing (2000) (Dublin: Stationery Office).
The Way Forward: National Economic Plan 1983–1987 laid by the Government before each house of the Oireachtas, October, 1982 (1982) (Dublin: Stationery Office).
Thomas, W. A. (1986) *The Stock Exchanges of Ireland* (Liverpool: Francis Cairns Publications).
Tobin, F. (1984) *The Best of Decades: Ireland in the 1960s* (Dublin: Gill & Macmillan).
Transparency International (2009) *Country Studies: Ireland* (Berlin: Transparency Secretariat).
Twining, W. (2000) *Globalisation and Legal Theory* (London: Butterworths).
Ua Maoileoin, P. (1989) *De Reir Uimhreacha* (Baile Atha Cliath: Sairseal – O Marcaigh).
Ussher, P. (1986) *Company Law in Ireland* (London: Sweet and Maxwell).
Vaughan, B. (2009) 'The Maginot line of Irish criminology: the rise of the regulatory impulse', *Irish Criminal Law Journal* 19.
Vaughan, B. and Kilcommins, S. (2008) *Terrorism, Rights and the Rule of Law: Negotiating Justice in Ireland* (Devon: Willan Publishing).
Vink, M. P. (2003) 'What is Europeanization? And other questions on a new research agenda', *European Political Science* 3.
Walsh, D. (2002) *Criminal Procedure* (Dublin: Thomson Round Hall).
Weber, M. (1968) *Economy and Society, An Outline of Interpretive Sociology* (Berkeley, CA: University of California Press).
Weisberg, D., Waring E. and Leeper Piquero, N. (2008) 'Getting beyond the moral drama of crime: what we learn from studying white-collar criminal

careers', in Minkes, J. and Minkes, L. (eds), *Corporate and White Collar Crime* (London: Sage).
Wells, C. (2001) *Corporations and Criminal Responsibility*, 2nd edn (Oxford: Oxford University Press).
Weston, R. (1980) *Domestic and Multinational Banking: The Effects of Monetary Policy* (London: Routledge).
Whitaker, T. K. (1958) *Economic Development* (Dublin: Stationery Office).
Whitaker, T. K. (1985) *Report of the Committee of Inquiry into the Penal System* (Dublin: Stationery Office).
White, F. (2011) *Commercial and Economic Law in Ireland* (Alphen aan den Rijn, The Netherlands: Kluwer International.
White, R. and Haines, F. (2000) *Crime and Criminology*, 2nd edn (Oxford: Oxford University Press).
Williams, G. (1955) 'The definition of a crime', *Current Legal Problems* 8.
Williams, G. (1961) *Criminal Law: The General Part*, 2nd edn (London: Stevens).
Wilson, S. V. and Matz, A. H. (1977) 'Obtaining evidence for federal economic prosecutions: an overview and analysis of investigative methods', *American Criminal Law Review* 14.
Wolgast, E. (1992) *Ethics of an Artificial Person: Lost Responsibility in Professions and Organisations* (Stanford ,CA: Stanford University Press).
Zedner, L. (2004) *Criminal Justice* (Oxford: Oxford University Press).

Index

EU authorised representative for GPSR:
Easy Access System Europe, Mustamäe tee 50,
10621 Tallinn, Estonia
gpsr.requests@easproject.com

www.ingramcontent.com/pod-product-compliance
Ingram Content Group UK Ltd.
Pitfield, Milton Keynes, MK11 3LW, UK
UKHW021840100926
8556IPUK00004B/450
9780719090660